from me
5 apr '81

MISSOURI PACIFIC

FREIGHT TRAINS

AND EQUIPMENT

PATRICK C. DORIN

2001
TLC Publishing, Inc.
1387 Winding Creek Lane
Lynchburg, Virginia 24503-3776

International Standard Book Number   1-883089-54-9
Library of Congress Catalog Card Number   00-108873

Design, Layout, Type, and Image Assembly by
Kevin J. Holland
type&DESIGN
Burlington, Ontario

Produced on the MacOS™

Printed by
Walsworth Publishing Company
Marceline, Missouri 64658

OTHER BOOKS BY PATRICK C. DORIN FROM TLC –

Chicago & North Western Passenger Service – The Postwar Years
Chicago & North Western Passenger Equipment
Louisville & Nashville Passenger Trains – The Pan-American Era (with Charles Castner and Bob Chapman)
Louisville & Nashville – The Old Reliable (with Charles Castner and Ron Flanary)
Western Pacific Locomotives and Cars

FRONT COVER – (Painting by Gil Bennett)

Alco FA's lead a Missouri Pacific "Perishable Freight" through the grandeur of an Ozark autumn.
The train's refrigerator cars are rushing Texas produce to markets in the Midwest and East.

Dedicated
to the
Memory of
Camille Chapuis

He provided a great deal of inspiration and encouragement for the creation of this book as well as other projects on the Missouri Pacific.

Camille was an extradordinary individual who is missed by many, not only for his knowledge of railroad operations, but most of all for his friendship.

THE AUTHOR

Patrick C. Dorin has been interested in railroads since the age of two.

While attending undergraduate school at Northland College, he worked for the Great Northern Railway. Later he worked for the Elgin, Joliet & Eastern Railway, the Duluth, Missabe & Iron Range, and the Milwaukee Road. His employment in the railroad industry included positions in operations, marketing research, customer service, and cost accounting.

He holds degrees in business administration, marketing, elementary education, and school administration including a Ph.D. from the University of Minnesota.

He is currently serving as a school principal for the Superior, Wisconsin, schools and has taught marketing, operations research, transportation, Japanese culture, and school administration courses on a part-time basis for both the University of Wisconsin–Superior and the University of Minnesota–Duluth.

Railroads continue to hold a strong fascination for Pat, and he has published over 25 books and nearly 30 articles on aspects of railroad service, companies, and equipment, as well as other subjects.

Pat lives in Superior, Wisconsin, with his wife Karen.

A C K N O W L E D G M E N T S

I wish to thank the following people who have assisted in a "thousand" ways (and more) in the research, writing, editing, and publishing of this book.

My wife Karen gave a substantial amount of her time during the original writing and the recent rewriting stages of the project, and provided assistance with reading and checking the manuscript as well as the proofs.

Thanks also to Mr. Tom Dixon of TLC Publishing and Mr. Kevin Holland for his design and layout work.

It is hard to believe that it was over twenty years ago when I worked with several people from the Missouri Pacific including: Mr. Harry Hammer, Assistant Vice President; Mr. Walter Fussner, Director Special Projects; Mr. D. M. Tutko, Chief Mechanical Officer; and many other staff members in the operating, mechanical, and public relations departments.

The Missouri Pacific Railroad photographs credited in the following pages include equipment photos from Thrall Car, Pacific Car & Foundry, Ortner, Greenville Steel Car, and General Steel Industries.

Also offering assistance with this book were members of the Missouri Pacific Railroad Historical Society. Mr. Ralph Barger, Mr. Jim Bennett, and the late Mr. Camille Chapuis assisted with a wide variety of information and photographs for the project.

Railroad photographers lending their support included Ron Merrick, Harold K. Vollrath, George C. Corey, A. Robert Johnson, W. C. Whittaker, A. C. Phelps, R. J. Wilhem, W. S. Kuba, J. W. Swanberg, Bob Lorenz, Ralph H. Carlson, Stan K. Bolton, Jr., Bill Pillard, Elmer Treloar, Howard S. Patrick, Scott Huch, Michael Burlaga, Dennis Roos, Thomas Dorin, Michael Dorin, Sy Dykhouse, William A. Raia, Allen Rider, David Schauer, Robert Blomquist, K. B. King (Dick Kuelbs Collection), and Lloyd Keyser.

Additional assistance with background information and research came from Mr. Luther Miller, Editor of *Railway Age*, and Mr. William J. Trezise, National Railway Publication Company and, later, Susan Murray, Primedia Directories Inc., publishers of the *Official Railway Equipment Register*.

Without the time and kind assistance of these individuals, the book would not have been completed. Should an acknowledgment have been inadvertently omitted, I apologize and trust that it will be found in the appropriate credit line within the text.

Again, *thank you*, each and every one!

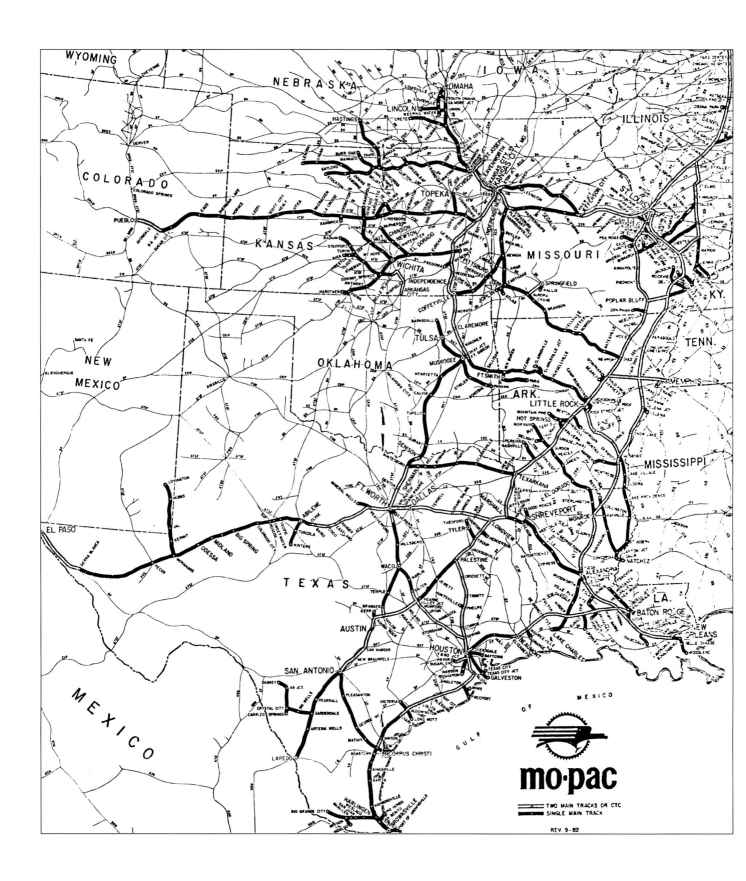

INTRODUCTION

The fifty years between the mid-1930s and the mid- to late 1980s marked an incredible period of time for the Missouri Pacific Railroad, and was perhaps the most dramatic period of the company's history, including the construction era and ownership by tycoons. The MoPac experienced a transformation from a complete and deep bankruptcy to one of the most financially healthy and service-minded transportation organizations in North America. It is the purpose of this book to review two very important parts of the MoPac story: Freight Train Services and Operations; and Freight Equipment.

The MoPac was a railroad which operated a wide variety of train services. It is probably most famous for its *Eagle* streamliner fleet because that was the most visible part of the railroad to the American public. A passenger train is a piece of rolling advertising for a railroad company since it is the closest connection with the geographical communities served by the company. Not too many people pay much attention to a unit coal train or an intermodal flyer unless they are complaining about being stopped at a crossing as the train passes by. Getting back on track, one could see coal trains, ore, fast manifest freights, secondary service freights, intermodal trains, and way freights throughout the system from Chicago to Mexico and New Orleans to El Paso.

Still another aspect about the MoPac was its once very complicated corporate structure. Since the 1920 through the 1970s, the Missouri Pacific Lines consisted of several railroads. There were several reasons for this, some of which had to do with various state laws requiring separate corporate organizations within those states; some had to do with the total reorganization process, while others were related to the process of expansion and merger of the railroad system. They system was quite complex, and it was not until the decade of the 1980s that the system was simplified into just the "Missouri Pacific." Gone were such railroads as the Texas & Pacific, the Chicago & Eastern Illinois as well as lesser-known properties, such as the Asphalt Belt Railway. Since the 1930s, there were thirty railroads that have operated as part of the Missouri Pacific Lines. This does not include the Alton & Southern, nor does it include the many short lines that were forged into the system during the 19th century. Following is a list of those railroads as well as the initials that are used throughout the book.

Railroad Company	Initials
Asherton & Gulf Railroad	A&G
Asphalt Belt Railway	AB
Beaumont, Sour Lake & Western Rwy	BSL&W
Chicago & Eastern Illinois Railroad	C&EI
Chicago Heights Terminal Transfer	CHTT
Fort Worth Belt Railway	FWB
Gulf Coast Lines:	
New Orleans, Texas and Mexico	NOT&M or NOTM
St. Louis, Brownsville & Mexico	St.LB&M
Houston & Brazos Valley	H&BV
Houston North Shore	HNS
Iberia, St. Mary & Eastern Railroad	IStM&E
International Great Northern	IGN or I-GN
Kansas, Oklahoma & Gulf Railway	KO&G
Midland Valley Railroad	MV
Missouri Illinois	MI
Missouri Pacific Railroad	MP
New Iberia & Northern Railroad	NI&N
New Orleans & Lower Coast	NO&LC
Oklahoma City–Ada–Atoka Railway	OC-A-A
Orange & Northwestern Railroad	O&N
Rio Grande City Railway	RGC
St. Joseph Belt Railway	StJB
St. Louis, Iron Mountain & Southern	StLIM&S
San Antonio Southern Railway	SAS
San Antonio, Uvalde & Gulf Railroad	SAU&G
San Benito & Rio Grande Valley Rwy	SB&RGV
Sugar Land Railway	SL
Texas & Pacific Railway	T&P
Texas Pacific–Missouri Pacific Terminal Railroad of New Orleans	TP-MP
Union Railway (of Memphis)	UR
Union Terminal Railway (of St. Louis)	UT

The Missouri Pacific Railroad Company was a transportation organization that deserves to be studied and re-studied by all people interested in transportation and railroads in particular.

This book, hopefully, provides a start by presenting the wide variety of freight services and equipment operated during the "transformation half-century" period between the 1930s and 1980s, with the arrival of the Union Pacific System closing the story.

Patrick C. Dorin
Superior, Wisconsin
December 1, 2000

Growing With HOUSTON

New Freight Terminal Enables Missouri Pacific to Keep Pace with Fast-Growing Texas City and Port

Anticipating the need for expanding transportation facilities to serve the busy port of Houston, Texas, as well as the city's booming industrial areas, Missouri Pacific recently completed and placed in service there a completely new freight terminal, named the Settegast yard for a prominent pioneer Houston family.

The new freight yard occupies a 375-acre site approximately six miles from the business center of Houston. It embraces 63 tracks totalling 34 miles in length and has a standing capacity of 2,320 cars. One section of the yard assigned to the handling of perishable freight has a capacity of 1,190 cars. Thirty-two cars may be accommodated on either side of the icing dock in this perishable yard.

Night illumination for the Settegast terminal is provided by batteries of huge floodlights mounted on five 100-foot steel towers. An extensive modern communication system, including loud speakers and hand telephones, enables the yardmaster to talk from his desk to yard and train crews at any point on the system. All train movements within the yard are governed by signal indication, no written train orders are needed.

Completion of the new Settegast facilities enabled the Missouri Pacific to concentrate all freight in one yard. This eliminated interchange switching movements between separate yards formerly operated by the I-GN and GCL (Missouri Pacific subsidiaries). For Houston it means speedier movement of shipments to and through the port, plus the alleviation of rail interference with city street and highway traffic.

Construction of the Settegast yard marks another step in a continuing program to keep Missouri Pacific equipment and facilities abreast of the growing transportation needs of the West-Southwest empire it serves.

Ads like this one from 1950 highlighted the role played by MoPac in the growth of the Southwest's post-war economy. (PCD Collection)

CONTENTS

CHAPTER ONE

Corporate Background

Every organization has an image, whether it is a school district, a steel company, a hospital, or even a family. Sometimes the image is genuine, whereas at other times the image is false. The Missouri Pacific Railroad, like other businesses, had a public image. It can be said that, during the half-century from the 1930s through to the UP merger, the MP's public image probably changed more than that of many other companies. It went from a very poor image during the 1920s and 1930s–complete with bankruptcy–to a very positive image in the 1980s. It was accomplished with both short- and long-term planning which actually began in the 1940s and continued through the next four decades.

The results of this type of planning by the MoPac were many–the *Eagle*, *Eagle* Less-than-Carload services, *Eagle* fast piggyback trains, reconstruction of trackage, successful consolidation of the corporate structure, and one of the most successful management training programs of almost any organization in North America, just to name a few. This is not to imply that the MP was without its problems, or that it no longer had to change train services or other functions to meet customer needs, but it did mean that the entire employee group had turned a losing railroad system into a winner.

Among the transportation companies in North America, the MP could be classified as one

of the more unusual properties. Looking back, the company had a rather humble beginning with the usual dreams. The discovery of gold in California in 1848 acted as an impetus for the people of the river town of St. Louis to push for a railroad. After all, what would be better than for St. Louis to be the starting point for the transcontinental railroad? The dreams grew to practical plans, and on July 4, 1851, ground was broken for the Pacific Railroad, which according to its Missouri charter granted in 1849, would extend from St. Louis to the western boundary of Missouri and then on to the Pacific Ocean.

Thomas Allen was the first president of the Pacific Railroad, with James P. Kirkwood as its first civil engineer. Kirkwood began work immediately, not only on the construction of the railroad, but also on the tunnels that were required on the main line to Kansas City.

The first locomotive arrived by river boat in August 1852. On December 9, 1852, a passenger train carrying the company's officers and leading citizens of St. Louis inaugurated the new Pacific Railroad with a trip to the end of the line. That train was the first to be operated west of the Mississippi River and ran over the five miles of completed track from the St. Louis depot to Cheltenham.

The first 38 miles of railroad were completed to Franklin, now known as Pacific, Missouri, in

July 1853. Financial difficulties slowed construction substantially. The tracks were not completed to Washington, Missouri, until almost January 1, 1855. It was not until late 1855 that the company reached the capital of Missouri at Jefferson City.

As the Pacific Railroad was building westward, still other Missouri railroad projects were either underway or in the planning stages, such as the St. Louis & Iron Mountain, the Cairo & Fulton, the Southwest Branch of the Pacific Railroad, the North Missouri, and the Hannibal & St. Joseph.

Still other railroads, such as the Houston Tap, the Galveston, Houston & Henderson and the Texas Western Railroads were underway in Texas in the early 1850s. The TW eventually became the Texas & Pacific Railroad, which in turn became a major component of the Missouri Pacific in later years.

The Civil War wrought a great deal of damage to the new railroad systems, but repairs were made and the different lines began to grow again. In fact, on September 19, 1865, the last spike was driven to unite Kansas City and St. Louis by rail. On the next day, the first train departed Kansas City at 3:00 a.m. and arrived in St. Louis at 5:00 p.m.

As the 1870s began, the T&P was expanding rapidly as well as the St. Louis & Iron Mountain, and the International-Great Northern (I-GN).

The Cairo & Fulton was working through Arkansas. The 1870s also brought financial difficulties to the Pacific Railroad, which was then reorganized as the Missouri Pacific Railroad Company in 1872.

No book on the Missouri Pacific would be complete without at least some mention of New York financier Jay Gould. In 1879, Gould purchased the controlling interest in the MP and became its president. This controlling interest was the start of a group of rail lines to be known as the Southwest System. In 1880 five smaller railroads were consolidated with the MP, and in 1881, the St. Louis, Iron Mountain & Southern was acquired. About the same time, Gould gained control of the Texas & Pacific and the MP leased the Missouri-Kansas-Texas Railroad (MKT). The International-Great Northern was also purchased and expanded to Laredo, Texas.

However, the system could not hang together and Gould began to loss control. In 1885, the T&P was separated from the MP and in 1888 the lease of the MKT was lost. This in turn caused the loss of the I-GN from the MP. Only the Iron Mountain Railroad remained part of the MP system at the end of 1888.

During the time period from 1885 to 1892, however, the MP was building far and wide into Kansas and Colorado. The Iron Mountain line was extended to Alexandria, Louisiana. Between

This painting depicts the building of the Pacific Railroad west from St. Louis. (Missouri Pacific Railroad, PCD Collection)

3

After the initial construction of the Iron Mountain Railroad between St. Louis and Iron Mountain, Missouri in 1858, the railroad continued south toward Poplar Bluff and Texarkana. This photo shows a work train loaded with ties and rails with a new track laying machine. Both ties and rail could be laid down, which in turn greatly speeded construction. This photo must be something of a festive occasion with the various ladies and gentlemen in dresses and suits. (Missouri Pacific Railroad, PCD Collection)

1892 and 1910, the Illinois Division was completed and several branch lines were also purchased. The main line of the road, later to be known as the Gulf Coast Lines, was extended to Houston and Brownsville, Texas.

A major merger took place in 1917 between the Missouri Pacific "Railway" and the St. Louis, Iron Mountain & Southern, which in turn created a new company, the Missouri Pacific Railroad Company.

The road's expansion was not yet complete and during 1923, the MP officially acquired the Gulf Coast Lines and the International-Great Northern. It was the second time that the I-GN had been part of the MP System. The San Antonio, Uvalde & Gulf was acquired to round out the system in southwest Texas. These various properties in Texas and Louisiana were formally merged in 1925 with the MP.

The MP adopted the name "Missouri Pacific Lines" in 1928 to cover the entire system of railroads under the MP management, ownership, and control. The T&P was also under MP control.

In many ways the 1920s were not as healthy as one might have expected. The Great Depression followed the stock market crash of October 1929, and the MP went bankrupt less than four years later. However, the MP bankruptcy was different from most railroad bankruptcies. Physical improvements and repairs were continued. In fact, in 1938 the Missouri Pacific Freight Transport Company was organized as a subsidiary of the railroad. Its truck routes were to supplement the railroad services, not compete with them.

The bankruptcy, actually the second since 1915, was unique in other ways. It extended throughout the Second World War and did not end for 23 years – one of the longest bankruptcies in U.S. railroading.

However, during that time the Missouri Pacific set up and incorporated Eagle Air Lines, a company that was to provide freight and passenger service in the same general territory as the railroad system. Due to federal restrictions, Eagle Air Lines never got off the ground. It is interesting to note that the MP ultimately operated a rather extensive air freight forwarding system.

From about 1935, the MP began a "system" of rebulding its railroad and total organization. Dieselization began in 1937 and was completed by 1955. A fleet of streamliners was placed in operation beginning in the early 1940s and proved to be very popular trains. Freight service was improved based on customer needs. Physical plant improvements included line changes on the Missouri Division, the installation of Centralized Traffic Control on many subdivisions. Several yards were rebuilt, and a new yard, Settegast, was placed in operation at Houston in 1950. All of this action and more provided the company with the ability to emerge from bankruptcy in 1956. Positive actions continued with a variety of new operations including new yards at Kansas City and North Little Rock in 1959 and 1961, respectively.

The expansion of the MoPac continued in 1967 with the addition of the Chicago & Eastern Illinois Railroad. Part of the agreement required that the C&EI sell its Evansville line to the Louisville & Nashville Railroad, retaining joint ownership and shared use of the Chicago-to-Woodland Junction line. The purchase of the C&EI gave the MP direct service between Chicago and the West and Southwest, bypassing the St. Louis Gateway via Thebes in southern Illinois. Furthermore, the MoPac now had a line to provide direct service between the important rail terminals of Chicago and St. Louis.

The MoPac started a rebuilding program on the C&EI as soon as they gained control in 1967. This involved the construction of new shops, yard and terminal expansions, heavier continuous welded rail, installation of CTC, rebuilding of many bridges and the purchase of new locomotives and freight cars. It took seven years to complete the rebuilding of the C&EI routings.

The Chicago & Eastern Illinois Railroad and the Texas & Pacific Railway were formally merged into the Missouri Pacific Railroad on October 15, 1976. The merger finalized the goals of the MoPac of assembling the component railroads into one 12,000-mile rail system.

In addition to the rail system, the Missouri Pacific Truck Lines operated an 18,000-mile system that provided both the rail and highway services with a great deal of intermodal capabilities. Although most of the MPTL paralleled the MoPac Rail System, a good deal of it provided scheduled freight services to places not reached by the railroad.

By 1980, the MP extended from the shores of Lake Michigan and the Mississippi River in the

"STEER" FOR THE IRON MOUNTAIN ROUTE

TO ARKANSAS, LOUISIANA, TEXAS, MEXICO AND CALIFORNIA

east to the Colorado Rockies, to the Gulf of Mexico and the Rio Grande River. It was an ideal spot geographically because much of the area was growing both in terms of population and industrial expansion. Because of its strategic location, the MP served as a vital link in Canadian-Mexican traffic between Laredo, Texas, and the Canadian railroads reaching Chicago.

During the last years of independent MoPac operation in the 1980s prior to the Union Pacific merger, the MP was separated into four districts known as the Eastern, Western, Southern, and the Texas as follows:

The Eastern District headquarters was located at North Little Rock. The district was in charge of four divisions: The Chicago, Illinois, Arkansas and the Louisiana. In addition, the district was also in charge of the Little Rock and St. Louis Terminals, which held the status of full "divisions" including a full complement of officers.

The Southern District, which included 4,710 miles of single main lines, was restructered into the Southern and Texas Districts on January 1, 1980. The Southern District was headquartered in Houston and included the Kingsville, New Orleans and the DeQuincy Divisions.

The Texas District was headquartered in Dallas and included the Palestine, Rio Grande, Red River, and the Dallas-Fort Worth Divisons.

The Western District, headquartered in

The St. Louis, Iron Mountain and Southern Railroad sought freight and passenger traffic through advertising like this 1884 example. (Missouri Pacific Railroad, PCD Collection)

The MoPac had a continuous program for track and roadbed maintenance and improvement. This 1980 photo was taken looking east near Webster, Missouri, on the Sedalia Subdivision of the Northern Division in CTC territory. (PCD Collection)

Kansas City, consisted of the Northern, Kansas, and Central Divisions plus the Kansas City Terminal Division.

The railroad in the 1980s was quite different from the company in the 1940s. One of the more obvious differences was the vast reduction in passenger services. Even in 2000, Amtrak trains are but a skeleton of the former *Eagle* streamliners let alone the company's passenger service as a whole.

Eagle-level performance "Piggyback" trains were traveling from Chicago to Texas on some of the fastest train schedules in existence at that time. Speaking of freight, chemicals had become the MP's largest traffic item and coal was becoming a larger and larger item in the company's marketing mix. Why was the MoPac doing so well as the company progressed through its last years as an independent railroad organization?

To answer that question in detail would require still another volume or two on the MoPac. This book provides only some of the answers, particularly in the area of freight services. Innovations alone, however, don't do the job. It takes people. People that are willing to work hard, think carefully, and above all co-operate. Morale is a key ingredient. Low morale at any point, whether it is train service personnel, senior or middle management can be damaging with long-lasting affects.

While the railroad was in bankruptcy, the groundwork was laid to improve the company. There were many problems, morale was bad, the corporate structure was complicated, maintenance was not what it should have been, service was often poorly supervised and car supply was erratic. It took the MoPac thirty years to change the company from one of ill health to one of top quality. It meant doing things differently, and spending more than $2 billion for new freight cars and locomotives and the modernization of the entire railroad plant. The company implemented a management training program that was open to employees as well as recent graduates from colleges and universities. This was a quiet program, not much fanfare, but a solid program. In fact so much so, that it can be said that the MP had one of the best management teams of any corporation. The concept of the management team is very important because it means co-operative works between and among departments. It sometimes means sacrifice, and sometimes means looking beyond the profit and loss statement.

This does not mean to imply that the MoPac had reached a stage of perfection in management affairs, but they had gone farther than most corporations. It also meant that the traffic and operting departments worked with each other instead of one dominating the scene.

Another problem with the industry was deferred maintenance. This was not tolerated by the MoPac management, and the company went to great lengths to improve the situation. For example, bridges were rebuilt and there were numerous construction and re-construction projects not only on the track, but signals too.

The MoPac also advertised their freight services and schedules in time tables and ads. This provided an opportunity for shippers to see what the company had to offer.

Car tracing for the shipper's inquiry was another top factor on the MoPac. The TCS System helped bring this about (more about this in Chapter 2).

The examples listed above were mostly behind the scenes. They were not something that the general public had a basic knowledge about. However, the company did have a project that was extremely visable, and became the subject of several newspaper articles, as well as an interesting ad campaign.

In regard to the MP's most visable project, it can be said that few such projects have been undertaken by the North American railroads during the past fifty years. In this case, a branch line had been converted to a second main line across eastern Arkansas. The purpose of the construction project between Jonesboro and McGehee was to relieve the traffic congestion on the main line through Little Rock, and to provide a shorter, faster route between the Gulf Coast and Chicago/St. Louis. In addition it placed the eastern Arkansas towns of Jonesboro, Forrest City, Marianna, Lexa, Elaine, Snow Lake, McGehee and Rohwer on a main line, which in turn greatly enhanced their economic future.

The line had once been a heavily traveled freight route until the late 1950s. Much of the traffic was moved off of the line when new yard facilities were completed at North Little Rock. With the old branch line upgraded to heavy main line status, there was improved service for existing shippers and local industrial developers had a new transportation selling tool for new prospects.

The first through train over the newly rebult line was a 109-car freight bound from St. Louis to Houston on February 15, 1982. Randy Tardy interviewed Tom Hogan, manager of public relations for the MoPac and reported the beginning of thru train services over the line in the February 21, 1982, edition of the *Arkansas Democrat*. According to Hogan, the train hit Paragould at 9:45 a.m. and Wynne at noon, where a red ribbon was broken to officially inaugurate the new line. Initially one train per day was run in each direction, but this was increased to two trains per day each way in a very short time.

Prior to the opening of the route for through train services, MP officials went up and down the Wynne Subdivision putting on a safety program called "Operation Lifesaver." This program stresses safe driving from a highway-rail crossing view point. Sixteen meetings were called, attracting several thousand people. This was but another example of the MP's positive approach to community relations.

The MoPac installed CTC on the line during 1983. Prior to the new CTC operation, trains were operated over the Wynne Subdivision under the direction of Voice Control Block Authority between Jonesboro Junction and North McGehee, otherwise known as VCBA.

The Missouri Pacific also ran ads in the *Wall Street Journal* and a number of industrial development publications. The purpose of the ad campaign was to call attention to the availability of new services, which was made possible by the extensive rebuilding of the trackage.

The company laid 115-pound welded rail, replaced 150,000 ties, enhanced the roadbed with more than 200,000 tons of stone ballast, strengthened bridges, stablized embankments, replaced many switches, improved nearly 200 street crossings and extended and/or upgraded the sidings at Harrisburg, Wynne, Caldwell, Marianna, Elaine, Snow Lake, and Watson.

These examples illustrate only a small part of the rebuilding process of the Missouri Pacific Railroad. The objective was improved service, which in turn meant greater rewards on the profit and loss statement. What did these freight services look like, and what types of equipment were needed to do the job? Roll over to the next chapter for the rest of the story.

Missouri Pacific placed ads like this in the *Wall Street Journal* and other publications in the 1980s. (Missouri Pacific Railroad, PCD Collection)

Prior to the MoPac merging with its subsidiaries, individual reporting marks identified rolling stock ownership. Kansas, Oklahoma & Gulf 251744 (251600-252099), was a 75-ton capacity, 50-foot box car with combination plug and conventional doors. (General American Tank Car Company, PCD Collection)

CHAPTER TWO

Red Ball, Tonnage, and Local Freight

It can be said that the Missouri Pacific Railroad operated one of the most interesting freight transport systems in the world. It was the culmination of a process begun during the Great Depression when the company went into bankruptcy in 1933.

MoPac management realized early in the situation that any overnight solution would only result in long-term failure. It was different thinking to say the least, and looking back over the past decades, it is obvious that it paid off. A series of customer service and operating innovations eventually led to a healthy railroad.

One of the first innovative projects was undertaken in 1938 and 1939. This involved less-than-carload traffic, otherwise known as LCL, and in particular the movement of perishables. Already looking forward to containerization, the company was using "Portakold" portable ice boxes in regular box cars and in road-haul trucks. These portable containers could be moved easily out of a box car and into a truck, along with other LCL traffic without the expensive use of refrigerator cars, which in turn could be operated for carload traffic more efficiently.

Because of the use of this type of equipment, the company was able to reverse the loss of business to non-rail competitors and increase their business 16 percent from 1938 to 1939.

The experience with the Portakold containers

prompted the company to expand their co-ordinated rail-highway systems in both Louisiana and Illinois. Freight from such cities as St. Louis, Kansas City, Memphis, Little Rock, and New Orleans was handled in freight cars to distribution centers, such as Kinder and DeQuincy. There the freight was reloaded into trucks for peddling from station to station. Through such an operation, the company was able to speed up freight shipments as well as cut many hours from the shipper's dock to the receiver.

During the first ten years of the bankruptcy, the MoPac worked on a variety of ways to improve freight service.

While the company was working to improve LCL service with co-ordinated rail-highway transport, the long haul services were also under scrutiny.

A new "Red Ball" freight train from St. Louis to Wichita, Kansas, was placed in service on February 24, 1941. The new train provided first-morning delivery, instead of second for the 481-mile run. The new overnight run to Wichita also served Joplin, Missouri, and Coffeyville, Kansas, and the contiguous territory to those three cities by highway truck distribution.

At the same time, the company revised its freight schedules entirely so that additional overnight service could be provided between St. Louis and Missouri River and Kansas points, as

well as to Memphis and Arkansas points for distances ranging from 280 to 500 miles.

Overnight freight service was also provided from Kansas City for distances of 200 to 300 miles, from Omaha for distances of 200 to 500 miles. Overnight Red Balls from Houston served the entire Lower Rio Grande Valley as well as Austin, San Antonio, Fort Worth, and Dallas, the distances ranging from 250 to 400 miles. Still other services were operated from Memphis, New Orleans, Little Rock, Fort Smith, Saline, and San Antonio to surrounding territories. The new trains brought back the business by the train load. For example, the company reported that the New Orleans-to-Louisiana service brought an increase of over 79 percent.

The transcontinental services were also improved. The St. Louis-Pacific Coast schedules were speeded up so that arrival in Los Angeles and Oakland was on the fourth evening for early fifth-morning delivery; and also provided sixth-morning delivery to Portland, Seattle, and Tacoma. The transcontinental schedules were improved in conjunction with the Southern Pacific, Union Pacific, Rio Grande, and Western Pacific railroads.

World War II literally doubled the MoPac's freight traffic volume and brought about some substantial changes. For years the line from Pueblo to Kansas City and St. Louis was predominantly loaded eastbound. After the war began,

the predominant direction of loads was westbound. Furthermore, the company had to move the war materials as fast as possible. Locomotives were run through intermediate terminals, as were cabooses system-wide. Changing cabooses had become a thing of the past. The freight traffic also had to contend with heavier passenger traffic, such as 68 troop trains in 72 hours between Kansas City and Pueblo. This meant that dispatchers had to be on their toes every single minute to avoid costly delays and maintain safe operations. There was very little margin for error but the company did the job safely.

An important source of revenue for the MoPac was the perishable traffic from the Rio Grande Valley in Texas. There were at one time 39 stations or towns served by the Missouri Pacific from which fruits and vegetables were shipped by rail. Each of these towns in the Rio Grande Valley had one or more loading sheds or packing plants.

After World War II, there was a wide variety of business generated from the various towns. Some would ship as many as 4,000 cars during a shipping season from October through the following June, while other towns would yield only a few cars.

There was, and still is, an enormous diversity of fruits and vegetables grown in the Valley. Grapefruit and oranges head the list of citrus fruits, while tomatoes led the vegetables with cab-

Missouri Pacific Extra 306 North rolls over the Illinois Division behind a new Alco FA-1/FB-1 duo in 1948. This particular train is handling perishables from the Rio Grande Valley. (Missouri Pacific Railroad, PCD Collection)

An eastbound time freight passes Reece, Kansas, on June 21, 1951, behind 2-8-2 No. 1524. Reece is just about midway between Durand and Wichita. (George C. Corey)

but also for the inbound movement of supplies and materials necessary for an agricultural area. The company also handled shiploads of bananas from Mexico and Central America through the port of Brownsville. In addition to the perishable traffic, the MoPac transported substantial amounts of crude petroleum out of the area.

Looking back to the days after World War II, the MoPac operated several special fruit switching runs to handle the perishables. Solid trainloads of empty reefers were operated from St. Louis and North Little Rock into the various centers from which the special traveling switch engines operated. The switch crews would distribute the empties to the loading sheds and packing plants and gather up the loads on the return trip.

Harlingen, located just north of Brownsville on the MoPac's Brownsville Subdivision, was one of the principal concentration points. Harlingen was also an important junction with the Mission Subdivision, which extended westward to Rio Grande City. This part of the MoPac's Kingsville Division was the main trackage serving the fruit and vegetable district. It might be added that much of the trackage in the Valley has been abandoned.

Getting back to the operations during the late 1940s, switch engines were located at Harlingen, San Benito, Raymondville, and Brownsville at the eastern end of the Valley. Except at Raymondville, all of the fruit switching runs were limited to 20 miles in each direction from the home terminal. For example, the San Benito switchers could run to Brownsville and Harlingen and also serve the Rio Hondo branch as well as the Port Isabel line and the line to Rangerville, both of which have been taken out of service.

Other switchers were located at Mercedes, Weslaco, McAllen, and Mission on the east-west Mission Subdivision. These switchers worked the Mission Sub but also did some branch line work as well. Except for a short industrial spur out of Mission, there were no other branch lines off the Mission Sub between Harlingen and Rio Grande City. The switchers at Mission literally worked in four directions on the main and two branches.

The switchers at Raymondville also worked the main line and the branches in both directions to Santa Monica and Hargill. These two branches are also gone with only a wye remaining to remind one of the former lines radiating out of Raymondville. The branch to Hargill, by the way, extended all the way to Mission with two additional branches that also joined the Mission Sub at Weslaco and San Juan.

bage, carrots, and potatoes following. This meant a relatively complicated operating procedure for the MoPac until the advent of mechanical refrigerator cars and the distribution of fruits and vegetables in frozen packages for the supermarket shelves.

These two developments changed the operations in the Rio Grande Valley completely to one of a year-round operation instead of the massive rush during October through June.

Historically, the "big rush" was very fascinating. The rail mileage in the Valley not only served for the outbound movement of the perishables,

The switchers gathered the loads and they were run to both Harlingen and Raymondville. Solid perishable trains were assembled at Harlingen into 85 to 100 car trains and moved northward. The trains often had cars added at Raymondville. The Brownsville Sub was the main line to Houston, and it paralleled the Gulf Coast along a flat coastal plain. The maximum grade along the entire line is not more than 0.2 percent. However, heavier trains could not be handled because of the prevailing high winds that blow in from the Gulf during the shipping season. These winds, often at gale force, could slow down trains.

No attempt was made at classifying the trains at either Harlingen or Raymondville. Diversion orders would render any classification nearly useless, and it would cut substantially into the speed the cars required en route to the market areas.

The 1945 schedule called for a 5:30 a.m. departure from Harlingen and arrival at Houston at 11:30 p.m. It was rather a slow schedule for the 346-mile run. Before trucks began to make substantial inroads into the perishable business, as many as seven solid trains would be dispatched northward from Harlingen in a 24-hour period. One or two additional trains would also operate out of Raymondville if the trains out of Harlingen were unable to add cars because of being at maximum tonnage.

From Houston the solid trains rolled northward and were iced as required along the way. One of the more important icing stations was Dupo, Illinois, an important St. Louis-area yard located on the Illinois Division 13 miles south of St. Louis. Most trains were iced at Dupo. The 2,284-foot-long dock could service cars on both sides of the dock. During the height of the season as many as 6,000 cars per month would be switched to and from the mammoth facility. This meant 200 cars per day, which in turn meant a 24-hour around-the-clock operation.

The icing stations were owned by the American Refrigerator Transit Company, a sub-

While diesel switch engines work at the Little Rock depot, a tank train of oil threads its way past in 1943. Running as Extra 1515 North, the train will run to Poplar Bluff. Tank trains were quite common on the railroads during World War II, carrying petroleum from the oil fields to refineries, and various oil and fuel products from the refineries to both the east and west coasts for the war effort when shipping by coastal tankers was threatened by U-boats. (Missouri Pacific Railroad, PCD Collection)

sidiary of the Missouri Pacific and Wabash Railroads. This company also provided the refrigerator cars for the perishable rush. After the Wabash became part of the Norfolk & Western in 1964, the N&W and MoPac jointly owned ART. Equipment carried the insignias of each road. ART was eventually owned soley by the MP.

After World War II, the MoPac turned its attention to a variety of improvement programs for their freight services. In December 1946 some of the first major steps were taken. During that month, train 67, which handled transcontinental traffic from St. Louis via southwestern connections, was divided into three sections and classified according to destination and routing. It provided a much faster service for southwestern traffic.

Six months later, in April 1947, a new train was added to the schedule departing East St. Louis at 3:00 a.m. to handle freight received too late for the three sections of train 67. The new train caught up with 67 at El Paso.

April 1947 also saw a new Red Ball morning high speed freight established from Kansas City to Fort Worth in connection with the Kansas, Oklahoma & Gulf, and the Texas & Pacific Railroads. This new schedule provided a brand-new double-daily fast freight schedule in both directions on this route.

Other improvements came at the same time. Train 61, a Red Ball transcontinental run from St. Louis to Pueblo, Colorado, began operating without stopping for picking up, setting out or classification work at Kansas City. A new train was established to handle the Kansas City traffic formerly handled by 61.

The company began a series of experiments to by-pass intermediate terminals and reduce overall transit time. Interestingly, there had been a trend shortly after World War II to speed up trains over the road, only to have them sit for additional hours in yards and terminals. The Missouri Pacific was aware of this fact, and made special arrangements for time precious cargo and merchandise to be placed at the receivers' and freight house sidings within one hour of the train's arrival. In most cases, this meant that the company was required to add switch crews to handle the arrangements. The cost of the crews was more than offset by the improvement in car- days (cars were unloaded faster and ready for the next load quicker), and the retention and addition of new business. It was another step toward the Missouri Pacific's goal of improving its service as well as its financial health.

The MoPac continued its postwar improvement program with not only new and faster train schedules, but also with new and improved facilities. In 1950 the company constructed a new yard at Houston for use by subsidiaries International-Great Northern and the Gulf Coast Lines. The new yard, named Settegast, was originally constructed as a flat-type yard with running tracks through the center and classification tracks on each side. The yard included 17 tracks for handling perishables and classification work with a maximum capacity for each track ranging from 60 to 147 cars. An icing dock was also constructed with space for 32 cars on each side of the facility.

The new yard permitted freight trains to bypass the congested parts of Houston and abandon the company's Percival and Congress Avenue Yards. A new LCL freight house was also constructed as part of the new complex. The entire yard was built with possible expansion in mind.

The year 1950 also saw the expansion of the company's new coordinated rail-truck services designed to ensure first-morning delivery of merchandise freight between St. Louis, Poplar Bluff, Charleston, and Jefferson City. The new services were placed on a daily except Saturday, Sunday, and holiday basis.

The Mopac, along with other railroads, was also concerned about car handling and routing. The step taken in 1951 with car handling by radio communications in the Kaw Yard at Kansas City was a humble beginning. However, with the newly installed radio in switch engine cabs, the yard masters were able to direct yard crews far faster and more efficiently than was previously possible. Again the savings in car-days was well worth the investment.

A westbound "Red Ball" freight en route from Kansas City to Wichita departs the junction point of Durand, Kansas, on June 21, 1951, with Mountain type MT-75 No. 5335 leading and Consolidation No. 43 pushing behind the caboose. The Mountain has been bumped from passenger service to fast freights on some of the secondary main lines, such as the route to Wichita. (George C. Corey)

(above) This publicity view symbolized a new generation of freight locomotives on the MoPac. (TLC Collection)

(left) This September 1958 freight, powered by a combination of two FTs and two GP7s, has stopped at the yard at Van Buren, Arkansas, on the route between Little Rock and Kansas City. (Louis A. Marre; Collection of W. S. Kuba)

Missouri Pacific's
Alco FA-1 and FB-1
road freight diesels
were delivered in
this stylish blue and
gray scheme,
accented by the red
"buzz saw" emblem
on the nose. (TLC
Collection)

Another interesting innovation during the early 1950s was the *Eagle Merchandise Service*. This service was basically an outgrowth of services found on other railroads, such as the New York Central's *Pacemaker* services. However, there was one big difference. The MoPac continued to maintain a quality control of its services as well as add coordinated rail-highway services and options. The company painted a series of box cars in its blue and gray streamliner colors and invested in small containers, known as "speedboxes," that could easily be used in either freight cars or trucks. The speedboxes improved service for the customer as well as improved handling at freight houses. Consequently, the MoPac continued in the LCL business especially with a greater role in truck services as the company approached 1980.

A new double hump yard was built in Kansas City during the period 1956-1959. Kansas City was one of the most important terminals of the MoPac. The new yard permitted switching and classification of trains in both directions and reduced freight car handling time by almost 12 hours. The new yard was named Neff Yard in honor of the road's president, Paul J. Neff.

Neff Yard was the company's first electronic yard, and it paved the way for a new yard at North Little Rock, which was completed in 1961. The North Little Rock yard was also on an important main line and served as the principal classification point between St. Louis and Texas points.

During the 1960s, the company tried a variety of systems to improve freight services. One

(above) For years, MoPac published condensed freight train schedules in its public passenger timetables. This edition appeared in December 1955. (TLC Collection)

(bottom) *Eagle Merchandise Service* provided priority handling over the road and in freight terminals. (Missouri Pacific, PCD Collection)

(above) Train 75 is preparing to depart St. Louis for Kansas City and Omaha in this 1961 view. The train will take nearly 11 hours to reach Kansas City, where extensive classification work will be done. (W. S. Kuba)

(below) Extra 528 West approaches Pacific, Missouri with a mixture of freight including coal, automobiles, general freight and empty refrigerator cars. The date is April 11, 1964, and the train is en route from St. Louis to Kansas City. (W. S. Kuba)

(bottom) In this April 1964 photo, Extra 513 East is struggling uphill past the Kirkwood, Mo., depot (to the right of the photo) with only a little more than 13 miles to go before terminating in the St. Louis yards. (W. S. Kuba)

system was the run-through New York Central-MoPac trains between Indianapolis and Little Rock. Locomotives and cabooses were pooled by both roads, and trains stopped only to change crews. This arrangement was not as successful as the MoPac would have liked it to be.

Another innovation was the "train-a-day" concept set up with Continental Grain Company during the late 1960s. This train was an effort to provide a fast, efficient movement of export corn from Southern Illinois to the port of New Orleans. In this case, Continental Grain Company paid a premium for the service, but the speed was necessary for the export movement. In fact, things went so well that Continental reported that the corn spent less than 48 hours in transit between East St. Louis and New Orleans and was delivered to Europe just 15 days later. The purpose of the train-a-day was to reduce intermediate switching. Another problem solved was the corn drying requirements prior to shipping. With the train-a-day, the company was always able to have room for the next batch of corn. It was always moving out. The system has been used for other grain handling moves since then.

In 1967, the MoPac began a program of rebuilding cabooses, labeling the upgraded cars, "Nice enough to make a man leave home." The cars were rebuilt at the Sedalia, Missouri, shops, and featured all-weather sliding metal windows and doors, a 200-gallon stainless steel water tank and sanitary water cooler, Caban oil heaters instead of the old coal stoves, stainless steel lavatory and flush-type toilets, three steel ice boxes and an all-steel cupola. Other additions included a new radio set, more exterior marker lights and a spotlight for track observation and back-up movements. A cushion underframe for greater safety and crew comfort was also added.

Each rebuilt caboose had 1,500 feet of electric wire, more than three times that in the old cars. Window areas were reduced because of the improved and expanded interior lighting. Lever controls made the step-over seats in the cupola face either direction with ease. Protective padding was also added to both ends of the cupola to protect the crew in case of sudden stops. The cars were painted in the traditional red caboose color scheme. (See Chapter 10 for a photo survey of caboose equipment.)

In addition to the new freight schedules, train-a-day concepts, coordinated rail-highway services and a whole host of other achievements, the Missouri Pacific made great strides in car control. Efficient freight car control has long been one of the most sought-after goals of the railroad industry, and the MoPac was definitely a leader and pioneer with its new computer applications.

THE TRANSPORTATION CONTROL SYSTEM

The Missouri Pacific devised a freight car control system that provided a means for dependable freight shipments. The system utilized a computer system as a powerful tool for providing up-to-date information for effective decision making by operating department personnel. The company developed the system over a period of ten years, and it became known as the Transportation Control System, or TCS.

TCS provided continuous information for decision making regarding individual car movements, generating switching instructions, handle empty car orders, produce bills of lading and way-bills, compute freight rates and produce current and predicted status reports on freight cars, yards and trains. The system monitored the quality of the entire transportation operation. This indeed was quite a task for on any given day in the early to the mid-1980s prior to the UP merger, the MoPac was handling over 95,000 freight cars over a 12,000-mile system in more than 800 trains. Add to this volume 124 stations and terminals with over 100,000 customer facilities and one begins to get an idea of the complexities of freight car control and utilization as well as quality control freight service. Had it not been for the development of the computer, the MoPac – or any other railroad for that matter – would not have been able to develop such a system. In actuality, there were several systems for TCS, all of which were interdependent.

One of the TCS systems was Car Scheduling. This system was developed not only as a management tool for the operating department decision makers, but also as a service for shippers. Car Scheduling included an operating plan, car shipment data, availability of a car for movement and the individual trip plan for the freight car itself.

The operating plan was the identification of all train schedules and switch engine assignments including blocking requirements. This aspect defined the kind of service a train handled and how the train picked up and set out cars during a run over a given route. The plan identified yard operating standards in terms of handling time for cars processed through the yard to outbound trains and switch engine moves.

The second element was the car shipment data. In this case, the car shipment data generated

Missouri Pacific's rapidly expanding fleet of specialized cars . . . 3,217 new ones in just the past two years . . . pampers your shipments with kid glove service. No matter how unusual your freight, how big or how bulky . . . if you're shipping it our way, we think we've got the car to get it there. Call your nearest Missouri Pacific or Texas & Pacific Freight Representative.

These 1963 trade ads promoted Missouri Pacific's diverse and growing freight car fleet and competitive service to points in California. (Kevin Holland Collection)

17

(above) As this 1963 trade ad shows, MoPac was serious about meeting truck competition–in this case for frozen food traffic. (Kevin Holland Collection)

(right) The MoPac relied on IBM's 370 computer system for its high quality car tracing and scheduling system. (Missouri Pacific Railroad, PCD Collection)

the waybill with such information as shipper, destination, consignee, origin, commodity description, weight, freight charges, routing, special handling instructions, and specific car type including weight, length, and other characteristics. This waybill information was entered into the system either through "Autobill" computer terminal input at one of the various customer service centers or automatically from the customer's own computer through "CoMPuBill."

The third component in car scheduling was the availability for movement reporting to TCS. This portion of TCS allowed identification and time a car is available for movement.

The waybill information and the availability for movement information was combined with the operating plan in terms of yard and train schedules to generate an individualized trip plan for a car from origin to destination on the MoPac. The origin could be a shipper's dock or a receipt from another railroad, while destination could be a receiver's dock or delivery to another carrier.

An important part of the car scheduling was that the objectives for each car on the railroad had to be communicated to the people who were responsible for moving or handling the cars, including yard switchman, yardmasters, or dispatchers. This meant that the trip plan had to be printed on switch lists to provide the knowledge to which tracks cars were to be switched. Trains, transfer, and/or traveling switch engine crews received work orders which specified the pickup and/or placement for individual cars.

TCS provided trip plans for all cars on the MoPac as well as the next scheduled move for cars located at various yards or in trains already. The next scheduled move meant the train and the block within the train in which a car was to move. In other words, the trip plan for individual cars was translated into individual yard objectives, handling requirements and train consists.

Management of freight car distribution was another facet of computer technology on the Missouri Pacific. Car distribution functions had been consolidated at the St. Louis headquarters since 1968.

All car control and empty car ordering was fully automated and centralized through car distribution. Customers could order cars by placing a car order with a MP clerk at a Customer Service Center. The clerk immediately transmitted the order to the computer system's central data base. The customer's request(s) were then identified on a real-time basis. The orders were met through a supply of freight cars on a system wide basis. The

System then generated trip plans and work orders so that operating crews could move the appropriate car(s) from one point to another on the MoPac System.

As the empty car moved to the shipper, spotting instructions went to the yardmaster responsible for the placement of the car(s) at the industrial siding for loading. Once a car had been spotted, feed back messages completed the transaction involving the placement of the empty car. The car distribution system allowed the MoPac to distribute the supply of empty cars efficiently as well as to assign cars to specific orders in an equitable manner.

The overall Transportation Control System had a direct effect upon yard operations. With up-to-date and advance information, yardmasters could plan the handling of inbound cars to outbound movements with greater efficiency. This substantially improved the overall speed of cars moving through the loaded/empty cycle. This in turn had a positive affect upon locomotive utilization. It was the goal of the MP to have at least 95 percent of their motive power fleet available for service at any given time.

The company was also able to use the data generated from TCS for marketing and traffic research. Consequently, the benefits were much

It is October 17, 1964, and train 80 is approaching the former Gulf, Mobile & Ohio crossing near Bixby, Illinois. The train is heading toward Dupo Yard with a mixed consist of freight from Louisiana, Arkansas, and Memphis, Tennessee. At the time this photograph was taken, the MP still identified their freight trains with numbers. In many instances, such trains operated as Second Class schedules in the various division timetables. (W. S. Kuba)

The Missouri Pacific pooled motive power with the service-conscious New York Central in the mid-1960s, by which time MoPac's attractive blue-and-gray paint had given way to more economical solid blue. This photo shows Extra NYC 2372 South moving through Poplar Bluff on its fast run from Indianapolis to North Little Rock. (Missouri Pacific Railroad, PCD Collection)

During the 1970s, the MoPac operated a special chemical train from Texas to Chicago. The train was established to speed chemical products from the Texas Gulf Coast for connections and destinations in both the St. Louis and Chicago areas. This edition was Extra 3234 North, passing a hotbox detector on the Chicago Subdivision of the Illinois Division in 1978. By the early 1980s, the MP no longer operated the chemical train as such because this important traffic moved north on other high-priority trains. (Missouri Pacific Railroad, PCD Collection)

wider than simply improved customer service, freight car control and utilization. Although the latter certainly would have been more than enough.

The system provided the company with still other benefits that cannot be measured in terms of the profit and loss statement. For example, they were able to secure new business, and come up with new ideas for securing hard to get traffic. Toys were strictly a truck item for years. With the MoPac's coordinated rail services, and the use of 85-foot box cars, toy traffic from California became a profitable item. Many companies began shipping via MoPac that otherwise would not have considered rail at all.

NEW TRAFFIC, NEW TRAINS

The new business meant many new trains. In the 1980s, there were more fast freight trains scheduled out of Chicago over the former C&EI than ever before. One fast freight was scheduled for just 28 hours between Chicago and Dallas.

The MP was an important link in transcontinental traffic moving from the south to the west. The MP served as a bridge route for transcontinental movements between the Southern and Seaboard (now Norfolk Southern and CSX) at Memphis and the Union Pacific at Kansas City.

Other transcontinental traffic, and also traffic from the Southwest, was handled in run-through

trains operated through the St. Louis Gateway in conjunction with the Norfolk & Western and the Baltimore & Ohio. Solid trains were also blocked for Conrail at North Little Rock and Kansas City.

MP freights ultimately were not numbered to the same extent that they once were. In the 1980s, letters indicated symbol freights and consisted of either two or three letter designations. Typically, a two-letter designation meant the "Origin-Destination" of a particular freight train, such as CF for Chicago-Fort Worth, or DH for Dupo-Houston and so on.

A third letter could mean several things, such as indicating more than one train scheduled in the same direction between a particular origin-destination set. In this case, a third letter was used to differentiate between two trains. It could be an arbitrary letter assignment, or a more specific letter designating a connection at either the origin or destination. For example, prior to the L&N and SCL merger into the Seaboard System Railroad, the L&N was designated "N" as a third letter for North Little Rock-Memphis trains, ie., LMN. The company also used three letters to designate route as well as origin-destination. For example, the CSP or PSC indicated Chicago-Pueblo or Pueblo-Chicago via St. Louis, respectively.

By 1983 all freight trains operated as extras. In other words, although the trains were run by a

(above and left) One can usually tell a local freight by the fact that it is shorter and normally powered by only one diesel unit. Such is the case with Extra 2042 North near Paola on the Kansas City Subdivision of the Kansas Division. The local is performing work between Osawatomie and Kansas City on a very bright and warm June 5, 1980. These overhead photos also illustrate the excellent quality of the MoPac trackage. (Dennis Roos)

(below) Because of its precision scheduling, train CSP was frequently called upon to handle MoPac business cars running to Kansas City or other points west. This photo shows CSP running as Extra 3306 West passing the famous Kirkwood, Missouri, depot on the evening of May 5, 1980. CSP's eastbound running mate was PSC for Pueblo-St. Louis-Chicago, an equally important train. (Thomas A. Dorin)

(above) Extra 2014 West, made up of auto-parts cars from Grand Trunk Western, Penn Central, Chesapeake & Ohio, and Detroit, Toledo & Ironton, moves through the cut near Eureka, Missouri, behind GP38s on the Northern Division's Sedalia Subdivision on May 25, 1975. (W. S. Kuba)

(opposite, top) One can often tell a great deal about a freight train by observing its motive power and consist. In this case, the motive power is a dead give away for train UMS, which operated from the Union Pacific at North Platte to the Southern Railway at Memphis via the MoPac. This photo shows the bridge-traffic train ready to depart Bailey Yard at North Platte with a mixture of UP, Southern, and MoPac power. The westbound symbol for this service was SMU. (Missouri Pacific Railroad, PCD Collection)

(opposite, bottom) During the 1980s the MoPac operated a vast network of scheduled freight trains throughout its system. Train CSP, shown here, was a top-priority run operating from Chicago to Pueblo via St. Louis. The train was blocked for St. Louis out of Chicago and reblocked at Lesperance Street Yard in St. Louis for Pueblo and Leeds, Missouri. After the train was reblocked in St. Louis with cars received from eastern rail carriers, it departed for Colorado. The train made one set out at Leeds and ran straight through to Pueblo. At that point, train CSP connected with Rio Grande's train 71 for California destinations on the Western Pacific.

This photo shows train CSP near Lindsborg, Kansas, on the Council Grove Subdivision of the Kansas Division in automatic block signal territory. At the time the photo was taken in 1979, train CSP operated as an "extra." In 1980, the train was given higher priority with a "First Class" timetable schedule, and operated as train 69 from St. Louis to Pueblo. The inclusion of the Union Pacific unit was part of the motive power pool between the UP and MP at that time. (Missouri Pacific Railroad, PCD Collection)

time schedule, they did not have timetable authority. Scheduling of freight trains was far more flexible with this type of operating philosophy. If a train had to be re-routed, or its schedule changed for whatever reason, it did not have an affect upon the timetable.

During the 1970s and parts of the 1980s, the MP from time to time did operate certain freight trains as "First Class" trains with timetable authority. There were certain advantages of doing this because it gave the train complete right over all other trains, except other first class trains. This is the reason passenger trains were run as first class trains in the operating timetables. In fact, in the Missouri Pacific Railroad Company Timetable No. 1 of April 28, 1985, the only first class trains were Amtrak passenger trains. Also, this timetable displayed the Union Pacific shield instead of the MoPac eagle.

The Missouri Pacific Railroad constantly endeavored to change freight schedules to improve services and to satisfy the needs of the wide variety of shippers throughout its territory. With the merging of the Missouri Pacific operations into the Union Pacific System, the company continued this approach with "new single system services" on the UP/MP.

Here are a few examples that took place during the 1980s. One of the first joint MP-UP trains was placed in service between Houston and North Platte, Nebraska. This new train, which began operations on February 4, 1983, was designated HKB, which stood for Houston-Kansas City-Baily Yard at North Platte. When the train transferred from the MP to the UP at Kansas City, it stopped only to make a set out and a pick up of pre-selected groups of cars. Crews were changed at Neff Yard and as soon as this was completed, the train moved west over the UP without further switching. The HKB, which operated via Fort Worth, was a combination piggyback and general freight train.

March 28, 1983, saw the beginning of still another fast train services, this time between St. Louis and Kansas City on the MP with through operations beyond to North Platte and connections with still other trains west. An eastbound service also went into effect. The trains, designated SBZ and BSZ, also offered overnight piggyback services between Kansas City and St. Louis in both directions. The symbols stood for St. Louis, Baily Yard with the third letter Z indicating expedited or fast train.

The service allowed a shipper to deliver a trailer to MP's Sarpy Yard in St. Louis as late as

(right) Symbol freight KSA was southbound at San Antonio on April 13, 1980, with one of MoPac's new cabooses bringing up the rear. (S. K. Bolton, Jr.)

(middle) Following KSA into San Antonio was another freight led by MoPac's 6050 and 3220. The first car of the train was loaded with oil well equipment. San Antonio is an important division point for the MoPac and was the southern end of the Austin Subdivison of the Palestine Division. (S. K. Bolton, Jr.)

(bottom) This photo portrays train 171 arriving in Omaha, Nebraska from Kansas City on September 10, 1972. This particular freight train handled freight for the Burlington Northern and the Chicago & North Western Railway connections. Train 171 itself was made up in Kansas City and served as a connection for a wide number of trains including 73, 75, and 77 from St. Louis. Trains 171 and 172 were later replaced by symbol freights KO and OK respectively between Kansas City and Omaha. (W. S. Kuba)

(left) Train KFY departs Neff Yard as Extra 3124 West en route from Kansas City to Fort Worth with 58 cars on a snow-less Christmas Day in 1979. This particular symbol freight stopped at Osawatomie, Durand, Coffeyville, Muskogee, and Denison during its run to Fort Worth. (Dennis Roos)

(below) During April 1980 the MoPac was leasing a substantial amount of motive power from other railroads, including Conrail and Grand Trunk Western. It was not uncommon to find such units together, as on this northbound freight at San Antonio on April 20. (S. K. Bolton, Jr.)

6:00 p.m. for loading onto the westbound SBZ, scheduled to depart at 8:00 p.m. The trailer would arrive in Kansas City by 3:00 a.m., and if it was destined for Kansas City, it would be available for pick up at 6:00 a.m. under the schedule originally designed for the train.

Trailers bound for points west of Kansas City continued to North Platte via the UP, and were scheduled to arrive there by 2:00 p.m. The first 679 miles of a trailer's transcontinental journey were completed in 18 hours.

At North Platte, the traffic connected with a fleet of Union Pacific trains with destinations including Salt Lake City, Los Angeles, Oakland, Seattle, and Denver. With the new westbound SBZ, the UP and MP could move intermodal traffic from St. Louis to Los Angeles in 54 hours, to Denver in 34 hours, Salt Lake City in 35-1/2 hours, Oakland in 66 hours, and to Portland in 59 hours.

The eastbound BSZ was also scheduled in such a way that shippers could take advantage of overnight, everynight services from Kansas City to St. Louis. Trailers could be delivered to Kansas City by 6:00 p.m. and be ready for pick up in St. Louis by 6:00 a.m. the next morning.

An MP-UP new release on May 12, 1983, made reference to Duke Ellington's jazz tune urging a person to take the "A" train, but proposed the idea that Idaho potatoes were finding that the Boise to Bourbon Street trip was much quicker on a "Z" train. In this case, the two railroads announced that two new trains went into service between New Orleans and Kansas City that cut transit time from the Pacific Northwest by three days.

The two new trains were designated KNZ and NKZ, meaning Kansas City to New Orleans and New Orleans to Kansas City respec-

tively. The reader will recall that the "Z" stands for expedited train service. The Union Pacific made direct connections in Kansas City with trains KNZ and NKZ in both directions. Running time for symbol freights KNZ and NKZ was improved even more when the MP completed extensive track rehabilitation work in Arkansas' White River country.

One of the most dramatic train schedule and service improvements in 1983 was the three-railroad operation of the new symbol freights BSN and NSB. These trains operated between Nashville, Tennessee and Baily Yard at

North Platte. The Seaboard handled the service between East St. Louis and Nashville via Evansville, Indiana; the MoPac between East St. Louis and Kansas City, and the UP between that point and Bailey Yard.

With the new BSN and NSB symbol freights, the UP-MP-Seaboard combination cut delivery time between the Pacific Northwest and the Southeastern states by one full day. In order to expedite the service, cars en route to the Southeast were pre-blocked at the UP's Bailey Yard into blocks destined for major rail centers on the

Seaboard System in the Carolinas, Tennessee, Kentucky, Georgia, and Florida.

This brings part of the MoPac freight history up to nearly 1985 when the Union Pacific began to make substantial changes in the freight service operations. A separate book would be required to fully describe the changes and freight service operations through the mega-merger era from the mid-1980s through the turn of the century. The table on page 31 lists the MP freight train symbols in the early 1980s prior to full inclusion into the new Union Pacific System.

(right) The MoPac's Chicago terminal comprised several yards for both freight and piggyback traffic. Yard Center was the former C&EI yard just south of Chicago. L&N (now CSX) trains also arrived and departed from this facility. The yard marked the south end of the Chicago & Western Indiana Railroad, over whose tracks MoPac trains ran into and out of Chicago. Indiana Harbor Belt and, at one time, Grand Trunk Western also visited this yard. This photo was taken from the yard tower at the south end of Yard Center. MP15 No. 1532 has just completed classifying a cut of cars destined for symbol freight CSK to St. Louis and Kansas City.

(right) This bird's-eye view of the 1532 was taken from the yard tower at the south end of Yard Center. (Both, PCD Collection)

(left) Switchers were used extensively system-wide for not only yard switching, but also for transfers, pick ups, and deliveries. The 1126 is shown here serving the grain elevators at Omaha in September 1970. (W. S. Kuba)

(middle and bottom) MoPac also operated Geeps of many different types for both yard switching and transfer runs. In this case, No. 1744 is meeting TRRA's No. 1509 near the Cotton Belt's Yard in East St. Louis. The objective of the 1744's crew is to pick up a transfer and bring it back to the MoPac's Dupo Yard, as can be seen in the bottom photo. These two views were taken on May 24, 1975. (Both, W. S. Kuba)

(right) A rather unusual train was Extra 6028 South at San Antonio on April 20, 1980. The entire consist of the train was the now-famous yellow Railbox cars. This train would have made a great publicity shot for both the MoPac and Railbox. (S. K. Bolton, Jr.)

(middle) A Work Extra in action arrives at Dupo yard with eight cars including the wrecker. The EMD switcher is more than ample power for the train. The first car in the train is a former 10-section sleeper converted to work train service. (W. S. Kuba)

(bottom) The end of the freight train appropriately enough was the caboose! Although this is the end of the freight train services chapter, MoPac freight service continued to roll under Union Pacific. In this 1979 view, train 70, departs Osawatomie en route from Pueblo to Kansas City. (Dennis Roos)

MISSOURI PACIFIC FREIGHT TRAIN SYMBOLS

In effect October 1983

Symbol	Origin	Destination
BHZ	North Platte (UP)	Houston
BKG	Kansas City	A&S at St. Louis
BSN	Kansas City	Nashville via St. Louis and the Seaboard System
BSZ	Kansas City	Nashville
CFZ	Chicago	Fort Worth
CHZ	Chicago	Houston
CKZ	Chicago	Kansas City
CL	Chicago	North Little Rock
CS	Chicago	St. Louis
CSP	St. Louis	Pueblo
DEZ	Fort Worth	El Paso
DFZ	Dupo	Fort Worth
DH	A&S (Dupo)	Houston
DMZ	A&S	Laredo to Mexico via NdeM
EFZ	El Paso	Fort Worth
FCZ	Fort Worth	Chicago
FH	Fort Worth	Houston
FIN	Fort Worth	Indianapolis
FK	Fort Worth	Kansas City
FL	Fort Worth	North Little Rock
FLY	Fort Worth	North Little Rock
FM	Fort Worth	Memphis
FNZ	Fort Worth	New Orleans
FSA	Fort Worth	San Antonio
FSW	Fort Worth	Sweetwater
HC	Houston	Chicago
HDC	Houston	Dupo
HF	Houston	Fort Worth
HKB	Houston	North Platte (UP)
HL	Houston	North Little Rock
HNS	Houston	New Orleans (to Southern)
HPI	Houston	Indianapolis
HSA	Houston	San Antonio
INF	Indianapolis	Fort Worth
INH	Indianapolis	Houston
KC	Kansas City	Chicago
KF	Kansas City	Fort Worth
KG	Kansas City	St. Louis (to A&S)
KL	Kansas City	North Little Rock
KNZ	Kansas City	New Orleans (Avondale)
KS	Kansas City	St. Louis
LCB	North Little Rock	Chicago (to BRC)
LCT	North Little Rock	Chicago
LG	North Little Rock	St. Louis (to A&S)
LH	North Little Rock	Houston
LK	North Little Rock	Kansas City
LM	North Little Rock	Memphis
LMN	North Little Rock	Memphis (to Seaboard)
MF	Memphis	Fort Worth
MLN	Memphis	North Little Rock
MLS	Memphis	North Little Rock
NF	New Orleans	Fort Worth
NG	New Orleans	St. Louis (to A&S)
NHS	New Orleans	Houston (from Southern)
NKZ	New Orleans	Kansas City
NSB	St. Louis	Kansas City (from Nashville to North Platte)
PK	Pueblo	Kansas City
SAF	San Antonio	Fort Worth
SAH	San Antonio	Houston
SAL	San Antonio	North Little Rock
SBZ	St. Louis	Kansas City (to N. Platte)
SC	St. Louis	Chicago (to BRC)
SK	St. Louis	Kansas City (Leeds)
SKY	St. Louis	Kansas City
SMU	Memphis	Kansas City (to N. Platte)
SWF	Sweetwater	Fort Worth
TAZ	Chicago	Fort Worth
UMS	North Platte (UP)	Memphis (to Seaboard)
YNL	Alexandria	New Orleans

Some MoPac freight trains continued to carry numbers as follows:

	Origin	Destination
106	North Little Rock	Coffeyville
107	Coffeyville	North Little Rock
110	Wichita	Durand, Kansas
111	Durand	Wichita
122	Fort Worth	Shreveport
123	Shreveport	Fort Worth
140	Houston	Texarkana
141	Texarkana	Houston
148	Laredo	San Antonio
150	North Little Rock	St. Louis
151	St. Louis	North Little Rock
152	Shreveport	North Little Rock
153	North Little Rock	Shreveport
156	North Little Rock	Chicago
170	Kansas City	Omaha
171	Omaha	Kansas City
180	Houston	Addis, Louisiana
181	Addis	Houston
182	Houston	Livonia, Louisiana
183	De Quincy, La.	Houston
185	Livonia	De Quincy
190	Corpus Christi	San Antonio
191	San Antonio	Corpus Christi
192	Harlingen	Kingsville
193	Houston	Harlingen
194	Kingsville	Houston
195	Houston	Bloomington
196	Vanderbilt	Houston
197	Houston	Angleton, Texas
198	Angleton	Houston
199	Avondale	Houston

The Missouri Pacific Railroad changed trains and train symbols as often as was necessary to reflect traffic levels and customer requirements. Consequently some symbols were dropped and new ones created on a month to month basis. This list provides a snapshot of the late 1983 symbols.

The use of the third letter in the symbol system generally (but not always) reflected different trains between the same origins and destinations. The use of the letter "Z" indicated piggyback trains.

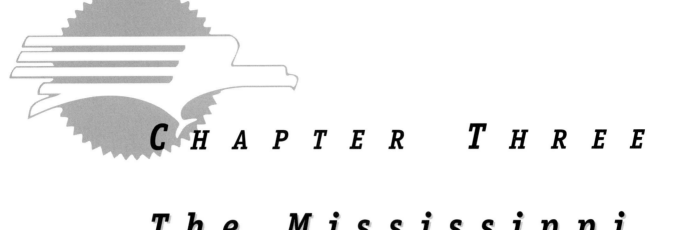

CHAPTER THREE

The Mississippi Transfer and Coal

The Missouri Pacific was not widely known as a coal hauler. Through its own branch lines or those of the Missouri-Illinois Railroad, however, the company served the Southern Illinois coal country. Although not to the same extent as the Chicago & North Western or the Burlington in the same area, the MoPac did handle a sizeable amount of traffic in the area. Later, after the C&EI merger, the MoPac began serving a wider area in Southern Illinois.

Traditionally, the MoPac served the coal mines at such cities as Bush, Pinckneyville, and Sparta areas. These branch lines extended in a northeast-southwest direction and joined the Thebes-East St. Louis (Dupo) line at Gorham, Chester, and Flinton.

Much of the coal shipped over the MP did not travel by rail routings to destination. Most of it moved to a coal transfer facility at Ford, Illinois, for movement on the Mississippi River barge systems both up and down river. The Ford Transfer facility was most interesting. It was the focal point for the MP coal operations for many years, and was one of the few innovative practices involving two different modes of transport operated over a long period of time.

The transfer facility at Ford (also known as Kirk's Landing) is on the east bank of the river some 70 miles south of St. Louis. The objective of building the facility in the early 1950s was to pro-

vide mine operators access to new and different market outlets for their products. From the water transfer point, the coal moved in barge tows to various destinations up and down the river as well as its northern and southern tributaries.

The MoPac built the facility in the Chester area in order to bring it as close as possible to the mines in order to avoid the long terminal delay in handling coal trains through the St. Louis area. Another reason for this location was to enable the company to control the car supply by handling its own cars from mine to transfer and back to the mines. A further advantage was that the MP could select the type of coal car which was best for the work performed. These two reasons had the effect of increasing the number of hopper cars available.

At the Mississippi River transfer, the cars were unloaded into a hopper at a tipple. There were two tracks through the tipple, each of which extended north and south. Cars moved into and out of the tipple by gravity and their speed was controlled by hand brakes.

Access to the tipple was by a running track which paralleled the main line of the Chester Subdivisoin of the Illinois Division, and by a lead track to the north of the two tracks leading into the tipple. Loaded cars were placed on these tipple tracks from the north end of the facility and empties were removed from the south. Coal trains from the Franklin and Williamson County mines

moved from south to north on the Illinois Division, while trains from the Pinckneyville and Sparta areas moved from north to south. Mines in the Sparta area shipping through the Ford intermodal transfer were located on the former Missouri-Illinois Railroad, which was part of the MoPac System.

Once the coal was unloaded in the tipple, it moved by conveyor belt system to riverside, where it was loaded directly into waiting barges.

During the dozen or so years after the Ford facility was built and placed into operation, the MP's coal business was relatively stable and the company really did not concern itself with expansion programs for such traffic. This began to change, however, after the mid-1960s.

The process actually began before 1966 with the construction of a new coal rail-to-water facility at Kellogg, Illinois, about 50 miles south of St. Louis. The new dock was built only a few hundred yards from the old Missouri-Illinois railroad ferry operaton to Ste. Genevieve, Missouri. Kellogg is next to Flinton on what became the Sparta Subdivision of the Illinois Division. This was the former Missouri-Illinois Railroad Company main line between Kellogg and Salem, Illinois, a distance of 83 miles.

Not only was this dock system a new operation for the MoPac, but it was the first time that the MP and M-I operated unit coal trains. As of

June 1966, two unit trains began working between the Kellogg dock and the mines in the Southern Illinois coal and soybean country. Each of the two trains, at that time, consisted of 63 rotary-coupler cars of 100-ton capacity, meaning that each train could handle 6,300 net tons of coal per trip.

The MoPac's partner in the new operation was the Truax-Traer Coal Company, a division of Consolidation Coal. The coal originally came from the Truax-Traer's Burning Star No. 3 mine near Sparta on the M-I, and the Burning Star No. 2 mine near Pinckneyville. The latter was on the Pinckneyville Sub of the MoPac's Illinois Division. In addition, the MoPac also handled coal from the United Electric Company mine, also near Pinckneyville, which used Truax-Traer facilities.

The MP and M-I supplied locomotives and crews for the unit trains, while Truax-Traer provided the cars. The coal from these mines was destined for use by riverside electric power plants.

The Burning Star No. 3 mine was 23 miles from the Kellogg dock. At the time the operation began, two roadswitcher-type diesel locomotives were assigned to each unit train. The trains were divided into two almost equal cuts of cars for loading at the No. 3 mine. The train crew would couple the two cuts together for the short run to the Kellogg dock. A Truax-Traer locomotive han-

Extra 3205 East, running over the Horace Subdivison of the Kansas Division, is a good example of the unit coal trains operating over the MoPac during the late 1970s and early 1980s. In this case, the coal train is symbol CUS with 80 cars. CUS trains were received by MoPac at Pueblo and ran all the way to St. Louis. The ultimate destination is East Alton, Illinois, for an Illinois power plant. (Missouri Pacific Railroad, PCD Collection)

MoPac operated two types of coal trains. One group carried coal for various customers from the Illinois coal fields, and the other handled company coal for steam locomotives. Extra 1318 South smoked it up just south of Jefferson Barracks on the line between St. Louis and Poplar Bluff. (Missouri Pacific Railroad, PCD Collection)

GP9 No. 4365 led a westbound mine transfer of Southern Illinois coal at Herrin, Illinois, in 1957. The train consists of 50- and 70-ton hoppers. (S. K. Bolton, Jr.)

dled the switching and spotting for emptying at the rotary dumper at Kellogg.

The two mines near Pinckneyville were located about 50 miles from the Kellogg dock, and the operations were similar. The knowledge gained from these operations, both the unit trains and the rail to water transfer facility would be highly utilized by the MP, which eventually involved the construction of a third coal dock operation on the Mississippi.

The third facility was planned, and construction began, in 1979. It was built by Pott Industries, and was operated by Federal Barge Lines of St. Louis. It was located at Cora, 11 miles south of Chester, the MoPac's Illinois Division headquarters.

The new dock had the capacity to handle 15 million tons annually of Illinois Basin and western coal. It could unload 110-car unit trains at the rate of 3,500 tons per hour, delivering the coal by conveyor belt to either barges or a storage area.

By early 1981 unit trains began operating from the Zeigler Coal Company mines in Illinois to the new high speed rail-to-water facility at Cora. The dock operations were among the most modern to be found anywhere, and could unload

as many as five (possibly even six) unit trains in a 24-hour period. Export coal for Europe was also being handled through the Cora dock. All three docks served by the MP were located on the Chester Subdivison. (Technically Kellogg was on the Sparta Sub, however Kellogg is only 2.8 miles from Flinton, which was located on the Chester Sub.)

The entire coal traffic picture had been changing on the Missouri Pacific. For many years, the MoPac handled about three to four million tons of coal annually. In fact, in 1970, the railroad moved 4-1/2 million tons. Part of this increase was due to the new Mississippi transfer operation at Kellogg. From that time on, the tonnage began increasing year after year. The tonnage handled annually increased to over 15 million tons by 1974, a 300-percent increase over the 1970 figure.

The company was serving a total of 31 mines in Illinois, Arkansas, Missouri, and Oklahoma in 1975. Much of this tonnage was handled in unit coal trains.

At the time, the company was operating 41 trains each week from the Southern Illinois coal fields to either the Mississippi transfers or directly to electric power generating plants. A smaller por-

The MoPac served several mines in Southern Illinois. Many unit trains served these mines, as in this photo with three units and their train going through the loading process at the Ziegler Mine No. 5. This mine is near Villa Grove, Illinois, on the MoPac's Westville Subdivision. (Missouri Pacific Railroad, PCD Collection)

(above) A coal mine near Sparta, Illinois. (Missouri Pacific Railroad, PCD Collection)

(right) A loaded coal train traveling as Extra 1644 North from the Captain Mine on the Pinckneyville Subdivision of the Illinois Division to the Ford Dock, the intermodal facility constructed on the Mississippi River for the MoPac's coal traffic. (Huch Photo, C. Chappuis Collection)

(left) An eastbound loaded coal train heels to the curve near Eureka, Missouri, in May 1976. Extra 3326 East is handling western coal and is traveling over the Sedalia Subdivision of the Northern Division between Kansas City and St. Louis. (W. S. Kuba)

(below) A MoPac unit coal train passes another coal mining operation near Sparta, Illinois. Note the size of the shovel. (Missouri Pacific Railroad, PCD Collection)

tion was moving north for interchange with the Elgin, Joliet & Eastern Railway.

One rather interesting operation began on September 1, 1975. At that time, only five percent of the MoPac's coal tonnage originated at the western gateways at Pueblo or Kansas City. However, that year a unit train of Utah coal was delivered to the MP at Pueblo for transfer to the Ford dock on the Mississippi River. From there the coal traveled by barge to an electric utility, reportedly the longest rail coal operation in the U.S. terminating at a rail-to-water transfer at the time.

From the mid-point of the 1970s, MP coal tonnage increased to 32.2 million tons in 1980. The figure topped 38 million tons in 1981 and approached 49 million tons by 1985 as ten more coal-fired utility plants were completed.

As of 1980, 33 percent of the MoPac's coal tonnage originated from the western gateways at Pueblo and Kansas City. This figure increased to nearly 50 percent by 1985. The coal originated from Wyoming, Montana, Colorado, New Mexico, and Utah and traveled to various utility plants located in the Midwest, Southwest, and Southeast.

The MP was operating a grand total of 56 unit trains in 1981. The consists of the trains var-

ied. Whereas some were totally MP operations with MoPac power, coal hoppers, and caboose; others consisted of pooled power with the Burlington Northern, BN coal cars or electric utility equipment, or even other railroad coal hoppers. In most cases, the equipment was 100-ton capacity cars, either of the solid-bottom or hopper design. Most MoPac hopper cars were painted box car red with white lettering.

Historically, MP coal traffic was handled in a variety of equipment ranging in capacity from 50 to 100 tons. The unit trains were basically the same with 100-ton-capacity equipment employed almost exclusively. Non-unit train operations had more of a mixture of both old and new equipment. The older MoPac hopper cars had been painted black with white lettering.

Since the 1980s and the UP merger, coal traffic has continued to grow on the MoPac routes. Trains originating in Wyoming from the Chicago & North Western (now UP) and the Burlington Northern (now Burlington Northern Santa Fe) operate to many destinations on the former MoPac trackage of the Union Pacific.

It could be said that the "Missouri Pacific" continues to grow as an important coal hauler under the "Union Pacific" banner. ●

(left) Texas and Pacific coal hopper 587053 is part of series 587000-587199, built in 1967 and lettered for both the MP and TP. All TP equipment carried the MoPac insignia. Inside length of this group is 47 feet, 11 inches long. (Missouri Pacific Railroad, PCD Collection)

(middle) Another group of the 587000 series, 100-ton capacity equipment was lettered for the Chicago & Eastern Illinois. Their MoPac buzz saw included the initials C&EI. (Missouri Pacific Railroad, PCD Collection)

(bottom) The latest scheme (late 1970s and 1980s) for the coal hoppers was box car red with white lettering. The newest insignia with the eagle and buzz saw was being applied to all coal hoppers being repainted. Car 582046 is from the series 582000-582499; 100-ton capacity equipment. (Missouri Pacific Railroad, PCD Collection)

The Mississippi coal transfer facility at Kellogg, Illinois, handled both hopper cars and gondolas. The coal was transferred from rail cars to river barges via the conveyor belt system and loading boom visible in the background.

This aerial photo of the Kellogg dock shows the barges being brought in for loading as well as the storage areas in the background. The dock switch engine is visible at left, next to the rotary car dumper. (Both, Missouri Pacific Railroad, PCD Collection)

(left) The MoPac operated coal trains to three intermodal facilities on the Mississippi River. The first constructed was at Ford. In this case, the coal trains are backed to the unloading station with the caboose being the first car through the unloader. This August 1981 photo shows the rear end of Extra 1644 at Ford. Upon arrival the train was cut in half and the first half was then shoved down the adjacent tracks.

(middle) To start the unloading process, the caboose was uncoupled from the loads and it rolled down the hill to join the empties. Note the unloading shed. The caboose has been uncoupled and is now attached to the empties in this near-dusk photo.

(bottom) This photo shows some of the trackage at the Ford Dock. The upper two tracks handle loads while the lower tracks handle the empty cars. (Three Huch photos, C. Chappuis Collection)

(right) Extra 1644 North, with coal headed for the Ford unloading facility, crosses the Mary's River south of Chester. The loaded train will soon slow to 10 miles per hour to negotiate the north leg of the wye at Chester. The locomotives will lead their train into the Chester yard, then back the entire consist about a mile to the Ford Dock. The wye south of Chester is where the Pinckneyville and Chester Subdivisions meet. The latter is the main line of the Illinois Division to Poplar Bluff. (Huch Photo, C. Chappuis Collection)

(below) The newest dock facility was built at Cora, south of Chester, and was operated by the Federal Barge Lines. This was the third dock served by the MoPac, all of which are in the Chester vicinity. This dock also has a storage area for coal, which permitted trains to be unloaded and dispatched immediately back to the mines, instead of waiting for barges. (Missouri Pacific Railroad, PCD Collection)

(left) The Missouri-Illinois was very much a coal hauler for the Missouri Pacific Lines. M-I 536252 was a 70-ton triple hopper (536200-536299). The series was built in 1948 and served in the Southern Illinois coal fields for most of their careers. The photo was taken in September 1976 at Bryan, Texas. (Allen Rider)

(middle and bottom) These two photos of Texas-New Mexico Railroad 70-ton coal hoppers illustrate the transfer from Texas & Pacific ownership to Missouri Pacific Lines jurisdiction. Some of the cars of the fleet (500000 to 500183) were rebuilt in the mid-1970s. The Texas-New Mexico was the 105-mile line from Monahans, Texas, to Lovington, New Mexico. This section of the former T&P Lines was operated as the T-NM Subdivision of the Rio Grande Division. T-NM No. 500068 was photographed at Bryan, Texas, in September 1976, and No. 500033 was at Texarkana on August 23, 1975. (Both, Allen Rider)

(above) MP 70-ton hopper 537518 (537300-537639) was built in 1950 and rebuilt at Desoto in 1973. The car was painted box car red with white lettering. MoPac also operated quad hopper cars of a similar style in series 55000-56499. This car was photographed at Austin, Texas, in 1975. (Allen Rider)

(below) Chicago & Eastern Illinois 70-ton triple hopper No. 522698 (522300-523049) reflects ownership by the Missouri Pacific with a new numbering system painted on. C&EI cars were painted red with white lettering and served the Southern Illinois coal fields. Photographed at Bryan, Texas, in September 1976. (Allen Rider)

(above left) Former C&EI hopper 587801 has had its C&EI reporting marks replaced with "MP". (Patrick Dorin)

(above) M-I 587407 (587200-587499) was a 100-ton car painted box car red with white lettering. (Sy Dykhouse, PCD Collection)

(left) MP 580695 (580400-580699) is a 100-ton quad hopper, painted box car red with white lettering. It was photographed in October 1981. (Patrick Dorin)

(below) For many years various railroad companies handled coke with containers. The Missouri-Illinois Railroad operated a small fleet of 300-series gondolas with open sides for the containers. (Missouri Pacific, PCD Collection)

CHAPTER FOUR

The Missouri Iron Rangers

Although iron ore traffic on the Missouri Pacific was of minor consequence during most of the 20th century, it is an important item in MoPac freight service history because of the types of trains operated and for the initial development of the St. Louis, Iron Mountain & Southern Railroad. It was the iron ore deposits that led to the development of the main line south and southwest from St. Louis to Arkansas and Texas.

These iron ore deposits were located in southeastern Missouri. To transport the ore to the new furnaces being constructed in St. Louis, the St. Louis & Iron Mountain Railroad was charted in 1851. This railroad was built specifically to tap the iron ore and other mineral deposits located in the Ozark foothills. The St. Louis & Iron Mountain was completed between St. Louis and Pilot Knob, a distance of 87 miles south of St. Louis and seven miles south of Iron Mountain, in 1858.

For the first few years of the StL&IM's existence, iron ore was the major source of traffic for the company. Later the line was extended further south into Arkansas and other southern points, not knowing that some day the route would become an important main line for the Missouri Pacific System.

The existence of the iron ore deposits in this section of Missouri influenced the naming of several towns. Ironton, Mineral Point, Hematite (a type of iron ore), and Iron Mountain clearly reflect the geology of the area. It is interesting to note that one can find identical names of towns and cities located in the iron mining regions of Minnesota, Ontario, Wisconsin, Michigan, Quebec, and Labrador.

The mining activity of the Ozark foothills never achieved a major status when compared to the Minnesota iron ranges. For several decades ore was handled from the small mines at Hemitite, Iron Mountain, Pilot Knob, and other locations until they either played out or became too expensive to mine. Most of the ore was handled in either regular coal hopper cars or gondolas. Specialized equipment, such as the Lake Superior type ore cars, was not be found in the Missouri iron ore country.

The Missouri Pacific served two iron mining facilities in this geographic area after the Korean War. The two mines and pelletizing plants were known as Pea Ridge and Pilot Knob. Both were relatively new as far as pelletizing operations are concerned. A pelletizing plant converts the raw iron ore into a higher-grade iron ore pellet about the size of a marble, which is far more suitable for iron and steel production.

The Pilot Knob mine and plant was located (naturally) at Pilot Knob, 87 miles south of St.

Louis on the DeSoto Subdivison of the Arkansas Division. The complex was located next to the main line and could be seen from passenger trains. Pilot Knob was a small facility and was served by a road crew.

The assignment also had the responsibility of switching the plant, including the placement of empties and picking up loads. The plant was served from a tri-weekly to a daily basis depending upon the business demands of the steel industry. Most of the pellet production moved to the St. Louis area and/or other destinations throughout the Midwest or West.

Pea Ridge has been in operation since 1963. In 1960, the MP began construction of a 26.7-mile branch line from Cadet (on the St. Louis-Poplar Bluff main line) to Pea Ridge. The new line was constructed to serve the then new Pea Ridge iron mine, which was developed by the Meremac Mining Company, a joint venture by Bethlehem Steel Company and St. Joseph Lead Company.

The new branch line was completed and ready for traffic by early 1961.

For the next two years, the MoPac operated the branch to deliver construction materials and equipment for the new mine and pelletizing plant. Actual production began in the second half of 1963.

In order to transport the iron ore, the MP and T&P originally purchased 400 open-top 100-ton cars from Bethlehem Steel Company at a cost of almost $15 million.

The ore from Pea Ridge moved from the mine and pelletizing plant over the Pea Ridge Subdivision to Cadet. For many years, most of the production went to the Chicago area. Bethlehem Steel Company had a large plant east of Gary, Indiana. The ore moved via the MP to a C&EI connection in Illinois, who in turn transported it to the Chicago area. The ore was then interchanged with the Chicago, South Shore & South Bend Railroad for delivery to the steel plant.

Around 1976, the Pea Ridge mine and pelletizing plant were closed. However, in 1978 the mine and plant were reopened, producing a substantial volume. Part of the production during the early 1980s moved to Texas in unit trains. The number of trains per week varied according to demand. The traffic continued through the Union Pacific merger.

The annual tonnage of iron ore transported by the MoPac varied from three to four million tons annually. This made up about three percent of the company's total revenues. Although the amount may have been small, the ore trains were among the heaviest operated by the Missouri Pacific. 🚂

Ore movements are heavy trains in any language on any railroad, and the MoPac's operation was no exception. In this view, three General Electric U30C's are handling an ore train from the Pea Ridge Mine. Extra 3306 North has just departed Pea Ridge near Potosi, Missouri, and will soon be running 30 miles per hour over the Pea Ridge Subdivision. The G-E motive power is well suited to the heavy train. The U30Cs were ultimately renumbered in the upper 2900s. (Missouri Pacific Railroad, PCD Collection)

(right) Electro-Motive SD40-2s were also well suited for heavy ore train movements. Three units were required since much of the Missouri ore moved to Texas during the 1980s. As soon as these ore trains turned south off the Pea Ridge Sub and onto the De Soto Sub of the Arkansas Division, they had two hills to climb: Tip Top and Gads Hill in the Ozark foothills. This photo shows a southbound ore train at Gads Hill. Notice how the pellets are heaped over the trucks in the 100-ton capacity ore cars. (Missouri Pacific Railroad, PCD Collection)

(below) This photo illustrates unit train ore cars being loaded at the Pea Ridge mine. The equipment carried both MP and T&P reporting marks since both railroads participated in the ownership of the cars. The MoPac ultimately owned over 600 of these cars, numbered in the series 575000-575649. (Missouri Pacific Railroad, PCD Collection)

(above) Side view of MP ore car 575 116. This equipment has a capacity of 100 tons with a double hopper bottom, and is 39 feet long. This particular car was photographed in a westbound train at Dallas, Texas, in October 1981. (Michael Dorin)

(below) Open-top hopper cars of various types were used for loading pelletized iron ore at the Pilot Knob facility, which is a smaller mine than the Pea Ridge operation. (Missouri Pacific Railroad, PCD Collection)

CHAPTER FIVE

A New Generation of Eagles

Missouri Pacific Railroad intermodal services began rather quietly, and much later than many other railroads. In fact, the MoPac did not begin such services until 1956. Interestingly enough, the railroad did not begin with conventional piggyback, but with containers. Using trailer bodies with detachable wheels, the railroad began a service in which gondola cars and/or flat cars could be used interchangeably.

The first services were provided between St. Louis-East St. Louis and Kansas City. Electrically operated gantry cranes lifted the trailer bodies off their chassis and placed them on a flat-bottom railroad car. The cranes were built at St. Louis and Kansas City in early 1956. During the latter half of that year, additional work began on terminals at Houston, San Antonio, Fort Worth, Corpus Christi, Dallas, Abilene, Little Rock, Wichita, Monroe, New Orleans, and Memphis. MP's use of cranes for their piggyback loading and unloading was in contrast to most other railroads, which were using drive-on ramp systems.

The new MP services were implemented over both the MP and Texas & Pacific lines. By late 1956 plans were being made for interchange services and participation in the Trailer-Train piggyback operations with the Pennsylvania and other railroads.

Piggyback in of itself cannot recapture freight traffic from the highway systems. Basically it is designed to provide the advantages of rail and highway in one neat package for the shipper. Through careful planning, the MP began to recapture perishable traffic that had virtually slipped away completely to the unregulated truck industry.

In 1958 the company purchased 50 mechanically refrigerator trailers for service to and from the Rio Grande Valley. The MoPac adjusted their rates for the Texas fruit and vegetables close to those being charged by the highway services at that time. By being able to offer "dependable" service, free refrigeration, split deliveries, and diversion and reconsignment en route, the MoPac was able to regain the lost traffic and make a profit.

The Missouri Pacific commented that the reason that they lost the perishable traffic was that it was their own fault. Mr. R. T. Watt commented to *Railway Age* (March 24, 1958, page 12) that the company had allowed the rail rates to become non-competitive and that the service itself left much to be desired. The important thing to recognize here is that the Missouri Pacific was not simply standing by and permitting things to deteriorate still further. The company was taking action.

By 1959 the perishable traffic was improving substantially. The company ordered 100 mechanically refrigerated containers (35 feet long) and 50 highway chassis from Trailmobile, a divi-

sion of Pullman, Inc. It is noteworthy that the MP was fully committed to the container concept before 1960. The company had also constructed a fleet of flat cars designed to carry containers (up to 37 feet long) that were designated as "cradle" cars. It was a simple task for the crane to transfer the containers from rail to truck and vice versa.

The concept was so well accepted that the company's revenues were always on the increase. For example, MoPac handled 12,170 loads in 1958, exactly double the 1957 traffic levels. (*Railway Age*, February 16, 1959, page 60.)

The Missouri Pacific's container service was not simply limited to the system described here and in use since 1956. In 1959, the MoPac purchased twenty 40-foot Flexi-vans and 22 bogies in order to provide interchange service with the New York Central. Oddly enough, the MoPac–like the Soo Line–purchased Flexi-van trucks, but did not purchase Flexi-van flat cars.

From 1959 to 1969, the MP's intermodal services continued to grow. During the 1960s, the company began operating conventional piggy-back service and joined Trailer-Train's flat car pool. It was a decade of growth with solid, all-piggyback trains. Train No. 69 between St. Louis and Dallas-Fort Worth was the first such train placed in service in the late 1960s. Little was it known at that time, No. 69 would soon lead a new fleet of "name" trains.

THE EAGLE FLEET

The year 1969 was a banner one for the MoPac as the company announced the establishment of five new TOFC/COFC (Trailer on Flat Car/Container on Flat Car) trains. All of these fast trains boasted precision scheduling and delivery, the key to a successful transportation operation. The new *Eagle* fleet consisted of the following intermodal trains:

THE WINDY CITY EAGLE

This train was billed as the fastest available rail freight service between Texas and Chicago. The *Windy City Eagle* originated at Fort Worth at 8:00 a.m. and departed Dallas at 10:15 a.m. (A Houston departure at 11:00 a.m.) with arrival in Chicago via the Chicago & Eastern Illinois at 4:00 a.m. the second morning.

THE GATEWAY EAGLE

The *Gateway Eagle* was a northbound intermodal train designed to operate on an interlocking schedule with arrival in St. Louis in time to make connections with the Penn Central and the Baltimore & Ohio Railroads.

The train departed Fort Worth daily at 8:00 a.m. with arrival in St. Louis at 10:30 a.m. the next morning. The *Gateway Eagle* traveled through Dallas and picked up sections from Houston, San Antonio, Texarkana, Beaumont,

The MP owned and operated a large fleet of trailers. In fact, as of 1980, the entire group numbered over 3,000. About half were owned by the Missouri Pacific Railroad, while the rest were owned by the Missouri Pacific Truck Lines. MPZ 200002 was a Trailmobile closed van, 40 feet in length, built in 1963. (Missouri Pacific Railroad, PCD Collection)

and Alexandria. This *Eagle* also stopped at Little Rock to pick up still other sections from Louisiana and Arkansas.

THE SOUTHWEST EAGLE

This was the famous train No. 69 which provided next-morning delivery from St. Louis through to Dallas-Fort Worth.

THE GULF COAST EAGLE

This *Eagle* originally operated as Second No. 69 and had been established to relieve No. 69 of its heavy load. The *Gulf Coast Eagle* departed St. Louis at 9:00 a.m. with arrival at Houston at 6:30 a.m. the next morning.

THE LONE STAR EAGLE

The *Lone Star* was established as a Chicago to Dallas-Fort Worth service. It departed Chicago at 10:30 p.m. daily and arrived at Dallas at 4:30 a.m. the second morning; Fort Worth at 6:00 a.m. with a Houston section arriving at 6:30 a.m. (all arrivals were second morning.)

MOPAC'S INTERMODAL PHILOSOPHY

The basic philosophy behind the company's service was dependability. The railroad invested millions of dollars into the intermodal terminals system wide in order to provide this "dependable" with precision scheduling marketing and operat-

(left) The early MoPac piggyback services involved the use of containers. Gantry cranes, like this first MoPac example in St. Louis, easily transferred the containers from trucks to gondolas or flat cars. Flatbed trailers were purchased for highway movements. Note the special corner posts on the blue and gray trailer.

(opposite top) MoPac GP7 No. 4160 was switching 14 forty foot container flat cars in the Rio Grande Valley in this 1960 view. Container shipments were handled in either time freights or fast perishable trains running as extras but with priority dispatching.

(opposite bottom) One of MoPac's 1958 refrigerated containers at the gantry. Once mated to their highway chassis, these containers were hard to distinguish from trailers. (All, Missouri Pacific Railroad, PCD Collection)

(above) MoPac piggyback equipment of the 1980s had a clean, progressive look. This 89-foot flat car No. 838310 (838215-838314) was leased from American Refrigerator Transit Company (ART).

(right) Missouri Pacific Truck Lines No. 37739 pulls the second semi-trailer to bear the number MPZ 200002. This trailer illustrates the markings applied to trucks in the mid-1970s, while the insignia on the tractor had been used on MoPac equipment from 1916 to 1925! (Both, Missouri Pacific Railroad, PCD Collection)

ing philosophy. Although not perfect, the company did have a closer working relationship between their marketing and operating departments.

The MoPac operated six different piggyback plans. However, that was only half of the services offered by the railroad. The MoPac also offered a concept called "Containerpak." In this case, containers were used in a variety of ways under four plans.

CONTAINERPAK I was a container on flat car "all of the way" plan. The shipper loaded the container at a container yard (or the container was offloaded from a ship) and moved directly to the receiver's siding.

CONTAINERPAK II was an over-the-highway plan at both ends of shipping and receiving, with rail transport providing most of the transport service.

CONTAINERPAK III was an "all-highway" service.

CONTAINERPAK X was a program that provided for the custom design of a particular type of service that a shipper-consignee required.

The small 20-foot containers used in the Containerpak service provided an opportunity for many smaller shippers to use the Missouri Pacific. Indeed with the use of both piggyback and containerpak, the MoPac remained in both the LCL and LTL services, whereas most of the other Class I railroads had given up such traffic.

The MoPac also operated an air freight forwarder business as part of their service offering in the intermodal concept. In fact, as the railroad moved into the 1980s, the company referred to the TOFC/COFC services as "Intermodal." The term was a far better description than the term "piggyback." Utilizing both highway and rail transport, the railroad also connected with ships at the ocean ports of the Gulf Coast including Houston, New Orleans, Baton Rouge, Brownsville, Galveston, and many others. On Lake Michigan, the MoPac also had connections with various terminals in Chicago.

The railroad also established a monitoring system to make sure that it continued to serve the needs of the customers. The MoPac continued this philosophy right through to the UP merger in 1982. Thus began a new chapter of continued high quality intermodal freight services.

MISSOURI PACIFIC—TEXAS PACIFIC OFFERS
ALL 5 PIGGYBACK PLANS
THROUGHOUT THE WEST—SOUTHWEST!!!

PUEBLO · KANSAS CITY · ST. LOUIS · LITTLE ROCK · MEMPHIS · FT. WORTH · DALLAS · EL PASO · SAN ANTONIO · HOUSTON · NEW ORLEANS · HARLINGEN

Fast and flexible! Dependable from door to door! Missouri Pacific—Texas & Pacific has a Piggyback plan to fit *your* shipping needs. Our operations include service under Plans 1, 2, 3, 4 and 5 and interline connections with principal railroads interchanging at all major junction points.

Under Plan 5, joint rail-motor rates with

motor carriers are offered from the Atlantic to the Pacific—Canada to the Gulf.

New and improved rail and highway equipment is constantly being added to our rapidly-expanding piggyback fleet. Don't wait. Call your nearest Missouri Pacific or Texas & Pacific Freight Representative. *He's a transportation specialist!*

MISSOURI PACIFIC—TEXAS & PACIFIC

(above) MoPac promoted its piggyback services to the Southwest in this 1963 trade ad. (Kevin Holland Collection)

(right) Intermodal train DMZ was running as Extra 2017 South in this 1977 view on the Hoxie Subdivision of the Arkansas Division. Train DMZ ran from Dupo Yard (Near St. Louis) to Laredo, Texas, with Mexican-bound freight, hence the symbol DMZ. (Missouri Pacific Railroad, PCD Collection)

INTERMODAL PLANS OFFERED BY MOPAC
Plan 1
Motor common carrier handles door-to-door services ... using MoPac Piggyback Rail Services as the long-distance carrier.

Plan 2
MoPac picks up trailers at shipper's door, delivers them to the ramp, handles rail transport and delivers trailers to final destination. Door-to-door service.

Plan 2-1/4
MoPac provides trailers, rail service and either door-to-ramp or ramp-to-door motor carriage.

Plan 2-1/2
MoPac provides trailers, flat cars, and rail transportation; shipper and consignee arrange motor pick up and delivery to or from ramps.

Plan 3
MoPac provides ramp to ramp rail transport ... shipper/consignee handles motor delivery of trailers to and from ramps.

Plan 4
MoPac provides ramp-to-ramp rail haul ... shipper provides motor delivery to and from ramps.

Plan 5
MoPac or common carrier provides trailers, pick-up or delivery. MoPac provides ramping and deramping.

Plan 8
U.S. Mail.

Land Bridge
A joint water-rail-water tariff to move containerized cargo from one foreign port to another through the United States. For example, shipment via steamship from Rotterdam to New Orleans, with rail transit from New Orleans to Los Angeles, and steamship from Los Angeles to Hong Kong.

Mini-Bridge
A joint water-rail or rail-water tariff on a single bill of lading for a through route from a foreign port to a U.S. port destination through an intervening U.S. port, or the reverse. For example, shipment via steamship from Tokyo to Seattle and then by rail from Seattle to Houston.

Micro-Bridge
A joint through water/rail or rail/water tariff and route on one bill of lading to or from a foreign port to or from an inland U.S. city. For example, a rail movement from St. Louis to Los Angeles then onward via steamship from Los Angeles to Seoul, South Korea.

Source: *MoPac Guide to Intermodal Services TOFC/COFC* (pages 3, 6 and 7).

(left) This July 1980 view was taken in Chicago from the cab of Extra 4649 North (running as a caboose hop). Approaching on the southbound main is the "City Job" running as Extra 1739 South en route with an all-piggyback consist from the downtown yards in Chicago. The northbound movement is from Yard Center to pick up piggyback symbol CFZ in Chicago. Both trains are on Chicago & Western Indiana trackage.

(middle) A Chicago switch crew with a pair of Geeps, Nos. 1989 and 1838, arrives at the 37th Street Yards with the second half of the CFZ, which will soon be picked up by the caboose hop shown in the view above.

(bottom) The three units of the caboose hop couple up to the consist of the CFZ. A yard crew places the caboose on the rear and CFZ officially becomes a train. The Chicago to Fort Worth piggyback consists of 36 flats and one caboose and is powered by three units, Nos. 2317, 1813, and 4649. The all-piggyback train will run like the *Eagles* of old all the way to the Lone Star State. (All, Patrick Dorin)

57

(above) MoPac's Chicago-Fort Worth CFZ is shown here running as Extra 3126 West on the Dallas Subdivision of the Dallas-Fort Worth Terminal Division in September 1976.

(right) This all-piggyback train, including automobiles from the Gulf Coast, was known as the *Gateway Eagle* and is shown here running as Extra 3215 North on the De Soto Subdivision of the Arkansas Division. The train is south of St. Louis along the Mississippi River. (Both, Missouri Pacific Railroad, PCD Collection)

(upper) MoPac's Chicago intermodal terminal was known as Canal Street Yard. It was a joint MP-L&N facility. The yard was close to several expressways and offered quick access for pick-up and delivery. This gave the MP a competitive edge in the handling of TOFC/COFC business. All of the outbound trains were built at Canal Street, and all of the inbound trains were placed there for unloading. Inbound trailers were delivered over the road to either customers or connections. The rail capacity of Canal Street in 1985 was 136 85-foot flat cars. Coupled with the "B Lot" at 34th Street and Normal, which was completed in 1977, there was storage for 950 trailers. Three traveling cranes loaded and unloaded trailers with a portable ramp for those loads needing special handling. The yard was leased from the C&WI, which was partially owned by the MP and the L&N in the 1980s. This photo shows the north end of the Canal Street Yard.

(lower) Some of the smaller intermodal terminals employed both gantry cranes and conventional circus loading ramps. North Little Rock was one such example. (Both, Missouri Pacific Railroad, PCD Collection)

C H A P T E R   S I X

B o x   C a r s   a n d
R e f r i g e r a t o r   C a r s

Box cars and refrigerator cars comprised a major portion of the Missouri Pacific freight car fleet. These cars provided the tools for a wide variety of rail service from machinery, paper, and lumber to perishables from the Rio Grande Valley.

MoPac box cars were painted box car red with white lettering. The individual subsidiary railroad reporting marks, such as I-GN and others, pro-

vided an interesting variation to the MoPac car fleet. In addition, many of the box cars carried the slogan "Route of the Eagles."

Box cars in special service, such as the *Eagle Merchandise Service*, were painted blue and gray. Refrigerator cars were painted yellow and carried the insignia of the dual owners of American Refrigerator Transit, the MP and Wabash (the latter was part of N&W after 1964).

(above) MoPac was part owner of the American Refrigerator Transit Company (ART) for many years. All ART cars carried the insignia of ART, MP, and Wabash (Norfolk & Western replaced Wabash in 1964). ART operated standard 40-foot cars ("icers") with conventional hinged doors, plug doors, and also combination hinged and plug door equipment. The ART cars were painted bright reefer yellow with black lettering and colorful insignia. (Pacific Car & Foundry, PCD Collection)

(opposite) Among the most colorful equipment operated by MoPac were the *Eagle Merchandise Service* cars. Forty-foot, single-door box cars from various series were repainted in the blue and gray *Eagle* colors. They were not interchanged with any other railroad except the Texas & Pacific. MP 42044 was originally built in 1924, and was rebuilt for dedicated service in 1951. (Missouri Pacific Railroad, PCD Collection)

(upper left) MP 114463 (114330-114679), shown in 1980, was a 40-foot, single 8-foot door, 50-ton car with 3,356 cubic feet of space, built in 1957.

(left) No. 255087 (255000-255299), also seen in 1980, is an example of the 50-foot, single-door cars with a capacity of 50 tons and 4,906 cubic feet of space. (Both, Patrick Dorin)

(right) MP No. 81169 was a 50-foot car with 9-foot doors (81100-81699) and a capacity of 50 tons. (Sy Dykhouse)

(below) MP 126761 (126585-127540), a single 6-foot door, 40-foot box car from a series built in 1952-53. As with most MP freight equipment, paint was box car red with white lettering. (Patrick Dorin)

(below right) C&EI No. 3747 was a 50-foot car from series 3735-3752, photographed in 1967.

(bottom) Forty foot, 8-foot door No. 131443 (128310-131762) was a typical MP rebuild. The series was built from 1955-59 and rebuilt in 1979. (Both, Missouri Pacific Railroad, PCD Collection)

(above) MoPac No. 98180 (98000-98100), shown in this rather heavily retouched builder's view, is an example of the 50-foot plug door insulated cars constructed by General American Tank Car in 1962. This car carried the lettering arrangement common at that time. (Missouri Pacific Railroad, PCD Collection)

(middle) T&P 366809 (366650-367099), a 70-ton capacity, 50-foot car with a 10-foot door, was photographed in May 1980. (Dennis Roos)

(bottom) Rebuilt in 1979, No. 354037 (354015-354339) was a 50-foot car with a 9-foot door, rated at 50 tons capacity and 4,845 cubic feet. It was built in 1959 and photographed in July 1980. (Patrick Dorin) (right) Fifty foot, double-door box car 250918 as it appeared in 1980. Series 250900-251099 was built in 1963 for general service. (Patrick Dorin)

(middle) Missouri-Illinois 251303 (251200-251395) was a 77-1/2-ton capacity, 50-foot car. Its double doors created a 16-foot opening. (Patrick Dorin)

(bottom) Fifty foot, double-door box cars No. 251070 illustrates the revised lettering arrangements on MP box cars adopted in the late 1970s. Series 250900-251099 was built in 1963 for general service. This car was photographed in 1980. (Patrick Dorin)

(top) Fifty foot car 253520 (253450-253749) was built by ACF in 1976.

(above) T&P 365423 (365226-365474) was a 50-foot, 70-ton car built by ACF in 1971 with Freightsaver equipment and 16-foot combination doors. (Both, Missouri Pacific Railroad, PCD Collection)

(left) Combination door car No. 365214 (365150-365224) was built in 1969 and rebuilt in 1976. (Dennis Roos)

(top) Fifty foot, combination double-door series 367100-367299 was built by ACF in 1974.

(above left) ACF built 60-foot No. 376738 (376700-376949) in 1978. (Both, Missouri Pacific Railroad, PCD Collection)

(above right) Cushion underframe, double plug door series 364775-364999 was built in 1971. (Patrick Dorin)

(middle right) MP purchased 100-ton, 60-foot, double-plug door series 267361-267860 in 1979. (Missouri Pacific Railroad, PCD Collection)

(right) MP 271010 (271000-271082) was assigned to auto parts service. (PCD Collection)

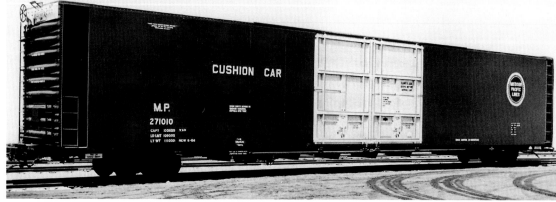

(top) T&P 272026 (272025-272044), photographed in August 1975, is another auto parts car, equipped with two 20-foot plug door openings per side. The total length of the car is 93 feet, 8 inches including the cushion underframe. (Allen Rider)

(middle) After the Wabash became part of the Norfolk & Western in October 1964, the ART cars carried MP and N&W insignia. (Patrick Dorin)

(bottom) The ART mechanical refrigerator cars, such as the 640, were painted reefer yellow with black lettering, ends, and underframes. (Missouri Pacific Railroad, PCD Collection)

CHAPTER SEVEN

Covered Hoppers

The MoPac's covered hopper car fleet ranged from conventional hoppers to the 70-ton capacity standard design as well as the 100-ton grain hoppers. Still other cars were designed for handling chemicals and other dry bulk cargo. Thus the MP had a variety of different types of cars with exterior posts as well as the cylindrical and CenterFlo designs. In most cases, the cars were painted gray with black lettering and insignia. Exceptions were the conventional open top cars with covers, which were painted black with white lettering.

(above) Some of the newest covered hoppers of the early 1980s were the 724000-series, 100-ton ACF CenterFlo cars. Built with a three-compartment design, the cars carried the new Eagle Buzz Saw insignia.

(opposite) MP 709756 (709600-709899) was a triple-hopper with a 3,700-cubic foot capacity. This series was built in 1965.

(left) MP 706800 (706500-706999) was a 2950-cubic foot twin-compartment ACF CenterFlo. The 35-foot car was painted light gray with black lettering. The series was built in 1977-78. (All, Missouri Pacific Railroad, PCD Collection)

(above) Hopper car 702303 (702200-702399) is an example of a coal hopper going through the rebuilding process and emerging as a "covered hopper." Note that the car still carried its black paint scheme with "Route of the Eagles" on the side in this 1975 view at Texarkana. (Allen Rider)

(below) MP 702798 was another conversion, with a ten-hatch roof and triple-hopper 2,680-cubic foot interior configuration. (M. D. McCarter, TLC Collection)

(left) The MP operated several basic types of grain-service covered hoppers, with some minor differences between manufacturers. C&EI covered hoppers took on the MoPac look with gray body paint, black lettering, and the Buzz Saw insignia. ACF CenterFlo car No. 718383 (718300-718574) was built in 1976 and photographed in 1980. (Dennis Roos)

(middle) Grain-service ACF CenterFlo covered hopper No. 711058 (711070-711097) was built in 1971 and photographed in 1980. (Dennis Roos,)

(below) CenterFlo car No. 710966 (710600-710999) was still another 4,460-cubic-foot car built for grain hauling in 1966. (Missouri Pacific Railroad, PCD Collection)

(right) Airslide™ car 720043 (720000-720174) had a 2,600-cubic-foot capacity and was intended for bulk flour loading only. (Patrick Dorin)

(middle) MP 700806 (700700-700899) was a 2,055-cubic-foot PS-2 covered hopper. It was photographed in 1979. Most covered hopper cars on the MoPac were painted light gray with black lettering. (Dennis Roos)

(bottom) PS-2CD covered hopper No. 711644 (711630-712054), built in 1971, as it appeared in May 1980. (Dennis Roos)

(left) PS-2CD covered hoppers, with their distinctive exterior post design, were an important part of the MoPac fleet. No. 722777 (722500-723099) was built in 1977.

(middle) Part of series 716050-716499, No. 716217 was built in 1970 for grain service.

(bottom) PS-2CD No. 712088 (712055-712254) was built in 1971. The three cars on this page were all photographed in 1980. (All, Dennis Roos)

CHAPTER EIGHT

Gondolas, Flats, and More

This chapter reviews the flat-bottom gondolas and flat cars as well as equipment not covered in previous chapters, such as wood chip cars, stock cars, and other miscellaneous rolling stock. ⬤

A dozen cars of pulpwood logs that have been loaded in Arkansas await movement to a paper mill. (Missouri Pacific Railroad, PCD Collection)

(above) Livestock handling, as here at Kansas City. in 1937, has virtually disappeared from the American railroad scene. Note the mixture of T&P and MP stock cars, both single and double deck. (Missouri Pacific Railroad, PCD Collection)

(left) Gondola No. 697118 (697050-697149) is a 52-foot covered car built by Ortner in 1969 for handling rolled steel products. (Ortner Car Co., PCD Collection)

MP 610090 and 611431 (610000-613675) represent the 70-ton, 52-foot low-side cars built from 1949 to 1958. Both were box car red with white lettering. No. 695026 was a 52-foot car from series 695000- 695099, built in 1958-59. No. 680041 (680000-680049) was a 65-foot drop-end mill gondola built in 1948. No. 614401 (614330-614424) is a 50-foot, bulkhead gondola built in 1966. Fifty two-foot, 100-ton No. 640250 (640250-640329) was built by Thrall Car in 1967. At the beginning of the 1980s, No. 642661 (642661-643049) represented the newest part of the MoPac gondola fleet. Five hundred cars were purchased from Greenville Steel Car in 1979. (Both below, PCD Collection; others Dennis Roos)

(left) Sixty-foot flat car No. 819813 (819840-819899) was built by Thrall Car in 1974. (Thrall Car, PCD Collection)

(below left) Coiled steel cars handle steel efficiently and with weather protection. MP 950004 (950000-950049) was built by Thrall in 1969. The 52-foot cars had a capacity of 93 tons. (Thrall Car, PCD Collection)

(lower left) Another unusual piece of Mopac equipment was this 45-foot flat car equipped with six containers for lead ore concentrate. Each container had 100 cubic feet of space. The car itself was part of series 99900-99919, built in 1954. The cars were assigned to service at Middle Brook, Missouri.

(below) The MoPac owned and operated three 300-ton capacity flat cars, numbered 865000 to 865002 and built in 1969. The length of the cargo space was 35 feet, 11 inches. (Both, Missouri Pacific Railroad, PCD Collection)

(top) This car was built for the International-Great Northern. I-GN 8589 was built in 1943, and was rebuilt at Palestine in 1955. (Missouri Pacific Railroad, PCD Collection)

(above) Bulkhead flat 822135 (822100-822159) was built in 1965.

(below left) Pulpwood flat 734816 (734800-734999) was 47 feet long and was built in 1967 by General Steel Industries. The group was originally built for the Texas and Pacific.

(below right) Still another group of pulpwood cars is represented by 728013 (728000-728099). Built in 1976 with a 100-ton capacity, the car was 53 feet, 6 inches long. Note the floor design. (Three photos, General Steel Industries, PCD Collection)

(above) These two photos illustrate two different configurations of tri-level auto rack cars. The racks themselves are either owned or leased by the railroad, while the flat car is frequently owned by Trailer-Train as is the case here. The enclosed rack offers greater protection from vandals and hail storms. (TTRX 965235, Dennis Roos; TTRX 911849, Missouri Pacific Railroad, PCD Collection)

(upper left) In 1969, the MoPac rebuilt a number of triple hoppers for wood chip service. No. 591110 (591000-591255) had an extension to increase its capacity from 2,760 to 4,525 cubic feet. (Allen Rider)

(middle) Wood chip hopper No. 592617 (592500-592799), had 12 hopper doors and 7,000 cubic feet of space. The inside length was 70 feet.

(bottom) C&EI 16250 was a 100-ton hopper designed for ballast or stone service for company or revenue operations, built by Bethlehem in 1972. (Both, Missouri Pacific Railroad, PCD Collection)

C H A P T E R   N I N E

Work Equipment and Cabooses

Work equipment plays a vital role in maintenance and construction projects for railroad companies. Some of the equipment is an "extended life" operation of former freight and passenger equipment. Work equipment can be divided into two classifications.

First there is the equipment that is purchased new for specific types of work, such as snow plows, Jordan spreaders, and wreckers. The second is equipment rebuilt from the former revenue freight and passenger equipment.

The caboose punctuated the end of Missouri Pacific freight trains through the company's entire history. The caboose has always seemed to mean more than just the end of the train, carrying with it a mystique that was part of railroading's appeal.

One of the interesting things about the MoPac caboose fleet was the different styles in operation. Wood cabooses, for example, sported both vertical siding as well as horizontal. The vertical was common to almost all railroads, while the horizontal was a bit more unusual. The company operated a superb fleet of steel cabooses with standard cupolas, wide-vision cupolas, and two basic types of bay-window cars—a standard size car and a shorter version. This makes the study of the company's cabooses all the more interesting.

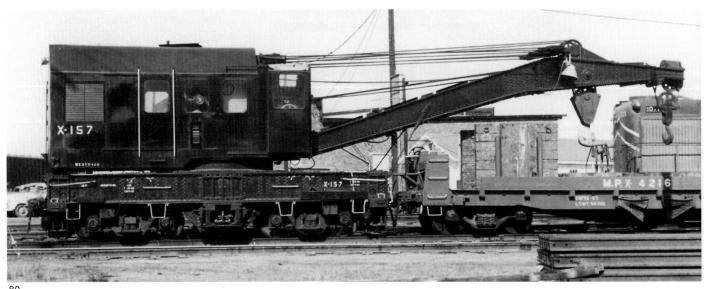

(above) Photos of work equipment in action are rare. Missouri Pacific recorded Weed Sprayer X-264 working a main line to rid the roadbed of weeds. Note the style and type of tank cars behind the X-264. (Missouri Pacific Railroad, PCD Collection)

(opposite) Wrecker X-157. Boom car X-4216 is partially visible at right in this February 21, 1970, view at Coffeyville, Kansas. (William A. Raia Collection)

(left) Wheel cars operated in interchange service to and from foundries for new wheels. (Missouri Pacific Railroad, PCD Collection)

(above) MP X3454, shown in 1980, was converted for maintenance of way service. (Dennis Roos)

(right) Also photographed in 1980, this former C&EI 40-foot box car had been assigned to work service with the number X93. (Dennis Roos)

(below right) Another converted box car, No. X4470 was designated as a Foreman's Car in this 1980 view. (Dennis Roos)

(upper left) The company owned and operated 12 snow plows at the beginning of 1980. Snow plow X183 (X181-X186) was photographed in strorage at Kansas City in May 1980. (Dennis Roos)

(middle left) Many tank cars found their way into work equipment service for carrying fuel, water, or other liquid commodities for weed spraying and other maintenance work. MP "MofW X-24" is one example of the tank work car fleet on the MP and T&P Systems. (William A. Raia Collection)

(left) MP X15101 was a flat car equipped to carry 39-foot lengths of rail. (Patrick Dorin)

(below) Sometimes wheel cars, such as MP's X-1064, could be used as boom cars, thus playing a dual role in wreck train service. (William A. Raia Collection)

(above) MP's X-1035, a locomotive crane with dual booms, was an American diesel-electric unit with a 30-mile-per-hour speed limit. The crane was photographed between job assignments at Dupo, Illinois, in October 1966. (William A. Raia Collection)

(middle) Wrecker X154 was photographed en route to a derailment. (Stan K. Bolton, Jr.)

(bottom) Hi-rail trucks and other vehicles used in maintenance service carried MoPac lettering on their doors. (Patrick Dorin)

(above) Cabooses played a key role in North American freight train operations for well over 100 years. The MoPac operated several different designs. No. 847 was built by ACF at Chicago in 1929. (Missouri Pacific Railroad, PCD Collection)

(left) Caboose No. 708 illustrates the opposite side of this type of car. The window configurations varied from one builder to another. These wooden cars were classics in their own right. (Ralph Carlson)

(bottom) Photographed in St. Louis in 1935, No. 411 looks like a rebuilt box car with a side door and cupola, and rode on arch bar trucks. (Ralph Carlson)

(top left) Side-door caboose No. 604 was at Kansas City on December 25, 1950.

(top right) Note the different lattering location on No. 657.

(middle) Note the different window layout on both sides of No. 948-R at Harlingen, Texas, in September 1960.

(lower left) No. 1013 is unusual in that it contains both a bay window and a side door for loading andunloading express and less than carload shipments. Topeka, Kansas, April 1948.

(lower right) No. 105 appears to be of similar construction to the 708 and 847, but without a cupola. It was likely assigned to assigned to transfer service when photographed at Omaha in April 1951. (Six photos, Ralph Carlson)

(bottom) Caboose 11959 (11958-11961) was built by International Car Company and assigned to yard and transfer duty in the Kansas City area when photographed in December 1979. The car has an inside length of 24 feet. (Dennis Roos)

(left) The MP still owned five cabooses with baggage doors in 1980. The cars were purchased from 1941 through 1944. This car was photographed in Lincoln, Nebraska, in May 1954, and had a 54 inch door for handling LCL and/or express traffic for both branch and mainline locals. (A. C. Phelps)

(middle) Bay window caboose No. 12512 (12509-12514) was assigned to the "City Run" between Yard Center and downtown Chicago when photographed in 1980. (Patrick Dorin)

(below) No. 13717 was one of a large series (13715-13964) built by MoPac between 1977 and 1981. They operated system-wide. (Missouri Pacific Railroad, PCD Collection)

(right) Note how the grab irons on caboose No. 910 extend beyond the body because the steps are narrower than the end platforms. (Ralph Carlson)

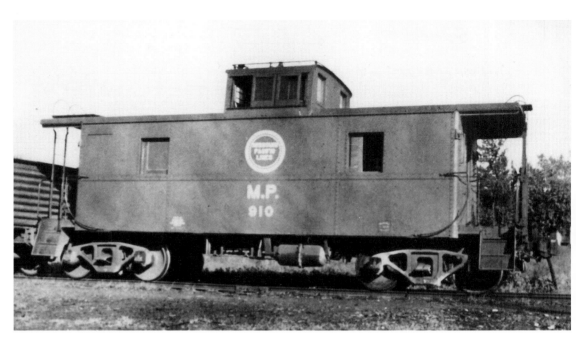

(middle) Caboose No. 13456 (13444-13493) is similar to the 12340 shown below. Again rebuilt with fewer windows, the series was originally built in 1950. (Dennis Roos)

(bottom) Caboose No. 12340 is one of two, the other being No. 12325. Originally built with four windows, the car has been rebuilt with fewer windows. One can see where the windows have been blocked out. The car was built in 1948, and was designated for local service only when photographed in December 1980. (Dennis Roos)

(left) MP No. 13613 (13605-13644) was one of 50 International Car Company extended-vision cupola cabooses in service on the MoPac. It was photographed in Chicago on a caboose hop from Yard Center in July 1980. The cars had an inside length of 30 feet. (Patrick Dorin)

(middle) MoPac pooled cabooses with other railroads including the Union Pacific. Such equipment traveled widely over the various main lines, such as UP 25587 photographed at Yard Center in July 1980. (Patrick Dorin)

(below) These three mainline cabooses illustrate dramatic differences in caboose design. All MoPac cabooses were painted red with white lettering and striping. In 1980, the MP was operating over 600 cabooses. (Missouri Pacific Railroad, PCD Collection)

C H A P T E R   T E N

S h a d e s   o f   B l u e

General Motors F-units were a common sight on MoPac freight trains well into the 1960s, when they were replaced by more-versatile road switchers. In the view below, F7A No. 880 posed at Little Rock in October 1964. On the facing page, F7A No. 916 led three mates with train 92 east through Fort Worth in June 1968. That same month, GP7 No. 256 led a trio of F-units on east-bound train 62. (All, TLC Collection)

(right) GP18 No. 440 was being serviced at Fort Worth in March 1964 (TLC Collection)

(middle) There is nothing better than a bright summer day for train watching at Dolton, Illinois. In this August 12, 1981, view a northbound intermodal train approaches the several sets of tracks at Dolton on what was once the Chicago & Eastern Illinois Railroad. (David Schauer)

(below) Three units led by SD40-2 No. 6014 power a northbound freight near Denison, Texas, in October 1982. (Lloyd Keyser)

(above) GP38-2 No. 2096 leads a train at Kansas City in May 1985. This photo illustrates two of the variations of number placement on the hoods of MoPac road switchers. The lead unit's small number is near the roof line, while the trailing unit's number is bold and very visible in the upper middle of the long hood. (Lloyd Keyser)

(left) A transfer and switch run moving north at Dolton, Illinois, with a short cut of cars on the afternoon of August 12, 1981. (David Schauer)

(above) A freight train arriving from Tulsa in May 1976 needed helpers from the yard as it crossed above the Rock Island yard at Fort Worth. It just goes to show that the switch engine, the unsung hero of the motive power fleet, could do just about any job on the railroad. (Lloyd Keyser)

(right) SW7s 1284 and 1285 worked the hump at Fort Worth Yard in April 1979. Notice the placement of the engine numbers on the hoods of the switchers. (Lloyd Keyser)

(left) SW9s 1230 and 1231 were in action with switching operations at Fort Worth, Texas, in April 1976. (Lloyd Keyser)

(below) The MoPac's Centennial Yard in Fort Worth had the latest in switching motive power in February 1982 with SW1500 No. 1552 and a slug. (Lloyd Keyser)

(above) SW1200s Nos. 1282 and 1283 were assigned to the hump at the Fort Worth yard in April 1976. (Lloyd Keyser)

(right) Although the Missouri Pacific never reached Denver over its own rails, MP freight power operated through to the "Mile High City" over the Denver & Rio Grande Western. No. 3172 was one of a group of locomotives laying over between runs on May 26, 1983. (David Schauer)

(bottom) Spring is well underway in April 1976 as a freight train with SD40-2 No. 3007 leading moves into the receiving yard at Fort Worth, Texas. (Lloyd Keyser)

Nos. 3147 and 3206 lead caboose 13844 across the diamonds at Dolton while running north for a transfer turn from Yard Center to downtown Chicago on August 12, 1981. (David Schauer)

(above) It is close to "sundown" as a westbound freight races through Kirkwood, Missouri, in May 1980 with a bright red caboose bringing up the rear. The Kansas City-bound freight will do the job overnight. (Thomas Dorin)

(below) Bay-window caboose No. 13669 was photographed at Itasca (Superior), Wisconsin, in July 1988 on the Chicago & North Western Railway. MP cabooses were a common sight in the north country, particularly on ore trains. (Robert Blomquist)

(tabove) No. 13907 illustrates the class CA-11 type of MoPac cabooses. (Robert Blomquist)

(left and below) Two different perspectives of a MoPac International Car Co. wide-vision caboose, No. 13519, in ore service on the C&NW at Superior, Wisconsin, in February 1985. (Both, Patrick Dorin)

(right) 40-foot box car No. 127104 was built in 1952 and was equipped with a 6-foot door. It was at Galveston, Texas, in June 1983. (Lloyd Keyser)

(middle) Displaying the "Route of the Eagles" slogan, 40-foot box car No. 131311 was equipped with an 8-foot door. Built in 1958, it was also at Galveston in June 1983. (Lloyd Keyser)

(below) 40-foot box No. 47119 clearly shows the "Route of the Eagles" slogan and buzz saw insignia. (From Lloyd Keyser, by K. B. King, Jr., Collection of Dick Kuelbs)

(above) MP No. 16267 displays the blue and gray scheme applied to cars in LCL service. It was photographed at Fort Worth, Texas, in April 1964. (K. B. King, Dick Kuelbs Collection)

(middle) MofW box car X4616 still proudly carries the "Route of the Eagles" slogan. The car was built in May 1924, but was still serving the railroad in October 1986 when its portrait was taken in Fort Worth. (Lloyd Keyser)

(left) MofW X-3207 was photographed at Mineola, Texas, in December 1982. (Lloyd Keyser)

(right) This 70-ton covered hopper was photographed at Oskaloose, Iowa, in June 1980. (Lloyd Keyser)

(middle) Covered hopper No. 2869 was recorded at Fort Worth in 1962. (K. B. King, Jr., Dick Kuelbs Collection)

(below) ARMN mechanical refrigerator No. 756094 bore a late-style MoPac Eagle insignia when it was photographed at Superior, Wisconsin, in July 1983. (Patrick Dorin)

(left) CenterFlo covered hopper No. 705903 as it appeared in March 2000. The car was showing its age but still displayed MP reporting marks. (Patrick Dorin)

(middle) Weather and age can take its toll on a paint scheme. Even this updated MP application with the UP insignia on CenterFlo No. 718194 was showing wear and tear in March 2000. The car was photographed in grain service on the ex-C&NW at Superior, Wisconsin. (Patrick Dorin)

(bottom) Two MoPac freights are lined up side by side at Dupo, Illinois. The locomotives on the left include one unit in Union Pacific colors – a sign of change on the horizon. (Camille Chapuis)

CHAPTER ELEVEN

The Union Pacific

Merger plans between the Missouri Pacific and Union Pacific were announced in 1980, and the two railroads came together in December 1982. In the immediate wake of the merger, the Missouri Pacific and the Union Pacific were sister companies with the Western Pacific Railroad a district of the Union Pacific Railroad. The entire system comprised over 22,000 route-miles and operated over 3,000 locomotives and 130,000 freight cars.

As a sister railroad, Missouri Pacific motive power and equipment was relettered and painted in the Union Pacific schemes, initially retaining "Missouri Pacific" lettering on motive power in the UP style. The practice, however, was short-lived and all motive power was eventually relettered "Union Pacific." This final chapter presents a sampling of MoPac equipment in the UP scheme as the Missouri Pacific began its own final chapter in railroad history.

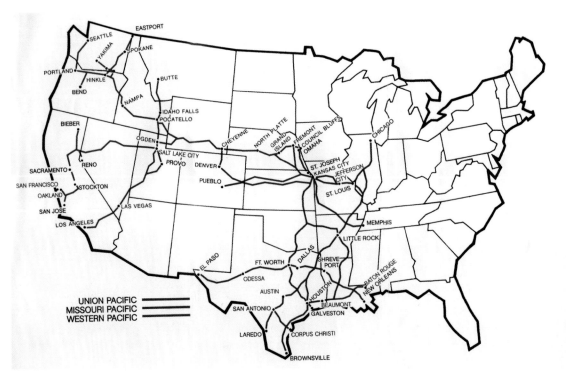

(above) As the months went by under the new Union Pacific System operation, more and more trains were powered with a mixture of UP and MP motive power. In this case, a new Union Pacific-Missouri Pacific single-system through train is ready to depart North Platte, Nebraska, for the Sunbelt. The new system delivered perishables from the Northwest nearly 24 hours sooner than previous freight schedules. (Missouri Pacific Railroad, PCD Collection)

(middle) Missouri Pacific CenterFlo covered hopper No. 717651 combined MP reporting marks with the UP insignia.

(bottom) All types of freight equipment repainted during the 1990s carried the MP-UP lettering combination, such as gondola No. 650584. (Both, Patrick Dorin)

(opposite) This map shows the result of the MP-WP-UP merger. (PCD Collection)

(above left) MoPac No. 367263 was repainted at Palestine in September 1987.

(above right) MP No. 375193 spotted for paper loading at the paper mill at Ashland, Wisconsin, on the Wisconsin Central on April 29, 1988.

(right) Hopper No. 588635 carries MP reporting marks as well as the UP insignia in March 1991. The car was in an all-rail ore service between the Minntac Plant at Mountain Iron, Minnesota, and Provo, Utah, via the DM&IR, C&NW, and UP. (Three photos, Patrick Dorin)

(below) One of the newest concepts in freight service in the late 1980s on the UP System was the 26-hour Chicago-Dallas "RoadRailer" on a C&EI-MP-T&P routing. (Union Pacific Photo, PCD Collection)

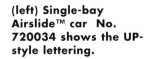

(left) Single-bay Airslide™ car No. 720034 shows the UP-style lettering.

(middle) MoPac cylindrical covered hopper No. 709663 carries the UP insignia in April 1991 at the Burlington Northern's 28th Street Yard in Superior, Wisconsin. (Both, Patrick Dorin)

(bottom) The mixture of UP power throughout the Missouri Pacific became more and more evident as time progressed into the late 1980s. A Missouri Pacific crew moves out of Avondale Yard at New Orleans with former MP GP15-1 No. 1738, painted in UP colors with "Union Pacific" lettering. The photo was taken in October 1987 at the western end of the yard on Alexandria Subdivision of the former New Orleans Division, which became part of the Louisiana Division. (Thomas Dorin)

A P P E N D I X   I

Equipment Rosters

The following two sets of rosters, reproduced with permission from the *Official Railway Equipment Register*, cover the Missouri Pacific's freight equipment in October 1956 and October 1976.

When reading over the 1956 roster (pages 109-114), the listed "outside length" of the equipment means "over the strikers," while in the 1976 roster the outside length means between the pulling faces of the couplers in normal positions.

The two sets of rosters were chosen to illustrate the changes and expansions that took place between the 1950s and into the late 1970s, leading up to the Union Pacific System mergers.

All pages from the *ORER* ar reprinted with the permission of Primedia Directories, Inc.

MISSOURI PACIFIC R. R. CO.

REPORTING MARKS—"M P", "I G N" AND "S B & M"

MISSOURI PACIFIC.

FREIGHT EQUIPMENT — Reporting Marks — "M P", "I G N" and "S B & M"

The freight cars of this Company are marked "Missouri Pacific Lines" and "M. P.", "I G N", "N O T M" or "St. L B M"
and are numbered and classified as follows:

Item No.	A.A.R. Mech. Desig.	Markings and Kind of Cars	Numbers	Inside Length	Inside Width	Inside Height	Outside Length	Width At Eaves or Top of Sides or Platform	Extreme Width	Height from Rail: To Extreme Width	To Eaves or Top of Sides or Platform	To Top of Running Board	To Extreme Height	Side Door Width of Open'g	Side Door Height of Open'g	End Door Width of Open'g	End Door Height of Open'g	Cubic Feet Level Full	Pounds or Gallons
1	FW	Well.....Note M	200, 201	42 3	10 2	......	46 2	10 2	......	......	4 5	......	7 7						100000 lb
2	FD	" .....Note F	210, 211	58 3	8 4	......	58 10	8 4	......	......	3 11	......	6 11						250000 lb
3	FD	" .....Note J	212	57 9	9 ...	......	58 4	9 ...	9 7	3 11	4 3	......	5 10						250000 lb
4	FM	Flat.....Note K	215	53 ...	9 9	......	54 1	9 9	10 3	3 6	3 8	......	5 5						250000 lb
5	LP	Rack	400 to 499	38 ...	8 8	7 6	43 4	8 8	9 3	10 9	11 7	......	11 7						100000 lb
6	LP	"	500 to 599	35 10	9 7	8 5	41 3	10 8	......	......	13	......	13						100000 lb
7	LP	"	600 to 699	38 ...	8 8	7 6	43 4	8 8	9 3	10 9	11 7	......	11 7						100000 lb
11	LP	" ...Note QQ	700 to 799	38 ...	......	7 ...	43 4	8 8	9 3	10 9	11 1	......	11 1						100000 lb
12	LP	"	800 to 999	37 6	9 5	8 4	42 11	10 6	......	......	12 7	......	12 7						100000 lb
13	LP	"	1000 to 1049	40 ...	9 1	......	40 2	10 ...	......	......	4 1	......	5 8						100000 lb
14	LP	" ....Note QQ	1050 to 1154	38 ...	......	7 ...	43 4	8 8	9 3	10 9	11 ...	......	11 ...						
15	LP	" ....Note QQ	1155 to 1299	38 ...	......	7 ...	43 4	8 8	9 3	10 9	11 ...	......	11 ...						100000 lb
16	LP	"	1394	35 6	9 4	7 8	37 6	9 4	......	......	11 1	......	11 1						80000 lb
17	LP	"	1400 to 1499	40 11	9 1	9 1	42 ...	9 10	10 2	3 6	12 11	......	13 7						100000 lb
21	LP	"	1500 to 1649	41 8	9 1	9 1	42 ...	9 9	10 ...	3 1	12 11	......	12 11						100000 lb
22	LO	Hopper, All Steel, with Steel Roof	1700 to 1724	31 4	10 ...	......	41 5	7 11 / 9 9	10 2	10 9	11 9 / 11 4	11 8	12 4					2200	140000 lb
23	HTR	" " "	1770 to 1799	40 5	10 ...	......	41 5	7 11 / 9 9	10 2	10 9	11 9 / 11 4	11 8	11 9					2755	140000 lb
24	HTR	" " "	1800 to 1981	40 5	10 ...	......	41 5	7 11 / 9 9	10 2	10 9	11 9 / 11 4	11 8	11 9					2755	140000 lb
25	LO	" " "	2000 to 2149	29 3	9 5	......	35 3	7 11 / 9 9	10 2	11 9	13 / 12 7	12 10	13					1892	140000 lb
26	LO	" " "	2150 to 2199	29 3	9 5	......	35 3	7 11 / 9 9	10 2	11 9	13 / 12 7	12 10	13					1892	140000 lb
27	LO	" " "	2200 to 2249	29 3	9 5	......	35 3	7 11 / 9 9	10 2	11 9	13 / 12 7	12 10	13					1892	140000 lb
31	LO	" " "	2250 to 2349	29 3	9 5	......	34 3	......	10 2	......	12 10	......						1892	140000 lb
32	LO	" " "	2350 to 2399	29 3	9 6	......	35 3	7 11 / 9 9	10 2	11 9	13 / 12 7	12 10	13					1892	140000 lb
33	LO	" " "	2400 to 2748	35 8	9 10	......	41 9	9 9	10 6	10 9	12 2	13 ...	13 4					2680	140000 lb
34	LO	" " "	2749 to 2870	35 8	9 7	......	41 9	9 8	10 6	10 8	12 1	13 ...	13 4					2680	140000 lb
35	XM	Box, Steel Underframe	2889 to 2899	40 ...	8 6	8 ...	41 11	9 7	9 9	12 7	12 7	13 2	14 10	6 ...	7 4			2740	80000 lb
36	XM	" "	2901 to 3400	40 ...	8 6	8 ...	41 7	9 6	9 10	12 7	12 1	13 ...	13 10	6 ...	7 5			2720	80000 lb
37	XM	" All Steel, Note UU	"	"	"	"	"	"	"	"	"	"	"	"	"			"	"
41	XME	" All Steel, Note TT	"	"	"	"	"	"	"	"	"	"	"	"	"			"	"
42	XM	" All Steel....	3601 to 3720	40 6	8 6	8 6	42 2	9 5	......	12 4	13 1	13 9	6 ...	8 2				2926	80000 lb
43	XME	" Note MM	"	"	"	"	"	"	"	"	"	"	"	"	"			"	
44	LO	Hopper, All Steel, with Steel Roof	4000 to 4299	39 10	9 9	......	45 11	8 8 / 10 6	10 6	12 10	13 1 / 12 10	13 ...	13 1					2828	140000 lb
45	LO	" " "	4600 to 4729	39 10	9 9	......	45 11	8 8 / 10 2	10 2	12 2	13 1 / 12 10	13 ...	13 1					2828	140000 lb
46	LO	" " "	4748 to 4799	35 8	9 7	......	41 9	9 8 / 10 6	10 6	10 8	12 1	13 ...	13 4					2680	140000 lb
47	LO	" " "	4800 to 4879	39 10	9 9	......	45 11	8 8 / 10 2	10 2	12 2	12 10 / 13 1	13 ...	13 1					2828	140000 lb
51	LO	" " "	4880 to 4929	39 10	9 9	......	45 11	8 8 / 10 2	10 2	12 2	12 10 / 13 1	12 11	13 1					2828	140000 lb
52	HT	Hopper, Aluminum.	5000 to 5009	43 11	10 4	......	45 1	10 5	......	10 8	......	10 8						3000	140000 lb
53	HT	" "	5010 to 5024	43 11	10 4	......	45 1	10 5	......	10 8	......	10 8						3000	140000 lb
54	GB	Gondola, All Steel, Flat Bottom, Drop Ends.	5100 to 5149	65 ...	7 9	3 6	67 11	8 7	8 10	6 10	7 8	......	7 5			7 2	3 6	1763	140000 lb
55	GB	Gondola, All Steel, Fixed Ends	5200 to 5499	52 6	9 5	3 9	53 9	10 5	10 5	7 4	7 4	......	7 5					1856	140000 lb
56	GB	Gondola, All Steel, Fixed Ends, Flat Bottom	5500 to 5999	52 6	9 5	3 9	53 9	10 5	10 5	7 4	7 4	......	7 5					1856	140000 lb
57	TM	Oil Tanks.......	6136 to 6185				31 5												10500 gal / 100000 lb
61	XM	Box, Steel Underframe	6202 to 6949	40 6	8 6	8 6	41 ...	8 11	......	12 4	13 1	13 9	6 ...	8 2				2926	80000 lb
62	XM	" All Steel Note FF①	"	"	"	"	"	"	"	......	"	"	"	"					"
63	XME	" All Steel Note AAA①	"	"	"	"	"	"	"	......	"	"	"						
		Forward....																	

MISSOURI PACIFIC FREIGHT EQUIPMENT—Continued.

Item No.	A.A.R. Mech. Desig.	MARKINGS AND KIND OF CARS.	NUMBERS.	Inside Length ft. in.	Inside Width ft. in.	Inside Height ft. in.	Outside Length ft. in.	Width At Eaves or Top of Sides or Platform ft. in.	Extreme Width ft. in.	Ht. To Extreme Width ft. in.	Ht. To Eaves or Top of Sides or Platform ft. in.	Ht. To Top of Running Board ft. in.	Ht. To Extreme Height ft. in.	Door Side Width of Open'g ft. in.	Door Side Height of Open'g ft. in.	Door End Width of Open'g ft. in.	Door End Height of Open'g ft. in.	Cubic Feet Level Full	Pounds or Gallons	No. of Cars
		Brought forward......																		4518
1	HK	Ballast, All Steel.	7000 to 7099	40 8	10 1	......	41 8	10 2	10 4		10 8		10 8					2505	140000 lb.	100
2	GS	Gondola.........	7100 to 7199	48 6	9 6	6	50 3	10 6	10 6	10 4	10 4		10 4					2765	140000 lb.	100
3	LO	Hopper, All Steel, with Steel Roof	7500 to 7899	39 10	9 9	......	45 11	9 7	10 2	12 2	12 8	13	13 3					2828	140000 lb.	400
4	FM	Flat, All Steel...	8000 to 8099	45	9 4	......	45 9	9 4	10 3	3 6	3 9		5 2						100000 lb.	85
5	FM	" " ..	8100 to 8199	50	9 4		50 9	9 3	10 2	3 5	3 9		5 2						100000 lb.	99
6	FM	" " ..	8200 to 8249	53 6	10 6		54 3		10 6		3 6								100000 lb.	25
7	FMS	" " Note Q	" "	"	"		"		"		"									10
11	FMS	" " Note O	" "	48 6	"	6 6	"	10 1	"	3 9	10 3		10 3							15
12	FM	" Steel Underframe	8300 to 8314	43	9		43	9 1			4		6 8						80000 lb.	7
13	FM	"	8315 to 8321	36	9						4 2								80000 lb.	1
14	FM	"	8330 to 8349	43 4	9 1		45	9 1	10	4 3									140000 lb.	20
15	FM	" Steel Underframe	8350 to 8399	50	9 4	5 2	50 9	9 4	10 3	3 2	3 9		5 2						100000 lb.	50
16	FM	" All Steel...	8400 to 8414	45	10 3		45 9	10 4	10 4	3 6	3 9		5 2						100000 lb.	14
17	FMS	" " Note S	8415 to 8449	53 6	10 6		54 2	10 6	10 6	3 8			3 8						100000 lb.	35
18	FM	" "	★ 8450 to 8483	45	10 6		46 2	10 6	10 6	4 2			4 2						140000 lb.	34
21	FM	" "	★ 8484 to 8499	43 4	10 6		44 6	10 6	10 6	4 3			4 3						140000 lb.	16
22	LP	Rack....Note QQ	8500 to 8550	50	9 4	7													100000 lb.	49
23	FM	Flat	8551 to 8599	53 6	9 4						3 8								100000 lb.	33
24	FMS	" ....Note CCC	" "	"	"		"				"									14
25	FM	" All Steel....	8600 to 8995	41 3	9 3		42	9 3	10 2	3 6	3 10		5 4						80000 lb.	395
26	FM	" "	9000 to 9199	41 3	9 3		42	9 3	10 2	3 6	3 10		5 4						80000 lb.	198
27	XM	Box, Steel Underframe	9401 to 9900	40 6	8 6	8 6	42 3	9 5	8 9		12 3	13 1	13 9	6	7 10			2935	80000 lb.	226
31	XM	" All Steel, Note FF②	" "	"	"	"	"	"	"		"	"	"	"	"			"	"	90
32	XME	" All Steel, Note AAA②	" "	"	"	"	"	"	"		"	"	"	"	"			"	"	20
33	TM	Tank Steel Uuderfr. Note WW	10553	......	......		34 10	8 11			10 8	12 8							80000 lb.	1
34	TM	" ..Note WW	10701 to 10800				32 2				9 2								80000 lb.	30
35	GB	Gond., Stl. Undfr., Fixed Ends, Wood Floor.	11001 to 11050	48	9 5	3 6	49 5	9 6	10 4	7 3	7 3		7 3					1582	140000 lb.	42
36	GB	" All Steel, Fixed Sides, Solid Ends, Solid Bottom.....	11100 to 11599	52 6	9 5	3 9	53 9	10 4	10 5	7 4	7 4		7 4					1856	140000 lb.	498
37	GB	" " "	11650 to 11899	52 6	9 5	3 9	53 9	10 4	10 5	7 4	7 4		7 4					1856	140000 lb.	250
41	GB	Gon. AllStl, Fixed Sides & Ends, Solid Bot..	12000 to 12499	52 6	9 5	3 9	53 9	10 4	10 5	7 4	7 4		7 4					1856	140000 lb.	499
42	GB	" " "	12550 to 12799	52 6	9 5	3 9	53 9	10 4	10 5	7 4	7 4		7 4					1856	140000 lb.	249
43	XM	Box, Steel Underframe	14002 to 14250	40 6	9	10	41	9 5			13 10	14 8	15 4	6	9 9			3611	80000 lb.	85
44	XM	" " Staggered Doors.	14251 to 14265	50 6	9	10 2	50 11	10			13 11	14 10	15 5	12 8	10 2	8 11	10 1	4653	100000 lb.	2
45	XM	Box, All Steel, Staggered Doors..	14300 to 14349	50 6	9 2	10 6	51 10	{9 4, 9 4}	10 8	3 4	{14 5, 13 6}	15	15	15 2	9 11			4860	100000 lb.	45
46	XAP	Auto, AllStl., Staggered Doors. Note XX①	" "	"	"	"	"	{9 4, 9 4}			{14 5, 13 6}			"	"			"	"	4
47	XM	Box, All Stl., Staggered Doors.....	14350 to 14399	50 6	9 4	10 6	51 10	{9 6, 10 7}	10 8	3 10	{14 5, 13 8}	15	15	15	9 9			4960	100000 lb.	37
51	XAP	Auto, AllStl., Staggered Doors. Note XX①	" "	"	"	"	"	{9 6, 10 7}	"	"	{14 5, 13 8}	"	"	"	"			"	"	12
52	XME	Box, All Steel....	14400 to 14424	50 6	9 3	10 6	51 10	{9 6, 10 7}	10 8	5 2	{14 5, 14 ..}	15 1	15 1	8	9 10			4916	100000 lb.	25
53	GB	Gondola, All Steel, Fixed Ends.	14920 to 14999	45	9 5	3 9	46 3	10 4	10 4	3 4			7 4					1634	100000 lb.	80
54	GB	Coal, All Stl., Fixed Sides & Ends, Solid Bottom	15000 to 15099	41 6	9 1		42 9		9 5				9 2					1855	100000 lb.	98
55	GB	Coal, Gond., Steel, Fixed Sides & Ends, Solid Bot.	15100 to 15274	45	9 5	3 9	46 3	10 2	10 4	3 4	7 4		7 4					1634	100000 lb.	174
56	GB	Coal, Gon. All Stl., Fixed Ends, Solid Bottom	15275 to 15624	45	9 5	3 9	46 3	9 5	10 4	7 4	7 4		7 4					1634	100000 lb.	347
57	GB	Coal, Gon. All Stl., Fixed Ends, Steel Floor.	15625 to 15704	45	9 5	3 9	46 3	10 4	10 4	3 4	7 4		7 4					1590	100000 lb.	79
61	XM	Box, Steel Underframe	16001 to 16318	40 6	8 6	8 6	41 3	8 11			12 4	13 1	13 9	6	8			2926	80000 lb.	210
62	XM	" All Steel, Note FF③	" "	"	"	"	"	"			"	"	"	"	"			"	"	79
63	XME	" All Steel, Note AAA③	" "	"	"	"	"	"			"	"	"	"	"			"	"	11
		Forward......																		9411

MISSOURI PACIFIC FREIGHT EQUIPMENT—Continued.

Item Number.	A.A.R. Mech. Designation.	MARKINGS AND KIND OF CARS.	NUMBERS.	INSIDE Length	INSIDE Width	INSIDE Height	OUTSIDE LENGTH	OUTSIDE WIDTH At Eaves or Top of Sides or Platform	OUTSIDE WIDTH Extreme Width.	HEIGHT FROM RAIL To Extreme Width.	HEIGHT FROM RAIL To Eaves or Top of Sides or Platform	HEIGHT FROM RAIL To Top of Running Board.	HEIGHT FROM RAIL To Extreme Height.	DOORS SIDE Width of Open'g	DOORS SIDE Height of Open'g	DOORS END Width of Open'g	DOORS END Height of Open'g	CAPACITY Cubic Feet Level Full.	CAPACITY Pounds or Gallons.	Number of Cars.
				ft. in.	ft. in.	ft. in.	ft. in.	ft. in.	ft. in.	ft. in.	ft. in.	ft. in.	ft. in.	ft. in.	ft. in.	ft. in.	ft. in.			
		Brought forward																		9411
1	XM	Box.............	17001 to 17300	40 6	8 9	9 4	41 9	8 8	10 2	....	13 2	13 10	13 10	6	8 10	....		3310	100000 lb.	266
2	XM	" Note DDD	" "	"	"	"	"	"	"	....	"	"	"	"	"	....		"	80000 lb.	28
3	XM	" All Steel...	17301 to 17500	40 6	8 9	9 4	41 10	8 8	10 2	13 2	13 10	13 10	13 10	6	8 10			3310	100000 lb.	194
4	XM	" " " ...	17501 to 17600	40 3	9 2	10 6	42 3	9 10	10 9	3 11	13 11	15 1	15 1	6	8 ...			3900	100000 lb.	100
5	XM	" " " ...	17601 to 17715	40 6	9 2	10 6	41 10	{9 4 / 10 5}	10 8	5 2	{14 5 / 14 ..}	15 1	15 1	6	9 10			3898	100000 lb.	115
6	XM	"	17751 to 17825	40 6	9 2	10 6	42 3	{9 4 / 10 5}	10 9	8 11	{14 5 / 13 10}	15 1	15 1	6	8 ...			3900	100000 lb.	73
7	XM	" All Steel..	17850 to 17999	40 6	9 2	10 6	41 10	{9 4 / 10 4}	10 8	3 10	{14 5 / 13 8}	15	15	6	9 10			3898	100000 lb.	149
11	XM	" " " .	18000 to 18449	40 6	9 2	10 6	41 10	{9 4 / 10 4}	10 8		{14 5 / 13 8}	15	15	6	9 10			3898	100000 lb.	446
12	XM	" " "	18465 to 18599	40 6	9 2	10 6	41 10	{9 4 / 10 5}	10 8	5 2	{14 5 / 14 ..}	15 1	15 1	6	9 10			3898	100000 lb.	135
13	XM	" " "	18800 to 18999	40 6	9 2	10 6	41 10	{9 4 / 10 4}	10 8	3 10	{14 5 / 13 8}	15	15	6	9 10			3898	100000 lb.	193
14	XM	" " "	19000 to 19499	40 6	9 2	10 6	41 10	{9 4 / 10 5}	10 8	5 8	{14 2 / 13 11}	15	15	6	9 10			3898	100000 lb.	498
15	XM	" " "	19500 to 19999	40 6	9 2	10 6	41 10	{9 4 / 10 4}	10 8	5 8	{14 2 / 13 11}	15	15	6	9 10			3898	100000 lb.	499
16	XM	" Steel Underframe	20001 to 20050	40	8 6	8	41 11	9 7	9 10	8 11	12 2	13 1	13 10	6	7 6			2740	80000 lb.	2
17	XM	" " " ..	20051 to 20550	40	8 6	10	41 7	9 6	....	9 6	14 1	14 11	15 10	6	9 5			8400	80000 lb.	151
21	XM	" " " ..	20551 to 20565	50 6	9	10 2	52 2	....		13 11	14 10	15 5	12 1	9 9	8 11	10 ...	4658	100000 lb.	13
22	XME	" All Steel....	20575 to 20599	50 6	9 3	10 6	51 10	{9 6 / 10 7}	10 8	5 2	{14 5 / 14 ..}	15 1	15 1	6	9 10			4906	100000 lb.	25
23	XM	" " "	20600 to 20699	50 6	9 2	10 6	51 10	{9 4 / 10 6}	10 8	3 4	{14 5 / 13 6}	15	15	15 2	9 11			4860	100000 lb.	99
24	XM	" " "	20700 to 20999	40 6	9 4	10 6	....	{9 6 / 10 7}	10 8	3 10	{14 5 / 13 8}	15	15	15 ...	9 9			3977	100000 lb.	295
25	GB	Log, Fixed Ends, Open Truss Sides, Rack Floor.	21000 to 21149	41 6	8 11	4 8	42 11	10 3	....	8 4			8 4						100000 lb.	2
26	GB	Gon., Fixed Ends, Flat Bot., Steel Floor.	22000 to 23774	45	9 5	3 9	46 3	10 2	10 4	3 4	7 4		7 4					1634	100000 lb.	1763
27	GB	" All Steel, Fixed Ends, Flat Bot.	23775 to 24614	45	9 5	3 9	46 3	10 4	10 4	3 4	7 4		7 4					1634	100000 lb.	837
31	GB	" All Steel, Fixed Ends, Flat Bot.	27900 to 27949	40	9 1	4 10	41 3	10	10 4	8 5	8 5		8 5					1770	100000 lb.	49
32	LG	" Note A	" "	"	"	"	"	"	"	"	"		"					"	"	1
33	GB	" Fixed Ends, Flat Bot., Steel Floor.	28000 to 28199	40	9 1	4 9	41 3	10	10 4		8 4		8 4					1751	100000 lb.	93
34	GB	" All Steel, Fixed Ends, Flat Bottom	28200 to 28899	40	9 5	4 10	41 3	10	10 4	8 5	8 5		8 5					1828	100000 lb.	381
35	LG	" "	" "	"	"	"	"	"	"	"	"		"					"	"	8
36	LG	" All Steel, Fixed Ends, Flat Bottom, Note B	" "	"	"	"	"	"	"	"	"		"					2680	"	2
37	GB	" All Steel, Fixed Ends, Flat Bottom	28900 to 29999	41 6	9 6	4 10	42 11	10 3	10 4	8 4	8 4		8 4					1885	100000 lb.	189
41	XM	Box, All Steel.....	30000 to 31399	40 6	8 9	9 1	41 10	{8 8 / 10 ..}	10 2	3 4	{13 2 / 12 5}	13 10	13 10	6	8 8			3233	100000 lb.	1372
42	XM	" "	31400 to 31499	40 6	8 9	9 1	41 10	{8 8 / 10 ..}	10 2	3 5	{13 3 / 12 6}	13 11	13 11	6	8 8			3233	100000 lb.	99
43	XM	" "	31500 to 32399	40 6	8 9	9 1	41 10	{8 8 / 10 ..}	10 2	3 4	{13 2 / 12 5}	13 10	13 10	6	8 8			3233	100000 lb.	878
44	XM	" "	32400 to 32499	40 6	8 9	9 4	41 10	{8 8 / 10 ..}	10 2	3 4	{13 2 / 12 5}	13 10	13 10	6	8 8			3310	100000 lb.	96
45	XM	" "	32500 to 33299	40 6	9 2	10 6	41 10	{9 5 / 9 11}	10 8	3 10	{14 4 / 13 10}	15	15	6	9 10			3898	100000 lb.	707
46	XAP	Auto., " Note L①	" "	"	"	"	"	{9 5 / 9 11}	"	"	{14 4 / 13 11}	"	"	"	"			"	"	81
47	XM	Box, "	34113 to 34287	40 6	9 2	10 6	41 10	{9 4 / 10 5}	10 8	3 10	{14 5 / 13 10}	15	15	8	9 10			3898	100000 lb.	169
51	XAP	Auto., " Note L②	" "	"	"	"	"	{9 4 / 10 5}	"	"	{14 5 / 13 10}	"	"	"	"			"	"	5
52	XM	Box, "	34300 to 34599	40 6	9 2	10 6	41 10	{9 4 / 10 4}	10 8	3 10	{14 5 / 13 8}	15	15	6	9 10			3898	100000 lb	291
53	XAP	Auto., " Note L③	" "	"	"	"	"	{9 4 / 10 4}	"	"	{14 5 / 13 8}	"	"	"	"			"	"	5
54	XM	Box, "	34600 to 35099	40 6	9 2	10 6	41 10	{9 4 / 10 5}	10 8	5 8	{14 2 / 13 11}	15	15	6	9 10			3898	100000 lb.	494
55	XM	" "	35100 to 35349	40 6	9 2	10 6	41 10	{9 4 / 10 5}	10 8	5 2	{14 5 / 14 ..}	15 1	15 1	6	9 10			3898	100000 lb.	248
56	XM	" "	35350 to 35824	40 6	9 2	10 6	41 10	{9 4 / 10 5}	10 8	5 2	{14 5 / 14 ..}	15 1	15 1	6	9 10			3898	100000 lb.	471
57	XM	" "	35825 to 36174	40 6	9 2	10 6	41 10	{9 4 / 10 3}	10 8	5 2	{14 5 / 13 7}	15 1	15 1	8	9 10			3898	100000 lb.	349
58	XM	" "	36175 to 37174	40 6	9 2	10 6	41 10	{9 4 / 10 5}	10 8	5 2	{14 5 / 14 ..}	15 1	15 1	8	9 10			3917	100000 lb.	165
		Forward....																....		21447

★ Denotes additions. ◆ Denotes increase. ♪ Denotes reduction.

MISSOURI PACIFIC FREIGHT EQUIPMENT—Continued.

Item No.	A.R. Mech. Desig.	MARKINGS AND KIND OF CARS.	NUMBERS.	Inside Length	Inside Width	Inside Height	Out. Length	Width At Eaves or Top of Sides or Platform	Extreme Width	Height To Extreme Width	To Eaves or Top of Sides or Platform	To Top of Running Board	To Extreme Height	Side Door Width of Open'g	Side Door Height of Open'g	End Door Width of Open'g	End Door Height of Open'g	Cubic Feet Level Full	Pounds or Gallons.	No. of Cars
		Brought forward																		21447
1	IM	Box, All Steel	41000 to 41799	40 6	8 8	8 6	42 3	9 1	9 10	11 8	12 5	13 1	13 1	6	7 10			2994	80000 lb.	399
2	IM	" Steel Underframe, Z-bar. Note HH①	" "	"	8 6	"	"	{8 11 / 10 ..}	10 3	4 1	{12 8 / 12 3}	13 2	13 2	"	"			2925	"	30
3	XME	" All Steel, Note AA①	" "	"	8 8	"	"	9 1	9 10	11 8	12 5	13 1	13 1	"	"			2994		163
4	IM	" Steel Underframe, Z-bar.	42000 to 42725	40 6	9 ..	10 ..	42 3	{9 5 / 10 6}	10 9	4 1	{14 4 / 13 6}	14 8	14 8	6	9 4			3645	80000 lb.	15
5	IM	" All Steel, Note GG	" "	"	9 2	8 6	"	9 7	10 4	11 8	12 5	13 1	13 1	"	7 10			3166	"	356
6	XME	" All Steel, Note KK	" "	"	9 2	8 6	"	9 7	10 4	11 8	12 5	13 1	13 1	"	7 10			3166		90
7	XAP	Auto., Stl. Underframe, Z-bar. Note L④	" "	"	9 ..	10 ..	"	{9 5 / 10 6}	10 9	4 1	{14 4 / 13 6}	14 8	14 8	"	9 4			3645		14
11	IM	Box, Steel Underframe, Staggered Doors	43000 to 43723	40 3	9 ..	10 ..	42 2	{9 5 / 10 6}	10 10	4 1	{14 4 / 13 6}	14 8	14 8	6	9 4			3626	80000 lb.	419
12	IM	"	44000 to 44410	40 4	9 1	10 2	42 2	{9 6 / 10 6}	10 10	4 1	{14 7 / 13 9}	14 10	14 10	6	9 9			3728	80000 lb.	334
13	IM	" Steel Underframe, Stagg. Doors, Z-bar	44500 to 44788	40 3	9 1	10 ..	42 2	{9 6 / 10 4}	10 8	5 3	{14 2 / 13 5}	14 8	14 10	6	9 9			3660	80000 lb.	248
14	IM	"	45251 to 45494	40 3	9 1	10 2	42 2	{9 6 / 10 6}	10 10	4 1	{14 7 / 13 9}	14 10	14 10	6	9 9			3724	80000 lb.	203
15	IM	" All Steel	46000 to 48749	40 6	8 8	8 6	42 3	9 1	9 10	11 8	12 5	13 1	13 1	6	7 10			2994	80000 lb.	1837
16	IM	" Steel Underframe, Z-bar. Note HH②	" "	"	8 6	"	"	{8 11 / 10 ..}	10 3	4 1	{12 8 / 12 3}	13 2	13 2	"	"			2925	"	93
17	XME	" All Steel, Note AA③	" "	"	8 8	"	"	9 1	9 10	11 8	12 5	13 1	13 1	"	"			2994		525
21	SM	Stock, Stl. Underframe, Z-bar	52000 to 52249	40 9	8 6	8 6	42 3	{9 7 / 10 ..}	10 5	4 3	{12 7 / 12 ..}	13 4	13 4	5	7 10			2969	80000 lb.	212
22	SM	" Steel Underframe, Z-bar	52250 to 52499	40 ..	8 6	8 6	41 5	{9 7 / 10 ..}	10 5	4 3	{12 7 / 12 ..}	13 4	13 4	5	7 10			2911	80000 lb.	204
23	SM	" Steel Underframe	52500 to 52999	40 ..	8 6	8 6	41 5	{9 7 / 10 ..}	10 5	3 11	{12 7 / 11 11}	13 4	13 4	5	8 ..			2911	80000 lb.	483
24	SM	" " "	53000 to 53214	40 ..	8 6	8 6	41 3	{9 7 / 10 ..}	10 5	4 ..	{12 5 / 11 11}	13 3	13 3	5	7 10			2947	80000 lb.	115
25	SC	" Steel Underframe, Double Deck	53500 to 53599	40 ..	8 6	8 6	41 3	{9 7 / 10 ..}	10 5	4 ..	{12 5 / 11 11}	13 3	13 3	5	{8 9 / 8 2}			2947	80000 lb.	96
26	SM	"	53850 to 53999	40 1	8 7	8 6	41 4	9 7	10 1	3 10	12 2	13 1	13 1	5	7 10			2947	80000 lb.	150
27	SM	"	54000 to 54099	40 1	8 7	8 6	41 5	9 7	10 1	3 10	12 6	13 3	13 3	5	7 10			2947	80000 lb.	97
31	SM	"	54100 to 54199	40 1	8 7	8 6	41 5	9 7	10 1	3 10	12 6	13 3	13 3	5	7 10			2947	80000 lb.	97
32	HT	Hopper, All Steel	55000 to 55499	40 5	10 ..		41 5	10 2	10 2	10 8	10 8		10 8					2755	140000 lb.	369
33	HT	" "	55500 to 56499	40 5	10 ..		41 5	10 2	10 2	10 8	10 8		10 8					2755	140000 lb.	871
34	HT	" "	56500 to 56597	40 8	10 4		41 9	10 6	10 6	10 9	10 9		10 9					2760	140000 lb.	96
35	HTR	" All Steel, with Roof	56598 to 56900	40 8	10 4		41 9	{7 11 / 9 9}	10 6	10 9	{12 6 / 12 3}	12 4	12 6					2955	140000 lb.	300
36	HT	" All Steel	56901 to 56999	40 8	10 4		41 9	10 6	10 6	10 9	10 9		10 9					2760	140000 lb.	99
37	HT	" "	57000 to 57499	40 8	10 4		41 9	10 6	10 6	10 9	10 9		10 9					2760	140000 lb.	493
41	HT	" "	57500 to 57899	40 8	10 4		41 9	10 6	10 6	10 9	10 9		10 9					2760	140000 lb.	398
42	HM	" "	58000 to 58749	30 6	9 5		31 11	10 1	10 1	10 9	10 9		10 9					1880	110000 lb.	137
43	HM	" " Note V	" "	"	"		"	"	"	"	"		"					1940	"	251
44	HM	" "	58750 to 60949	33 ..	10 4		34 1	10 5	10 5	10 8	10 8		10 8					2191	110000 lb.	2167
45	HT	" "	61000 to 61999	40 8	10 4		41 9	10 6	10 6	10 8	10 8		10 8					2760	140000 lb.	995
46	HT	" "	62000 to 62739	40 8	10 4		41 9	10 6	10 6	10 8	10 8		10 8					2760	140000 lb.	737
47	HT	" "	63000 to 64199	40 8	9 6		41 9	10 5	10 5	10 8	10 8		10 8					2650	140000 lb.	842
51	HT	" Composite	65000 to 65099	40 8	9 6		41 9	10 5	10 5	10 8	10 8		10 8					2580	140000 lb.	47
52	HT	" All Steel	65250 to 65499	40 8	9 6		41 9	10 5	10 5	10 8	10 8		10 8					2580	140000 lb.	126
53	HT	" "	65500 to 65699	40 8	10 4		41 9	10 5	10 5	10 8	10 8		10 8					2760	140000 lb.	198
54	GS	Gondola, Drop Bot., Steel Underframe	66001 to 68000	40 ..	9 1	4 10	41 3	10 ..	10 4	8 5	8 5		8 5					1770	100000 lb.	31
55	LG	Gon., Solid Bot., Steel Underfrme. Note E	" "	"	"	"	"	"	"	"	"		"					"	"	14
56	LG	Gon., Solid Bot., Steel Underfrme. Note G	" "	"	"	"	"	"	"	"	"		"					"	"	2
57	LG	Gon., Solid Bot., Steel Underfrme. Note DD	" "	"	"	"	"	"	"	"	"		"					"	"	5
61	GB	Gond., All Steel, Fixed Ends	70501 to 73500	41 6	9 6	4 10	42 11	10 3	10 4	8 4	8 4		8 4					1885	100000 lb.	160
62	GB	Gond., All Steel, Fixed Ends	73501 to 74250	41 6	9 ..	4 11	42 9	10 3	10 4	8 7	8 7		8 7					1914	100000 lb.	175
		Forward																		36140

MISSOURI PACIFIC FREIGHT EQUIPMENT—Continued.

Item Number	A.A.R. Mech. Designation	MARKINGS AND KIND OF CARS.	NUMBERS.	Inside Length	Inside Width	Inside Height	Outside Length	Outside Width At Eaves or Top of Sides or Platform	Outside Width Extreme Width	Height from Rail To Extreme Width	Height from Rail To Eaves or Top of Sides or Platform	Height from Rail To Top of Running Board	Height from Rail To Extreme Height	Side Door Width of Open'g	Side Door Height of Open'g	End Door Width of Open'g	End Door Height of Open'g	Cubic Feet Level Full	Pounds or Gallons	Number of Cars
				ft. in.	ft. in.	ft. in.	ft. in.	ft. in.	ft. in.	ft. in.	ft. in.	ft. in.	ft. in.	ft. in.	ft. in.	ft. in.	ft. in.			
		Brought forward........																		36140
1	XAR	Auto., Stl. Underframe, Stag. Doors, Z-bar. Note NN①	75280 to 75479	40 6	9 ...	10 8 / 10 2	42 2	9 3 / 9 6	10 10	4 1	15 .. / 13 7	15 4	15 4	12 1	9 9	......		3921 / 3563	80000 lb.	130
2	XM	Box, Stl. Underfr., Stag. Doors, Z-bar. Note N	75480 to 75999	40 6	9 ...	10 8	42 2	9 3 / 10 6	10 10	4 1	15 .. / 13 7	15 4	15 4	12 1	9 9	......		3921	80000 lb.	94
3	XAR	Auto., Steel Underfr., Stag.Doors, Z-bar. Note W	" "	"	"	10 8 / 10 2	"	9 3 / 9 6	"	"	15 .. / 13 7	"	"	"	"			3921 / 3563	"	228
4	XAR	Auto., Stl. Underframe, Stag. Doors, Z-bar. Note NN①	76150 to 76999	40 6.	9 ...	10 8 / 10 2	42 2	9 3 / 10 6	10 10	4 1	15 .. / 13 7	15 4	15 4	12 1	9 9	......		3921 / 3563	80000 lb.	58
6	XM	Box, Steel Underfr., Stag. Doors, Z-bar.	79000 to 79199	40 6	9 ...	10 ...	42 2	9 6 / 10 4	10 10	4 1	14 2 / 13 5	14 8	14 8	12 ..	9 7	......		3677	80000 lb.	29
7	XM	Box, All Steel...	80000 to 80499	40 6	9 4	10 6	41 10	10 7 / 10 7	10 8	3 10	14 5 / 13 8	15 ...	15 ...	15 ...	9 9	......		3977	100000 lb.	301
11	XME	" " Note T	" "	"	"	"	"	9 6 / 10 7	"	"	14 5 / 13 8	"	"	■	"			"	"	60
12	XAP	Auto., All Steel, Note L②	" "	"	"	"	"	9 6 / 10 7	"	"	14 5 / 13 8	"	"	"	"			"	"	132
13	XM	Box, Steel Underfr., Stag. Doors. Z-bar.	84000 to 84099	40 6	9 ...	10 2	42 2	9 3 / 10 6	10 10	4 1	15 .. / 13 7	15 4	15 4	12 1	9 9	......		3921	80000 lb.	99
14	XM	Box, Steel Underfr., Stag. Doors. Z-bar.	84100 to 84480	40 6	9 ...	10 8	42 2	9 6 / 10 6	10 10	4 1	15 .. / 13 7	15 4	15 4	12 1	9 9	......		3921	80000 lb	312
15	XM	Box, Steel Underfr., Stag. Doors. Z-bar.	84481 to 84663	40 6	9 1	10 8	42 2	9 3 / 10 6	10 10	4 1	15 .. / 13 7	15 4	15 4	12 1	9 9	......		3921	80000 lb.	107
16	XM	Box, Steel Underfr., Stag. Doors. Z-bar.	84664, 84710	40 3	9 1	10 6	42 2	9 6 / 10 6	10 10	4 1	14 9 / 13 6	15 2	15 2	12 1	9 9	......		3841	80000 lb.	2
21	XM	Box, Steel Underfr., Stag. Doors. Z-bar.	85000 to 85449	50 6	8 11	10 ...	52 3	9 5 / 10 6	10 9	4 1	14 2 / 13 5	14 8	14 8	10 ...	9 4	......		4545	100000 lb.	63
22	XAP	Auto. Stl. Undfr., Stag. Doors, Z-bar. Note L⑤	" "	"	"	"	"	9 5 / 10 6	"	"	14 2 / 13 5	"	"	"	"			"	"	17
23	XM	Box, Steel Underfr., Stag. Doors, Z-bar.	85450 to 85949	50 6	8 11	10 ...	52 2	9 5 / 10 6	10 9	4 1	14 2 / 13 5	14 8	14 8	11 ...	9 4	......		4545	100000 lb.	55
24	XAP	Auto., All Steel, Stag. Doors, Z-bar, Note LL	" "	50 4	9 2	"	"	9 5 / 10 6	10 6	3 6	14 2 / 13 5	"	"	8 ...	9 6	......		4648	"	85
25	XM	Box, Steel Underfr., Stag. Doors, Z-bar.	86000 to 86149	50 6	9 ...	10 2	52 2	9 6 / 10 6	10 9	3 11	14 7 / 13 7	14 10	14 10	12 ...	9 9	......		4669	100000 lb.	37
26	XM	Box, All Steel, Staggered Doors.	86200 to 86399	50 6	9 2	10 6	51 9	9 4 / 10 6	10 8	3 4	14 5 / 13 6	15 ...	15 ...	15 1	9 10	......		4860	100000 lb.	21
27	XAP	Auto., All Steel, Stag. Doors. Note L⑦	" "	"	"	"	"	9 4 / 10 6	"	"	14 5 / 13 6	"	"	"	"			"	"	175
31	XM	Box, All Steel...	86400 to 86999	50 6	9 4	10 6	51 9	9 6 / 10 6	10 8	3 10	14 5 / 13 8	15 ...	15 ...	15 ...	9 9	......		4960	100000 lb.	19
32	XME	" All Steel.. Note BB①	" "	"	9 3	"	"	9 6 / 10 6	"	"	14 5 / 13 8	"	"	"	"			4860	"	220
33	XAP	Auto.. All Steel Note L⑧	" "	"	9 4	"	"	9 6 / 10 6	"	"	14 5 / 13 8	"	"	"	"			4960	"	156
34	XAP	Auto., All Steel Note R	" "	"	9 4	12 2	"	9 6 / 10 6	"	"	16 1 / 15 4	16 8	16 8	"	"			5795	"	40
35	XAR	Auto., All Steel Note EE	" "	"	9 4	10 6 / 9 8	"	9 6 / 10 6	"	"	14 5 / 13 8	15 ...	15 ...	,	"			4960 / 4587	"	156
36	XM	Box, All Steel...	87000 to 87249	50 6	9 4	10 6	51 9	9 6 / 10 6	10 8	3 10	14 5 / 13 8	15 ...	15 ...	8 ...	9 9	......		4960	100000 lb.	34
37	XME	" " Note BB②	" "	"	9 3	"	"	9 6 / 10 6	"	"	14 5 / 13 8	"	"	"	"			4860	"	169
41	XAP	Auto., All Steel Note L⑨	" "	"	9 4	"	"	9 6 / 10 6	"	"	14 5 / 13 8	"	"	"	"			4960	"	
42	XM	Box, All Steel....	87250 to 87349	50 6	9 4	10 6	51 10	9 6 / 10 6	10 8	5 2	14 5 / 13 8	15 1	15 1	8 ...	9 10	......		4960	100000 lb.	
43	XAP	Auto., All Steel Note L⑩	" "	"	"	"	"	9 6 / 10 6	"	"	14 5 / 13 8	"	"	"	"			"	"	
44	XME	Box, All Steel.. Note BB③	" "	"	9 3	"	"	9 6 / 10 6	"	"	14 5 / 13 8	"	"	"	"			4860	"	
45	XME	" All Steel..	87350 to 87829	50 6	9 3	10 6	51 10	9 6 / 10 6	10 8	5 2	14 5 / 13 8	15 1	15 1	8 ...	9 10	......		4906	100000 lb.	
46	XME	" "	87830 to 87979	50 6	9 2	10 6	51 10	9 6 / 10 6	10 8	5 2	14 5 / 13 8	15 1	15 1	8 ...	9 10	......		4906	100000 lb.	
47	XAR	Auto., Stl. Underframe, Stag. Doors, Z-bar. Note NN①	88000 to 88099	50 6	9 ...	10 8 / 9 8	52 2	9 2 / 10 6	10 9	3 11	14 11 / 13 7	15 4	15 4	14 6	9 9	......		4892 / 4453	100000 lb.	
51	XAR	Auto., Steel Underframe, Stag. Doors, Z-bar. Note NN③	88100 to 88149	50 6	9 ...	10 8 / 9 8	52 1	9 4 / 10 4	10 10	4 1	14 11 / 14 1	15 4	15 4	14 6	9 6	......		4861 / 4424	100000 lb.	
52	XAR	Auto., Stl. Underframe, Stag. Doors, Z-bar. Note NN④	88150 to 88199	50 6	9 ...	10 8 / 9 8	52 3	9 5 / 10 4	10 10	4 1	14 11 / 14 1	15 4	15 4	14 7	9 6	......		4818 / 4412	100000 lb.	
53	XME	Box, All Steel, Stag. Doors, Z-bar. Note RR	88325 to 88339	50 6	9 2	10 6	51 11	9 4 / 10 ..	10 8	4 7	14 7 / 14 ..	15 ...	15 ...	15 ...	9 10	......		4860	100000 lb.	
		Forward......																		

MISSOURI PACIFIC FREIGHT EQUIPMENT—Continued.

A.A.R. Mech.	MARKINGS AND KIND OF CARS.	NUMBERS.	Inside Length	Inside Width	Inside Height	Outside Length	Outside Width At Eaves or Top of Sides or Platform	Outside Extreme Width	Height To Extreme Width	Height To Eaves or Top of Sides or Platform	Height To Top of Running Board	Height To Extreme Height	Side Door Width of Open'g	Side Door Height of Open'g	End Door Width of Open'g	End Door Height of Open'g	Cubic Feet Level Full	Pounds or Gallons.	Number of Cars.
	Brought forward																		39684
XM	Box, All Steel, Stag. Doors, Z-bar.	88372 to 88399	50 4	9	10 6	52 2	9 3 / 10 4	10 6	5 6	14 8 / 13 8	15 2	15 2	15 ...	9 10			4760	100000 lb.	14
XAP	Auto, All Steel, Stag. Doors, Z-bar. Note P	" "	"	9 2	"	"	9 3 / 10 4	"	"	14 8 / 13 8	"	"	"				4880	"	12
XM	Box, All Steel, Stag. Doors, Z-bar. Note RR	88400 to 88434	50 6	9 2	10 6	51 11	9 4 / 10 ..	10 8	4 7	14 7 / 14 ..	15	15	14 6	9 10			4860	100000 lb.	35
XAR	Auto, Stl. Undfr., Stag. Drs, Z-bar. Note NN (5)	88501 to 88803	50 6	9	10 6 / 9 6	52 3	9 5 / 10 4	10 6	3 5	14 8 / 13 3	15 2	15 2	14 7	9 4			4785 / 4420	100000 lb.	233
XAR	Auto, Stl. Undfr., Stag. Drs, Z-bar. Note NN (6)	88825 to 88849	50 6	9	10 8 / 9 8	52 2	9 2 / 10 6	10 9	3 11	14 11 / 13 7	15 4	15 4	14 6	9 9			4892 / 4453	100000 lb.	18
XM	Box, Steel Underfr., Stag. Doors, Z-bar.	89000 to 89069	50 6	9 1	10 2	52 2	9 6 / 10 6	10 9	3 11	14 7 / 13 6	14 10	14 10	12 1	9 9			4681	100000 lb.	23
XM	Box, Steel Underfr., Stag. Doors, Z-bar.	89070 to 89169	50 6	9 1	10 2	52 2	9 6 / 10 6	10 9	3 11	14 7 / 13 6	14 10	14 10	12 1	9 9			4681	100000 lb.	50
XM	Box, All Steel	89200 to 89499	50 6	9 5	10 7	51 10	9 6 / 10 6	10 8	5 2	14 5 / 13 8	15 1	15 1	8	9 10			4984	100000 lb.	300
XM	" "	89500 to 89568	50 6	9 5	10 7	51 10	9 6 / 10 6	10 8	5 2	14 5 / 13 8	15 1	15 1	15 ...	9 9			4984	100000 lb.	69
XME	" "	89569 to 89599	50 6	9 3	10 7	51 10	9 6 / 10 6	10 8	5 2	14 5 / 13 8	15 1	15 1	15 ...	9 9			4906	100000 lb.	31
XME	" "	89600 to 89699	50 6	9 2	10 6	51 10	9 6 / 10 6	10 8	5 2	14 5 / 13 8	15 1	15 1	15 ...	9 9			4906	100000 lb.	100
XM	" "	*89700 to 89949	50 6	9 4	10 6	51 10	9 6 / 10 6	10 8	5 2	14 5 / 13 8	15 1	15 1	15 ...	9 9			4984	110000 lb.	250
XM	Box, Steel Underfr., Stag. Doors, Z-bar.	90000 to 91249	40 6	9	9 3	42 3	9 5 / 10 6	10 9	4 1	13 6 / 12 9	13 11	13 11	6	8 7			3371	100000 lb.	873
XM	Box, Stl. Underfr., Stag. Doors, Z-bar. Note C	" "	40 4	"	"	"	9 5 / 10 6	"	"	13 6 / 12 9	"	"	"	"			3360	"	95
XM	Box, Steel Underframe	93000 to 95249	40 6	9	9 3	42 2	9 5 / 10 5	10 7	3 11	13 6 / 12 10	13 11	13 11	6	8 10			3371	100000 lb.	2164
XI	" All Steel, Insulated	96000 to 96024	40 1	9 2	9 8	41 10	9 10 / 10 5	10 5	4 10	15 .. / 14 2	15 1	15 1	8	9 8			3569	100000 lb.	25
XM	" Stl. Underframe, Z-bar.	120000 to 120849	36 3	8 6	8 2	38 3	9 6 / 10 2	10 5	4 2	12 8 / 12 2	18 ...	13 ...	6	7 6			2563	80000 lb.	29
XM	" Stl. Underframe, Z-bar. Note X	" "	36	"	"	"	9 6 / 10 2	"	"	12 8 / 12 2	"	"	"	"			2546	"	7
XME	" All Steel, Note U (1)	" "	36 4	8 7	8 4	"	8 11 / 9 1	9 10	11 6	12 2 / 12 1	12 10	12 10	"	7 9			2645	"	238
...	Coke, Roofless Box, Stl. Underframe. Note VV	" "	36 3	8 6	8 2	"	9 6 / 10 2	10 5	4 2	12 8 / 12 2	13 ...	13 ...	"	7 6			2503	"	9
XM	Box, Stl. Underframe, Z-bar.	120850 to 121149	36 4	8 6	8 2	38 3	9 6 / 10 2	10 5	4 2	12 8 / 12 2	18 ...	13 ...	6	7 6			2572	80000 lb	2
XM	" Stl. Underframe, Z-bar. Note Z	" "	36 3	"	"	"	9 6 / 10 2	"	"	12 8 / 12 2	"	"	"	"			2563	"	3
XME	" All Steel, Note U (2)	" "	36 4	8 7	8 4	"	8 11 / 9 1	9 10	11 6	12 2 / 12 1	12 10	12 10	"	7 9			2645	"	84
...	Coke, Roofless Box, Stl. Underframe. Note OO	" "	36 3	8 6	8 2	"	9 6 / 10 2	10 5	4 2	12 8 / 12 2	13 ...	13 ...	"	7 6			2563	"	2
XM	Box, Stl. Underframe, Z-bar.	121150 to 121749	36 4	8 6	8 2	38 3	10 .. / 10 1	10 1	4 2	12 9 /	13 ...	13 ...	6	7 6			2572	80000 lb	9
XM	" Stl. Underframe, Z-bar. Note H	" "	36 3	"	"	"	10 .. /	"	"	12 9 /	"	"	"	"			2563	"	1
XM	" Stl. Underframe, Z-bar. Note CC	" "	36	"	"	"	10 .. /	"	"	12 9 /	"	"	"	"			2546	"	3
XME	" All Steel, Note U (3)	" "	36 4	8 7	8 4	"	8 11 / 9 1	9 10	11 6	12 2 / 12 1	12 10	12 10	"	7 9			2645	"	175
...	Coke, Roofless Box, Stl. Underframe. Note PP	" "	36 3	8 6	8 2	"	9 6 / 10 2	10 5	4 2	12 8 / 12 2	13 ...	13 ...	"	7 6			2563	"	3
...	Caboose	150 to 243																	16
...	"	250 to 284																	35
NM	"	401 to 529																	78
NM	"	700 to 934																	195
NM	"	935 to 954																	19
NM	"	970 to 999																	80
...	" Merchandise	1000 to 1015																	16
NM	"	1016 to 1080																	65
NM	" Drover	1100 to 1119																	20
NM	"	1125 to 1149																	25
...	"	1150 to 1167																	18
NM	"	1170 to 1256																	90
	Total																		45148

2300

10-76

MISSOURI PACIFIC RAILROAD COMPANY
MISSOURI PACIFIC LINES
Reporting Marks and ACI Nos.—"ARMN"- 0 048; "MP"- 0 494
Uniform Alphabetic Code and ACI No.—"MP"- 0 494

GENERAL OFFICES: Telex 44-7105; 44-7382

Do not confuse with Maryland and Pennsylvania Railroad Company.

FREIGHT EQUIPMENT
Cars are marked "ARMN" or "Missouri Pacific Lines" and "MP" and are numbered and classified as follows:

Line No.	A.A.R. Mech. Desig.	DESCRIPTION (See Explanation Pages for Abbreviations & Symbols)	A.A.R. Car Type Code	NUMBERS ▶Change from Previous Issue	INSIDE Length	INSIDE Width	INSIDE Height	OUTSIDE Length	Width At Eaves or Top of Sides or Platform	Extreme Width	Height To Extreme Width	Height To Eaves or Top of Sides or Platform	Height To Extreme Height	Door Width of Open'g	Door Height of Open'g	CAPACITY Cubic Feet Level Full	CAPACITY Lbs. (000)	No. of Cars
		"ARMN"																
1	RP	Refrig., Cush. Underfr., Permanent Flr. Racks, Side Wall Flues, Special Service, 140000 lb. Cap. Journals, 25K ... Note 1	R104	80-89	44 9	8 8	8 3	59 3	9 9	10 8	13 10	14 4	15 1	8....	8 4	3280	130	9
2	RP	Refrig., Permanent Flr. Racks, Side Wall Flues, Special Service, 140000 lb. Cap. Journals, 25K ... Note 1	R104	90-99	45 6	8 6	8 6	56 2	9 10	10 8	13 9	14 3	15 1	8....	8 8	3316	130	10
3	RP	Refrig., Permanent Flr. Racks, Side Wall Flues, Special Service, 140000 lb. Cap. Journals, 25K ... Note 1	R104	175-324	45...	8 7	8 3	56....	9 11	10 8	13 10	14 3	15 1	8....	8	3187	130	143
4	RPL	Refrig., Cush. Underfr., Permanent Flr. Racks, Side Wall Flues, Special Service, 140000 lb. Cap. Journals, 25K ... Note 1	R110	325-464	44 9	8 8	8 3	59 3	9 9	10 8	13 10	14 4	15 1	8....	8 4	3280	130	133
5	RPL	Refrig., Cush. Underfr., Movable Blkhds, Permanent Flr. Racks, Side Wall Flues, Special Service, 140000 lb. Cap. Journals, 25K .. Note 1	R210	500-599	49 4	8 9	8 7	63 8	10....	10 8	13 10	14 1	15 1	8 1	8 7	3766	130	95
6	RPL	Refrig., Cush. Underfr., Movable Blkhds, Permanent Flr. Racks, Side Wall Flues, Special Service, 140000 lb. Cap. Journals, 25K .. Note 1	R210	600-700	49 10	9....	8 11	63 8	10....	10 8	13 10	14 1	15 1	9....	8 8	4011	130	99
7	RPL	Refrig., Cush. Underfr., Movable Blkhds, Permanent Flr. Racks, Side Wall Flues, Special Service, 140000 lb. Cap. Journals, 25K .. Note 1	R210	701-715	50...	9...	8 11	61 8	10....	10 8	13 10	14 1	15 1	9....	8 8	4022	130	14
8	RPL	Refrig., Cush. Underfr., Movable Blkhds, Permanent Flr. Racks, Side Wall Flues, Special Service, 140000 lb. Cap. Journals, 25K .. Note 1	R210	716-745	50...	9...	8 11	61 8	10....	10 8	13 10	14 1	15 1	9....	8 8	4042	130	30
9	RPL	Refrig., Cush. Underfr., Movable Blkhds, Permanent Flr. Racks, Side Wall Flues, Special Service, 140000 lb. Cap. Journals, 25K .. Note 1	R210	746-775	50...	9...	8 11	63 8	10....	10 8	13 10	14 1	15 1	9....	8 8	4042	130	30
10	RPL	Refrig., Cush. Underfr., Movable Blkhds, Permanent Flr. Racks, Side Wall Flues, Special Service, 140000 lb. Cap. Journals, 25K .. Note 1	R210	776-850	50...	9...	8 11	63 8	10....	10 8	13 10	14 1	15 1	9....	8 8	4022	130	71
11	RPL	Refrig., Cush. Underfr., Movable Blkhds, Permanent Flr. Racks, Side Wall Flues, Special Service, 140000 lb. Cap. Journals, 25K .. Note 1	R210	851-1050	50...	9...	8 11	63 9	10....	10 7	4 4	14 4	15...	9....	8 10	4021	130	197
		"MP"																
12	XP	Box, Stl., 2 Doors Each Side, Originally Mail & Baggage in Passenger Service Now Frt. Service Only, (Bulky Frt. Such as Hay Bales & Cotton Bales Etc.)	A300	135-184	70...	9...	8...	71 3		10 3	4 4 / 6 10		13 7	9...	6 6	5040	75	47
13	XP	Box, Stl., 1 Door Each End: Width 2'7" & Height 6'4", Originally Mail & Baggage in Passenger Service Now Frt. Service Only, (Bulky Frt. Such as Hay Bales & Cotton Bales Etc.)	A400	213	80 7	9 2	7 5 / 9 5	85....	10...	10 6	4 6 / 6 8		13 9	8...	6 5	5480	90	1
14	XP	Box, Stl., 1 Door Each End: Width 2'7" & Height 6'4", Originally Mail & Baggage in Passenger Service Now Frt. Service Only, (Bulky Frt. Such as Hay Bales & Cotton Bales Etc.)	A400	250-276	80 7	9 2	7 5 / 9 5	85....	10...	10 6	4 6 / 6 8		13 9	8...	6 5	4945	60	18
15	GBS	Gond., Stl. Flr., Fixed Ends, Flat Bottom, (Pipe)	E130	▶1300-1399	45...	9 5	3 9	48 9	10 2	10 4	3 4	7 4	7 4			1634	110	32
16	LP	Rack	L026	1431, 1442, 1499	36 8	9 1	4 1	44 6	9 8	9 4	7 8	11 9	12 7				110	3
17	LP	Rack	L026	1642	37 6	9 1	4 1	44 6	9 11	11 9	7 8	11 9	12 8				110	1
18	LO	Hop., Stl., Stl. Roof	L151	2822	35 8	9 10		44 3	9 9	10 6	10 9	12 2	13 4			2680	154	1
19	GBS	Gond., Stl. Flr., Fixed Ends, Flat Bottom, (Pipe)	E130	3400-3499	45...	9 5	3 9	48 9	10 2	10 2	7 4	7 4	7 4			1634	110	46
20	LO	Hop., Stl., Stl. Roof	L151	4684	39 10	9 9		48 5	8 8 / 10 2	10 2	12 2	13 1 / 12 10	13 1			2828	154	1
21	LO	Hop., Stl., Stl. Roof	L151	4786	35 8	9 7		44 3	9 8 / 10 6	10 6	10 8	12 1	13 4			2680	154	1
22	GB	Gond., Stl., Fixed Ends, Flat Bottom	G212	▶5200-5999	52 6	9 5	3 9	56 3	10 5	10 5	7 4	7 4	7 5			1856	154	5
23	GB	Gond., Stl., Fixed Ends, Flat Bottom	G412	6079	65...	7 9	3 6	68 9	8 7	8 8	4 3	7 1	7 3			1763	154	1
24	HK	Hop., Ballast, Stl.	H230	6832	40 8	9 8		44 3	10 7	10 7	11 1	11 1	11 1			2795	154	1
25	GS	Gond.	G282	7114, 7120	48 6	9 6	6...	52 9	10 6	10 6	10 4	10 4	10 4			2765	154	2
26	GBSR	Gond., 3 Section Removable Roof, Blkhd. (Stl. Mill Products), Inside Width Between Rails 9'1"	E340	7331	52 5	9 6	4 6	56 3	10 8	10 8	8 9	8 9	9 8			2242	150	1
27	FM	Flat, Stl.	F101	8019, 8047, 8050	45...	9 4		48 3	9 4	10 3	3 6	3 9	5 2				110	3
28	FM	Flat, Stl.	F201	8347	45...	9 1		49 2	9 1	10...	4 2	4 2	4 2				154	1
29	FM	Flat, Stl.	F101	8403	45...	10 3		48 3	10 4	10 4	3 6	3 9	5 2				110	1
30	FM	Flat, Stl.	F201	8495	43 4	10 6		47...	10 6	10 6	4 4	4 4	4 4				154	1
31	FM	Flat, Stl.	F101	8600-8995	41 3	9 3		44 6	9 3	10 2	3 6	3 10	5 4				88	33
32	FM	Flat, Stl. ■	F101	9000-9199	41 3	9 3		44 6	9 3	10 2	3 6	3 10	5 4				88	12
33	FC	Flat, Tie Down Equipment, (Containers)	F971	9003, 9062	41 3	9 3		44 6	9 3	10 2	3 6	3 10	5 4				88	2
34	FM	Flat, Stl.	F103	9914, 9970	60...	10 6		63 5	10 6	10 6	3 9	3 9	3 9				110	2
35	GB	Gond., Stl., Fixed Sides, Solid Ends, Solid Bottom	G312	11112	52 6	9 5	3 9	56 3	10 4	10 5	7 4	7 4	7 4			1856	154	1
36	LG	Gond., Stl., Fixed Sides, Solid Ends, Solid Bottom, 9 Containers, Cap. 135 Cubic ft. Each, (Dolomite)	L016	11538	36 9	9 5	3 9	56 3	10 4	10 5	7 4	7 4	7 4				154	1
37	GB	Gond., Stl., Fixed Sides, Solid Ends, Solid Bottom	G312	11544	52 6	9 5	3 9	56 3	10 4	10 5	7 4	7 4	7 4			1856	154	1
38	GB	Gond., Stl., Fixed Sides, Solid Ends, Solid Bottom	G312	11666-11874	52 6	9 5	3 9	56 3	10 4	10 5	7 4	7 4	7 4			1856	154	5

Line No.	A.A.R. Mech. Desig.	Description (See Explanation Pages for Abbreviations & Symbols)	A.A.R. Car Type Code	Numbers (▶Change from Previous Issue)	Inside Length	Inside Width	Inside Height	Outside Length	Outside Width At Eaves or Top of Sides or Platform	Outside Extreme Width	Height from Rail To Extreme Width	Height To Eaves or Top of Sides or Platform	To Extreme Height	Doors Side Width of Open'g	Doors Side Height of Open'g	Capacity Cubic Feet Level Full	Capacity Lbs. (000)	No. of Cars
		"MP"																
1	GB	Gond., Stl., Fixed Sides & Ends, Solid Bottom	G312	12465, 12466	52 6	9 5	3 9	56 3	10 4	10 5	7 4	7 4	7 4			1856	154	2
2	GB	Gond., Stl., Flat Bottom, Drop Ends: Width 8'10"	G322	12915, 12981	52 6	9 5	3 9	57 2	10 5	10 8	5 6	7 4	7 7			1856	154	2
3	XM	Box, Stl., Stagg. Doors	B209	14338, 14595	50 6	9 2	10 6	54 4	9 4 / 10 6	10 8	3 4	14 5 / 13 6	15 ...	15 2	9 11	4860	110	2
4	LG	Gond., Stl., Fixed Ends, 10 Containers, (Dolomite & Lime)	L016	14946	45 ...	9 5	3 9	48 9	10 4	10 4	3 4	7 4	7 4			1590	110	1
5	GB	Gond., Stl., Fixed Ends, Solid Bottom, (Coal)	G112	15495	45 ...	9 5	3 9	48 9	9 5	10 4	7 4	7 4	7 4			1634	110	1
6	GB	Gond., Stl., Fixed Ends, Flat Bottom	G312	▶ 21028-21865	52 6	9 5	3 9	56 3	10 5	10 5	7 4	7 4	7 4			1856	154	2
7	GB	Gond., Stl. Flr., Fixed Ends, Flat Bottom ■	G112	22000-23774	45 ...	9 5	3 9	48 9	10 2	10 4	3 4	7 4	7 4			1634	110	29
8	GB	Gond., Stl. Flr., Fixed Ends, Flat Bottom	G112	22013, 22069, 22384, 22478, 23035, 23077, 23210, 23288, 23310, 23346, 23353, 23416, 23615	45 ...	9 5	3 9	48 9	10 2	10 4	3 4	7 4	7 4			1590	110	13
9	GB	Gond., Stl., Fixed Ends, Flat Bottom ■	G112	23841-24614	45 ...	9 5	3 9	48 9	10 4	10 4	3 4	7 4	7 4			1590	110	6
10	LG	Gond., Stl. Flr., Fixed Ends, Flat Bottom, 10 Containers, (Dolomite & Lime)	L016	24373, 24435	45 ...	9 5	3 9	48 9	10 4	10 4	3 4	7 4	7 4			1590	110	2
11	GB	Gond., Stl., Fixed Ends, Flat Bottom	G312	25000-25499	52 6	9 5	3 9	56 3	10 5	10 5	7 4	7 4	7 4			1856	154	6
12	XM	Box, Stl.	B107	35998, 36119	40 6	9 2	10 6	44 4	9 5 / 10 3	10 8	5 2	14 4 / 13 7	15 1	8 ...	9 10	3898	110	2
13	XM	Box, Stl.	B107	37179, 37427, 37962	40 6	9 2	10 6	44 4	9 4 / 10 5	10 8	5 2	14 5 / 14 ...	15 1	8 ...	9 10	3917	110	3
14	XL	Box, Stl., DF Loaders	A130	38561, 38563	40 6	9 2	10 6	44 4	9 4 / 10 5	10 8	5 2	14 5 / 14 ...	15 1	8 ...	9 10	3917	110	2
15	XM	Box, Stl.	B107	38635	40 6	9 4	10 6	44 4	9 6 / 10 8	10 8	5 2	14 5 / 13 6	15 1	8 ...	9 11	4000	110	1
16	XM	Box, Stl.	B107	38974	40 6	9 4	10 6	44 4	9 6 / 10 8	10 8	6 8	14 5 / 13 7	15 1	8 ...	9 10	3952	110	1
17	HT	Hop., Stl.	H250	56537	40 8	10 4		44 3	10 6	10 6	10 9	10 9	10 9			2760	154	1
18	HTR	Hop., Stl., Roof	K230	56808-56799	40 8	10 4		44 3	3 ... / 10 3	10 6	10 8	12 3 / 11 ...	12 3			2760	154	6
19	HTR	Hop., Stl., Roof	K230	56823, 56877, 56882, 56895	40 8	10 4		44 3	7 11 / 9 9	10 6	10 8	12 6 / 11 6	12 6			2955	154	4
20	HM	Hop., Stl.	H140	60647	33 ...	10 4		36 7	10 5	10 5	10 8	10 8	10 8			2191	110	1
21	HT	Hop., Stl.	H250	61020, 62451	40 8	10 4		44 3	10 6	10 6	10 8	10 8	10 8			2760	154	2
22	HT	Hop., Stl.	H250	64003, 64065	40 8	9 10		44 3	10 5	10 5	10 8	10 8	10 8			2650	154	2
23	HT	Hop., Stl.	H250	65524, 65580	40 8	10 4		44 3	10 5	10 5	10 8	10 8	10 8			2760	154	2
24	HT	Hop., Stl.	H350	▶ 67000-67299	47 11	9 9		51 8	10 6	10 7	3 6 / 10 8	11 ...	11			3209	200	5
25	XM	Box, Stl.	B208	82172	50 6	9 2	10 6	54 4	9 4 / 10 6	10 6	6 8	14 5 / 13 7	15 ...	9 ...	9 9	4845	110	1
26	XL	Box, Stl., DF Loaders	A230	82416	50 6	9 2	10 6	54 4	9 7 / 10 8	10 8	5 2	14 5 / 13 6	15 1	9 ...	9 11	4878	110	1
27	XM	Box, Stl., Stagg. Doors	B209	86204	50 6	9 2	10 6	54 4	9 4 / 10 6	10 8	3 4	14 5 / 13 6	15 ...	15 1	9 10	4860	110	1
28	XL	Box, Stl., DF Loaders	A230	87130, 87158	50 6	9 3	10 6	54 4	9 6 / 10 6	10 8	3 10	14 5 / 13 8	15 ...	8 ...	9 9	4860	110	2
29	XL	Box, Stl., DF Loaders	A230	87875	50 6	9 3	10 6	54 4	9 6 / 10 6	10 8	5 2	14 5 / 13 8	15 1	8 ...	9 11	4906	110	1
30	FC	Flat, Stl., ACF 1 Trailer Hitch ■	F871	▶ 99325-99412	45 ...	8 2		48 3	9 4	10 3	3 5	3 9	7 9				110	46
31	FC	Flat, Stl., ACF 1 Trailer Hitch, Leased to Arkansas Power & Light	F871	99326	45 ...	8 2		48 3	9 4	10 3	3 5	3 9	7 9				110	1
32	XP	Box, Stl., Special Interior Coating, (Flour) ■	A100	▶ 112000-112499	40 6	9 3	9 ...	44 11	9 5	10 5	5 ...	12 9	13 6	8 ...	8 4	3356	88	283
33	XM	Box, Stl.	B102	112011, 112018, 112025, 112029, 112038, 112045, 112058, 112099, 112101, 112104, 112106, 112107, 112109, 112110, 112112-112116, 112118, 112120-112122, 112129, 112132, 112133, 112135-112141, 112143-112145, 112148, 112150-112157, 112161-112167, 112169-112171, 112173-112176, 112178, 112180-112189, 112191, 112192, 112196, 112198-112201, 112204, 112205, 112207, 112208, 112210, 112212, 112214, 112216, 112218, 112220, 112224, 112227, 112228, 112238, 112239, 112249, 112254, 112255, 112280, 112295, 112296, 112318, 112330, 112331, 112334, 112335, 112337-112339, 112341-112345, 112347-112349, 112351, 112353, 112354, 112357, 112358, 112360, 112362-112364, 112366, 112367, 112369-112371, 112374, 112376-112378, 112385-112388, 112390-112392, 112394, 112396, 112397, 112399, 112401, 112403, 112405, 112409-112414, 112416-112420, 112422-112426, 112428, 112429, 112431, 112433, 112438, 112439, 112441, 112443-112445, 112448-112453, 112459-112461, 112465, 112466	40 6	9 3	9 ...	44 11	9 5	10 5	5 ...	12 9	13 6	8 ...	8 4	3356	88	188
34	XP	Box, Stl., Supplemental Blkhds Consisting of Corrugated Spacers & Pressboard Sheets, [Proctor & Gamble]	A100	112202, 112203, 112206, 112211, 112217, 112219, 112222, 112223, 112225, 112229	40 6	9 3	9 ...	44 11	9 5	10 5	5 ...	12 9	13 6	8 ...	8 4	3356	88	10
35	XM	Box, Stl. ■	B102	112500-113049	40 6	9 3	9 ...	44 11	9 5	10 5	5 ...	12 9	13 6	8 ...	8 4	3356	88	539
36	XP	Box, Stl., (Flour)	A100	112907	40 6	9 3	9 ...	44 11	9 5	10 5	5 ...	12 9	13 6	8 ...	8 4	3356	88	1
37	XM	Box, Stl.	B102	113085-113332	40 6	9 3	9 ...	44 11	9 5	10 5	5 ...	12 9	13 6	8 ...	8 4	3356	88	243
38	XM	Box, Stl.	B102	114000-114329	40 11	9 3	9 ...	44 9	9 5	10 5	12 6	12 6	13 4	8 ...	8 4	3350	110	314
39	XM	Box, Stl.	B102	114330-114730	40 10	9 4	9 2	44 9	9 10 / 10 1	10 4	5 7	12 8 / 13 ...	15 ...	8 ...	8 5	3356	100	347
40	XM	Box, Stl.	B106	120400-120599	40 6	9 3	10 6	43 10	9 10 / 10 7	10 7	14 ...	14 ... / 3 8	14 10	7 ...	9 11	2300	110	157
41	XM	Box, Stl.	B105	▶ 123384-123410	40 6	9 2	10 6	44 5	9 4 / 10 4	10 9	5 9	14 5 / 13 8	15 ...	6 ...	9 10	3903	110	24
42	XM	Box, Stl.	B105	▶ 123411-123444	40 6	9 2	10 6	44 10	9 4 / 10 4	10 9	5 9	14 5 / 13 7	15 ...	6 ...	9 10	3903	110	28
43	XM	Box, Stl.	B105	123481, 123527	40 3	9 2	10 6	44 4	9 10	10 9	3 11	13 11	15 1	6 ...	9 10	3900	110	2
44	XM	Box	B105	123586, 123595	40 6	9 2	10 6	44 4	9 10 / 10 5	10 9	3 11	14 5 / 13 10	15 1	8 ...	9 10	3900	110	2
45	XM	Box, Stl.	B105	123606-124539	40 6	9 2	10 6	44 4	9 5 / 9 11	10 8	3 10	14 4 / 13 11	15 ...	6 ...	9 10	3898	110	17
46	XM	Box, Stl.	B105	124540-125118	40 6	9 2	10 6	44 4	9 4 / 10 4	10 8	3 10	14 5 / 13 8	15 ...	6 ...	9 10	3898	110	86
47	XM	Box, Stl.	B105	125119-125308	40 6	9 2	10 6	44 4	9 4 / 10 4	10 8	3 10	14 5 / 13 8	15 ...	6 ...	9 10	3898	110	26
48	XM	Box, Stl. ■	B105	125310-126329	40 6	9 2	10 6	44 4	9 4 / 10 4	10 8	3 10	14 5 / 13 8	15 ...	6 ...	9 10	3898	110	625
49	XL	Box, Stl., (Flour)	A130	125421	40 6	9 2	10 6	44 4	9 4 / 10 8	10 8	3 10	14 5 / 13 8	15 ...	6 ...	9 10	3898	110	1

MISSOURI PACIFIC RAILROAD COMPANY — Continued

See Explanation Pages for Abbreviations & Symbols

▶Change from Previous Issue

"MP"

Line No.	A.A.R. Mech. Desig.	Description	A.A.R. Car Type Code	Numbers	Inside Length ft. in.	Inside Width ft. in.	Inside Height ft. in.	Outside Length ft. in.	Width At Eaves or Top of Sides or Platform ft. in.	Extreme Width ft. in.	To Extreme Width ft. in.	To Eaves or Top of Sides or Platform ft. in.	To Extreme Height ft. in.	Door Width of Open'g ft. in.	Door Height of Open'g ft. in.	Cubic Feet Level Full	Lbs. (000)	No. of Cars
1	LC	Box, Stl., Roof Hatches, (Alumina), [Alcoa at Point Comfort-TX]	L070	125776, 126089, 126155	40 6	9 2	10 6	44 4	9 4 / 10 4	10 8	3 10	14 5 / 13 8	15 ...	6 ...	9 10	3898	110	3
2	XM	Box ■	B105	▶126330-126469	40 6	9 2	10 6	44 4	9 4 / 10 5	10 8	5 2	14 5 / 14 ...	15 1	6 ...	9 10	3898	110	100
3	LC	Box, Stl., Roof Hatches, (Alumina), [Alcoa at Point Comfort-TX]	L070	126347, 126435	40 6	9 2	10 6	44 4	9 4 / 10 5	10 8	5 2	14 5 / 14 ...	15 1	6 ...	9 10	3898	110	2
4	XM	Box, Stl.	B105	▶126470-126584	40 6	9 2	10 6	43 10	9 4 / 10 5	10 8	5 2	14 5 / 14 1	15 1	6 ...	9 10	3898	110	103
5	XM	Box, Stl. ■	B105	▶126585-127549	40 6	9 2	10 6	44 4	9 4 / 10 5	10 8	5 8	14 2 / 13 11	15 ...	6 ...	9 10	3898	110	809
6	LC	Box, Stl., Roof Hatches, (Alumina), [Alcoa at Point Comfort,-TX]	L070	126681, 126899, 127536	40 6	9 2	10 6	44 4	9 4 / 10 5	10 8	5 8	14 2 / 13 11	15 ...	6 ...	9 10	3898	110	3
7	LC	Box, Stl., Roof Hatches	L070	126729, 126858	40 6	9 2	10 6	44 4	9 4 / 10 5	10 8	5 8	14 2 / 13 11	15 ...	6 ...	9 10	3898	110	2
8	XM	Box, Stl.	B109	▶127550-127835	40 6	9 4	10 6	43 10	9 6 / 10 7	10 8	3 10	14 5 / 13 8	15 ...	15 ...	9 9	3977	110	87
9	XM	Box, Stl. ■	B109	▶127836-128309	40 6	9 4	10 6	43 10	9 6 / 10 7	10 8	3 10	14 5 / 13 8	15 ...	15 ...	9 9	3977	110	190
10	XL	Box, Stl., DF Loaders	A130	127884, 127929, 128051, 128069, 128070, 128175, 128181, 128254	40 6	9 4	10 6	43 10	9 6 / 10 7	10 8	3 10	14 5 / 13 8	15 ...	15 ...	9 9	3977	110	8
11	XM	Box, Stl.	B107	▶128310-128769	40 5	9 2	10 6	44 4	9 4 / 10 5	10 8	5 2	14 5 / 14 ...	15 1	8 ...	9 10	3898	110	400
12	LC	Box, Stl., Roof Hatches, (Alumina), [Alcoa at Point Comfort-TX]	L070	128391, 128414	40 5	9 2	10 6	44 4	9 4 / 10 5	10 8	5 2	14 5 / 14 ...	15 1	8 ...	9 10	3898	110	2
13	XM	Box, Stl.	B107	▶128770-129108	40 6	9 2	10 6	44 4	9 5 / 10 3	10 8	5 2	14 4 / 13 7	15 1	8 ...	9 10	3898	110	301
14	LC	Box, Stl., Roof Hatches, (Alumina), [Alcoa at Point Comfort- TX]	L070	128788, 128964, 129036	40 6	9 2	10 6	44 4	9 5 / 10 3	10 8	5 2	14 4 / 13 7	15 1	8 ...	9 10	3898	110	3
15	XM	Box, Stl.	B107	▶129109-131388	40 6	9 2	10 6	44 4	9 5 / 10 3	10 8	5 2	14 4 / 13 7	15 1	8 ...	9 10	3917	110	2146
16	XL	Box, Stl., DF Loaders	A130	131389-131466	40 6	9 2	10 6	44 4	9 4 / 10 5	10 8	5 2	14 5 / 14 ...	15 1	8 ...	9 10	3917	110	56
17	XL	Box, Stl., DF Loaders ■	A130	▶131467-131515	40 6	9 4	10 6	44 4	9 6 / 10 8	10 8	5 2	14 5 / 13 6	15 1	8 ...	9 11	4000	110	34
18	XM	Box, Stl.	B107	131487, 131495, 131496, 131498, 131499, 131507, 131510	40 6	9 4	10 6	44 4	9 6 / 10 8	10 8	5 2	14 5 / 13 6	15 1	8 ...	9 11	4000	110	7
19	XL	Box, Stl.	A130	131516	40 6	9 2	10 6	44 4	9 4 / 10 5	10 8	5 2	14 5 / 14 ...	15 1	8 ...	9 10	3898	110	1
20	XL	Box, Stl., DF Loaders ■	A130	131517-131611	40 6	9 4	10 6	44 4	9 6 / 10 8	10 8	5 2	14 5 / 13 6	15 1	8 ...	9 11	4000	110	79
21	XM	Box, Stl.	B107	131517, 131522-131524, 131526, 131537, 131539, 131549, 131562, 131571, 131578, 131593, 131598, 131600, 131603, 131606	40 6	9 4	10 6	44 4	9 6 / 10 8	10 8	5 2	14 5 / 13 6	15 1	8 ...	9 11	4000	110	16
22	XL	Box, Stl., DF Loaders ■	A130	131612-131664	40 6	9 4	10 6	44 4	9 6 / 10 8	10 8	5 2	14 5 / 13 6	15 1	8 ...	9 11	4000	110	36
23	XM	Box, Stl.	B107	131621, 131625, 131628, 131629, 131633, 131635, 131638, 131641, 131643, 131650, 131652, 131658, 131660-131662, 131664	40 6	9 4	10 6	44 4	9 6 / 10 8	10 8	5 2	14 5 / 13 6	15 1	8 ...	9 11	4000	110	16
24	XM	Box, Stl. ■	B107	▶131665-131762	40 6	9 4	10 6	44 4	9 6 / 10 8	10 8	5 2	14 5 / 13 6	15 1	8 ...	9 11	4000	110	25
25	XL	Box, Stl., DF Loaders	A130	131665, 131667, 131671, 131674, 131676, 131678-131686, 131689-131702, 131704, 131705, 131707, 131709, 131710, 131713-131720, 131723, 131724, 131726, 131727	40 6	9 4	10 6	44 4	9 6 / 10 8	10 8	5 2	14 5 / 13 6	15 1	8 ...	9 11	4000	110	45
26	XM	Box, Stl. ■	B107	131765-131904	40 6	9 4	10 6	44 4	9 6 / 10 8	10 8	6 8	14 5 / 13 7	15 1	8 ...	9 10	3952	110	106
27	XL	Box, Stl., Belt Rails, [Kansas Milling Company]	A130	131773, 131784, 131785, 131824, 131840, 131841, 131846, 131861, 131864, 131881, 131890-131904	40 6	9 4	10 6	44 4	9 6 / 10 8	10 8	6 8	14 5 / 13 7	15 1	8 ...	9 10	3952	110	25
28	XM	Box, Stl. ■	B107	▶131905-132079	40 6	9 4	10 6	44 4	9 4 / 10 6	10 6	6 8	14 5 / 13 7	15 ...	8 ...	9 9	3952	110	155
29	XL	Box, Stl., DF Loaders	A130	131906, 131911, 131943, 131952, 131956, 131977, 131999, 132007, 132030, 132039, 132044	40 6	9 4	10 6	44 4	9 4 / 10 6	10 6	6 8	14 5 / 13 7	15 ...	8 ...	9 9	3952	110	11
30	LC	Box, Stl., DF Loaders, Roof Hatches	L070	▶ 132076	40 6	9 4	10 6	44 4	9 4 / 10 6	10 6	6 8	14 5 / 13 7	15 ...	8 ...	9 9	3952	110	1
31	XL	Box, Stl., DF Loaders	A130	▶132080-132104	40 6	9 4	10 6	44 4	9 4 / 10 6	10 6	6 8	14 5 / 13 7	15 ...	8 ...	9 9	3952	110	23
32	XL	Box, Stl., Cush. Underfr., Sparton Easy Loaders, 50K ■	A230	250000-250049	50 6	9 3	10 6	56 ...	9 7 / 10 8	10 8	5 2	14 5 / 13 6	15 1	9 ...	9 11	4972	154	45
33	XL	Box, Stl., Cush. Underfr., DF Loaders, Considered Part of Car: 60 Shipper Owned Pallets & 40 Separators & 20 Dividers, 50K, Assigned Service	A230	250029	50 6	9 3	10 6	56 ...	9 7 / 10 8	10 8	5 2	14 5 / 13 6	15 1	9 ...	9 11	4972	154	1
34	XL	Box, Stl., Cush. Underfr., DF Loaders, 50K ■	A230	250050-250149	50 6	9 2	10 6	56 ...	9 7 / 10 8	10 8	5 2	14 5 / 13 6	15 1	9 ...	9 11	4910	154	61
35	XL	Box, Stl., Cush. Underfr., Sparton Easy Loaders, 50K	A230	250075, 250077-250081, 250085-250089, 250103, 250105-250108, 250111, 250113, 250115, 250116, 250121, 250124, 250136, 250145, 250147	50 6	9 3	10 6	56 ...	9 7 / 10 8	10 8	5 2	14 5 / 13 6	15 1	9 ...	9 11	4972	154	25
36	XL	Box, Stl., Cush. Underfr., DF Loaders, Considered Part of Car: 60 Shipper Owned Pallets & 40 Separators & 20 Dividers, 50K, Assigned Service	A230	250082-250084, 250090	50 6	9 2	10 6	56 ...	9 7 / 10 8	10 8	5 2	14 5 / 13 6	15 1	9 ...	9 11	4910	154	4
37	XM	Box, Stl., Cush. Underfr., Combination Plywood & Alum. Side Lining, Lading Strap Anchors, 50K	B208	250097, 250098, 250100	50 6	9 4	10 6	56 ...	9 7 / 10 8	10 8	5 2	14 5 / 13 6	15 1	9 ...	9 11	4988	154	3
38	XL	Box, Stl., Cush. Underfr., DF Loaders, 25K ■	A230	250150-250349	50 6	9 4	10 5	58 ...	9 6 / 10 ...	10 8	5 8	14 6 / 14 ...	15 ...	9 ...	9 10	4902	154	51

CONTINUED ON FOLLOWING PAGE

Line No.	A.A.R. Mech. Desig.	DESCRIPTION (See Explanation Pages for Abbreviations & Symbols)	A.A.R. Car Type Code	NUMBERS (▶Change from Previous Issue)	INSIDE Length	INSIDE Width	INSIDE Height	OUTSIDE Length	OUTSIDE Width At Eaves or Top of Sides or Platform	OUTSIDE Extreme Width	Height from Rail To Extreme Width	Height from Rail To Eaves or Top of Sides or Platform	Height from Rail To Extreme Height	DOORS Side Width of Open'g	DOORS Side Height of Open'g	Cubic Feet Level Full	Lbs. (000)	No. of Cars
		"MP"																
1	XM	Box, Stl., Cush. Underfr., 25K	B208	250151–250154, 250156, 250157, 250160, 250161, 250164–250167, 250171–250175, 250177–250181, 250183, 250185, 250190, 250192–250195, 250197–250199, 250203, 250205–250208, 250210, 250211, 250214–250222, 250224, 250225, 250229, 250230, 250232–250235, 250237, 250239, 250241, 250242, 250244, 250247–250249, 250251, 250252, 250254, 250257–250260, 250262–250269, 250273, 250275, 250278–250281, 250284–250286, 250288, 250290, 250292–250294, 250297, 250300–250302, 250305, 250307–250322, 250324–250339, 250342, 250344, 250345	50 6	9 4	10 5	58	9 6 / 10	10 8	5 8	14 6	15	9	9 10	4902	154	133
2	XL	Box, Stl., Cush. Underfr., Sparton Easy Loaders, 25K ■	A230	▶250600–250899	50 6	9 4	10 6	58 1	9 6 / 10 7	10 8	3 8	14 5 / 13 10	15 1	16	9 10	4941	154	133
3	XM	Box, Stl., Cush. Underfr., 25K	B209	250600–250604, 250606, 250623, 250625, 250627–250629, 250632, 250634, 250635, 250637, 250638, 250643, 250649, 250664, 250665, 250687, 250689–250691, 250693, 250696–250699, 250716, 250718, 250719, 250721, 250723, 250727, 250728, 250731–250733, 250737–250739, 250741, 250744, 250747, 250750, 250751, 250753–250755, 250759, 250761, 250763, 250765, 250766, 250768, 250769, 250771, 250773, 250774, 250776, 250780–250784, 250787, 250788, 250791, 250793, 250795, 250797, 250798, 250800, 250808, 250809, 250812, 250816, 250818, 250820, 250822–250824, 250827, 250831, 250833, 250835, 250841, 250845, 250846, 250850–250853, 250856–250861, 250863–250866, 250869–250874, 250878, 250880, 250882, 250883, 250885, 250886, 250888–250894, 250897	50 6	9 4	10 6	58 1	9 6 / 10 7	10 8	3 8	14 5 / 13 10	15 1	16	9 10	4941	154	124
4	XL	Box, Stl., Cush. Underfr., DF Loaders, 25K	A230	250607, 250618, 250622, 250855	50 6	9 4	10 6	58 1	9 6 / 10 7	10 8	3 8	14 5 / 13 10	15 1	10	9 10	4941	154	4
5	XP	Box, Stl., Cush. Underfr., Racks, 25K, (Auto Transmissions)	A200	250608, 250609, 250611, 250614–250616	50 6	9 4	10 6	58 1	9 6 / 10 7	10 8	3 8	14 5 / 13 10	15 1	16	9 10	4941	154	6
6	XP	Box, Stl., Cush. Underfr., Racks, 25K, (Misc. Auto Parts)	A200	250612, 250613, 250617, 250651	50 6	9 4	10 6	58 1	9 6 / 10 7	10 8	3 8	14 5 / 13 10	15 1	16	9 10	4941	154	4
7	XP	Box, Stl., Cush. Underfr., Racks, 25K, (Auto Axles)	A200	250619, 250620, 250624	50 6	9 4	10 6	58 1	9 6 / 10 7	10 8	3 8	14 5 / 13 10	15 1	16	9 10	4941	154	3
8	XL	Box, Stl., Cush. Underfr., Sparton Easy Loaders, Considered Part of Car: 60 Shipper Owned Pallets & / or 40 Separators & 20 Dividers, 25K, Assigned Service	A230	250645–250647, 250657, 250658, 250662, 250663, 250678, 250667	50 6	9 4	10 6	58 1	9 6 / 10 7	10 8	3 8	14 5 / 13 10	15 1	16	9 10	4941	154	9
9	XP	Box, Stl., Cush. Underfr., Racks, 25K, (Auto Control Arm)	A200	250661	50 6	9 4	10 6	58 1	9 6 / 10 7	10 8	3 8	14 5 / 13 10	15 1	16	9 10	4941	154	1
10	XP	Box, Stl., Cush. Underfr., Racks, 25K, (Auto Mufflers & Tail Pipes)	A200	250681	50 6	9 4	10 6	58 1	9 6 / 10 7	10 8	3 8	14 5 / 13 10	15 1	16	9 10	4941	154	1
11	XM	Box, Stl., 25K ■	B209	251400–251414	50 6	9 4	10 6	54 4	9 6 / 10 7	10 8	5 2	14 5 / 14	15 1	15	9 9	4959	154	8
12	XP	Box, Stl., Racks, Cush. Underfr., 25K, (Auto Motors)	A200	251401, 251404, 251414	50 6	9 4	10 6	54 4	9 6 / 10 7	10 8	5 2	14 5 / 14	15 1	15	9 9	4959	154	3
13	XP	Box, Stl., Racks, 25K, (Auto Transmissions)	A200	251402, 251406	50 6	9 4	10 6	54 4	9 6 / 10 7	10 8	5 2	14 5 / 14	15 1	15	9 9	4959	154	2
14	XL	Box, Stl., 25K	A230	251403	50 6	9 4	10 6	54 4	9 6 / 10 7	10 8	5 2	14 5 / 14	15 1	15	9 9	4959	154	1
15	XP	Box, Stl., Racks, 25K, (Auto Axles)	A200	251405	50 6	9 4	10 6	54 4	9 6 / 10 7	10 8	5 2	14 5 / 14	15 1	15	9 9	4959	154	1
16	XL	Box, Stl., Cush. Underfr., Load Dividers, Plug Doors, 50K ■	A230	▶252350–252449	50 6	9 4	9 11	58 2	10	10 4	14 1	14 4	14 11	10 6	9 10	4710	150	54
17	XL	Box, Stl., Cush. Underfr., Load Dividers, Plug Doors, Considered Part of Car: 47 Shipper Owned Pallets &/or Separators & Dividers, 50K, Assigned Service	A230	252354, 252355, 252357, 252361, 252367, 252380, 252389, 252413, 252416, 252418, 252420, 252438	50 6	9 4	9 11	58 2	10	10 4	14 1	14 4	14 11	10 6	9 10	4710	150	12
18	XL	Box, Stl., Cush. Underfr., Load Dividers, Plug Doors, Considered Part of Car: 66 Shipper Owned Pallets, 50K, Assigned Service	A230	252356, 252362, 252375, 252376, 252379, 252381, 252391, 252405, 252423, 252426	50 6	9 4	9 11	58 2	10	10 4	14 1	14 4	14 11	10 6	9 10	4710	150	10
19	XL	Box, Stl., Cush. Underfr., Load Dividers, Plug Doors, Supplemental Blkhds Consisting of Corrugated Spacers & Pressboard Sheets, Considered Part of Car: 80 Pieces Corrugated Cardboard, 50K, [Proctor & Gamble]	A230	252358, 252365, 252368, 252392, 252399, 252424, 252432, 252437	50 6	9 4	9 11	58 2	10	10 4	14 1	14 4	14 11	10 6	9 10	4710	150	8
20	XL	Box, Stl., Cush. Underfr., Load Dividers, Plug Doors, Considered Part of Car: 52 Pallets, 50K, [Cargill]	A230	252360, 252363, 252369	50 6	9 4	9 11	58 2	10	10 4	14 1	14 4	14 11	10 6	9 10	4710	150	3
21	XL	Box, Stl., Cush. Underfr., Load Dividers, Plug Doors, Considered Part of Car: 48 Shipper Owned Pallets & 24 Separators, 50K, Assigned Service	A230	252372	50 6	9 4	9 11	58 2	10	10 4	14 1	14 4	14 11	10 6	9 10	4710	150	1
22	XL	Box, Stl., Cush. Underfr., Load Dividers, Plug Doors, Considered Part of Car: 60 Shipper Owned Pallets, 50K, Assigned Service	A230	252373, 252377, 252382, 252398, 252400, 252411, 252412	50 6	9 4	9 11	58 2	10	10 4	14 1	14 4	14 11	10 6	9 10	4710	150	7
23	XL	Box, Stl., Cush. Underfr., Load Dividers, Plug Doors, Considered Part of Car: 67 Shipper Owned Pallets, 50K, Assigned Service	A230	252385, 252390, 252407	50 6	9 4	9 11	58 2	10	10 4	14 1	14 4	14 11	10 6	9 10	4710	150	3
24	XL	Box, Stl., Cush. Underfr., Plug Doors, 2 Blkhds, 50K ■	A230	▶252775–252849	50 6	9 4	9 10	58 4	10 4	10 8	3 6 / 13 8	14	15	10 6	9 9	4655	146	33
25	XL	Box, Stl., Cush. Underfr., Load Dividers, Plug Doors, Considered Part of Car: 56 Shipper Owned Pallets, 50K, Assigned Service	A230	252777	50 6	9 4	9 10	58 4	10 4	10 8	3 6 / 13 6	14	15	10 6	9 9	4655	146	1
26	XL	Box, Stl., Cush. Underfr., Plug Doors, Considered Part of Car: 60 Shipper Owned Pallets & 40-40"x48" & 30-4'x8' Dividers Per Car, 50K, Assigned Service	A230	252779, 252781	50 6	9 4	9 10	58 4	10 4	10 8	3 6 / 13 8	14	15	10 6	9 9	4655	146	2
27	XL	Box, Stl., Cush. Underfr., Plug Doors, Considered Part of Car: 60 Shipper Owned Pallets & 40 Separators & 20 Dividers, 50K, Assigned Service	A230	252786, 252820	50 6	9 4	9 10	58 4	10 4	10 8	3 6 / 13 8	14	15	10 6	9 9	4950	140	2
28	XL	Box, Stl., Cush. Underfr., Plug Doors, 2 Blkhds, Considered Part of Car: 47 Shipper Owned Pallets &/or Separators & Dividers, 50K, Assigned Service	A230	252791–252794, 252796, 252797, 252804, 252805, 252807–252809, 252811–252816, 252823, 252825, 252827, 252829, 252833–252835, 252838, 252839, 252841, 252843–252849	50 6	9 4	9 10	58 4	10 4	10 8	3 6 / 13 8	14	15	10 6	9 9	4950	140	34
29	XL	Box, Stl., Cush. Underfr., Load Dividers, Plug Doors, Considered Part of Car: 48 Shipper Owned Pallets & 24 Separators, 50K, Assigned Service	A230	252803	50 6	9 4	9 11	58 2	10	10 4	14 1	14 4	14 11	10 6	9 10	4710	150	1
30	XL	Box, Stl., Cush. Underfr., Load Dividers, Plug Doors, Considered Part of Car: 66 Shipper Owned Pallets, 50K, Assigned Service	A230	252836	50 6	9 4	9 10	58 4	10 4	10 8	3 6 / 13 6	14	15	10 6	9 9	4655	146	1
31	XL	Box, Stl., Cush. Underfr., Plug Doors, 2-1 Piece Blkhds, 50K ■	A230	▶253200–253449	50 6	9 4	9 10	57 10	10 3	10 6	12 7	14 1	14 11	10 6	9 10	4948	145	228
32	XL	Box, Stl., Cush. Underfr., Plug Doors, Considered Part of Car: 27 to 48 Pallets Per Car, 50K, Assigned Service	A230	253221, 253234, 253284, 253358, 253398, 253419	50 6	9 4	9 10	57 10	10 3	10 6	12 7	14 1	14 11	10 6	9 10	4948	195	6
33	XL	Box, Stl., Cush. Underfr., Plug Doors, 2-1 Piece Blkhds, Considered Part of Car: 56 Shipper Owned Pallets, 50K, Assigned Service	A230	253227, 253236, 253238, 253246, 253271, 253396, 253417	50 6	9 4	9 10	57 10	10 3	12 6	12 7	14 1	14 11	10 6	9 10	4948	145	7
34	XL	Box, Stl., Cush. Underfr., Plug Doors, 2-1 Piece Blkhds, Considered Part of Car: 66 Shipper Owned Pallets, 50K, Assigned Service	A230	253257, 253325, 253371	50 6	9 4	9 10	57 10	10 3	10 6	12 7	14 1	14 11	10 6	9 10	4948	145	3

Line No.	A.A.R. Mech. Desig.	Description	A.A.R. Car Type Code	Numbers ▶Change from Previous Issue	INSIDE Length ft. in.	INSIDE Width ft. in.	INSIDE Height ft. in.	OUTSIDE Length ft. in.	OUTSIDE Width At Eaves or Top of Sides or Platform ft. in.	OUTSIDE Width Extreme Width ft. in.	Height from Rail To Extreme Width ft. in.	Height from Rail To Eaves or Top of Sides or Platform ft. in.	Height from Rail To Extreme Height ft. in.	DOORS Side Width of Open'g ft. in.	DOORS Side Height of Open'g ft. in.	CAPACITY Cubic Feet Level Full	CAPACITY Lbs. (000)	No. of Cars
		"MP"																
1	XL	Box, Cush. Underfr., Plug Doors, 2-1 Piece Blkhds, Considered Part of Car: 60 Shipper Owned Pallets & 40 Separators & 20 Plywood Dividers, 50K, Assigned Service	A230	253280, 253392, 253415	50 6	9 4	9 10	57 10	10 3	10 6	12 7	14 1	14 11	10 6	9 10	4948	145	3
2	XL	Box, Cush. Underfr., Plug Doors, 2-1 Piece Blkhds, 50K	A230	▶253450-253749	50 6	9 6	9 10	57 10	10 3	10 6	12 7	14 1	14 11	10 6	9 10	4948	145	300
3	XL	Box, Stl., Cush. Underfr., Load Dividers, Plug Doors, 50K ■C	A230	253929-253999	50 8	9 4	11 3	60	9 1	10 8	3 5 / 14 1	14 8	15 4	10 6	10 1	5380	145	66
4	XL	Box, Stl., Cush. Underfr., Load Dividers, Plug Doors, Considered Part of Car: 48 Pallets, 50K, Assigned Service C	A230	253979, 253980, 253983, 253985	50 8	9 4	11 3	60	9 1	10 8	3 5 / 14 1	14 8	15 4	10 6	10 1	5380	145	4
5	XL	Box, Stl., Cush. Underfr., DF Loaders, 50K ■	A230	254100-254324	50 6	9 4	10 6	58 2	10	10 7	13 10	14 4	14 11	10	9 11	4960	154	204
6	XL	Box, Stl., Cush. Underfr., DF Loaders, Considered Part of Car: 60 Shipper Owned Pallets, 50K	A230	254111, 254113, 254126, 254129, 254154, 254175, 254184, 254196, 254216, 254228, 254233, 254241, 254243	50 6	9 4	10 6	58 2	10	10 7	13 10	14 4	14 11	10	9 11	4960	154	13
7	XL	Box, Stl., Cush. Underfr., DF Loaders, Considered Part of Car: 25 Shipper Owned Pallets, 50K	A230	254207	50 6	9 4	10 6	58 2	10	10 7	13 10	14 4	14 11	10	9 11	4960	154	1
8	XP	Box, Stl., Cush. Underfr., 50K, (Steering Gears) ■	A200	254989-254999	44 3	9 2	11 1	58 2	10	10 7	5 5	14 8	15	16	10 9	4510	189	8
9	XP	Box, Stl., Cush. Underfr., [St. Joe Lead Mining]	A200	254996, 254998, 254999	44 3	9 2	11 1	58 2	10	10 7	5 5	14 8	15	16	10 9	4510	189	3
10	XL	Box, Stl., DF Loader ■	A230	▶255000-255299	50 6	9 3	10 6	54 4	9 6 / 10 6	10 8	5 2	14 5 / 13 8	15 1	8	9 11	4906	110	275
11	XM	Box, Stl.	B207	255112, 255211	50 6	9 3	10 6	54 4	9 6 / 10 6	10 8	5 2	14 5 / 13 8	15 1	8	9 11	4906	110	2
12	XL	Box, Stl., DF Loader	A230	▶255300-255398	50 6	9 2	10 6	54 4	9 7 / 10 8	10 8	5 2	14 5 / 13 6	15 1	9	9 11	4878	110	92
13	XL	Box, Stl., Sparton Easy Loaders	A230	255399-255494	50 6	9 2	10 6	54 4	9 7 / 10 8	10 8	5 2	14 5 / 13 6	15 1	9	9 11	4938	110	91
14	XL	Box, Stl., DF Loaders ■	A230	255500-255547	50 6	9 4	10 6	54 4	9 7 / 10 8	10 8	5 2	14 5 / 13 7	15 1	15	9 11	4910	110	46
15	XL	Box, Stl., DF Loaders, Considered Part of Car: Shipper Owned Pallets &/ or Separators & Dividers, Assigned Service	A230	255527	50 6	9 4	10 6	54 4	9 7 / 10 8	10 8	5 2	14 5 / 13 7	15 1	15	9 11	4910	110	1
16	XL	Box, Stl., DF Loaders ■	A230	255548-255595	50 6	9 2	10 6	54 4	9 7 / 10 8	10 8	5 2	14 5 / 13 7	15 1	15	9 11	4922	110	20
17	XM	Box, Stl.	B209	255548, 255550, 255555-255557, 255560, 255561, 255564, 255567-255570, 255572, 255575, 255577-255579, 255583-255587, 255591, 255593	50 6	9 2	10 6	54 4	9 7 / 10 8	10 8	5 2	14 5 / 13 7	15 1	15	9 11	4922	110	24
18	XP	Box, Stl., Cush. Underfr., Plug Doors, 25K ■C	A300	260000-260099	60 9	9 2	10 9	67 11	9 10	10 4	2 8	14 8	15 4	16	10 9	6232	200	21
19	XP	Box, Stl., Cush. Underfr., Plug Doors, Racks, 25K, (Auto Bumpers) C	A300	260000, 260002, 260004, 260006, 260008, 260010-260014, 260017-260020, 260023, 260025-260027, 260029-260032, 260034	60 9	9 2	10 9	67 11	9 10	10 4	2 8	14 8	15 4	16	10 9	6232	200	23
20	XP	Box, Stl., Cush. Underfr., Plug Doors, Racks, 25K, (Auto Transmissions) C	A300	260003, 260005, 260037, 260042, 260044, 260047, 260049, 260052, 260057, 260058, 260060-260062, 260064, 260066, 260067, 260069, 260084, 260092	60 9	9 2	10 9	67 11	9 10	10 4	2 8	14 8	15 4	16	10 9	6232	200	19
21	XP	Box, Stl., Cush. Underfr., Plug Doors, Racks, 25K, (Auto Axles) C	A300	260015	60 9	9 2	10 9	67 11	9 10	10 4	2 8	14 8	15 4	16	10 9	6232	200	1
22	XP	Box, Stl., Cush. Underfr., Plug Doors, Racks, 25K, (Misc. Auto Parts) C	A300	260016, 260035, 260036, 260038, 260045, 260046, 260053, 260074, 260099	60 9	9 2	10 9	67 11	9 10	10 4	2 8	14 8	15 4	16	10 9	6232	200	9
23	XP	Box, Stl., Cush. Underfr., Plug Doors, Racks, 25K, (Auto Engines) C	A300	260022, 260024, 260051, 260070, 260075, 260076, 260083, 260085-260087, 260089, 260094, 260096, 260098	60 9	9 2	10 9	67 11	9 10	10 4	2 8	14 8	15 4	16	10 9	6232	200	14
24	XP	Box, Stl., Cush. Underfr., Plug Doors, Racks, 25K, (Auto Motors) C	A300	260080, 260093	60 9	9 2	10 9	67 11	9 10	10 4	2 8	14 8	15 4	16	10 9	6232	200	2
25	XL	Box, Stl., Cush. Underfr., Plug Doors, 25K ■C	A330	260100-260124	60 8	9 1	10 9	67 11	9 10	10 4	2 8	14 8	15 4	16	10 9	6232	200	30
26	XL	Box, Stl., Cush. Underfr., Plug Doors, Considered Part of Car: 25 Stl. Flo-Bins, Leased from American Minerals Incorporated, 25K, Assigned Service C	A330	260109	60 8	9 1	10 9	67 11	9 10	10 4	2 8	14 8	15 4	16	10 9	6232	200	1
27	XP	Box, Stl., 50K ■C	A300	▶260125-260194	60 8	9 2	10 9	68	10 6	10 6	3 10	14 7	15 4	16	10 9	6340	200	10
28	XP	Box, Stl., Racks, 50K, (Auto Engines) C	A300	260125, 260131, 260138, 260141, 260145, 260147, 260148, 260150, 260152, 260155, 260157, 260159, 260181, 260182, 260185, 260189, 260190	60 8	9 2	10 9	68	10 6	10 6	3 10	14 7	15 4	16	10 9	6340	200	17
29	XP	Box, Stl., Racks, 50K, (Auto Bumpers) C	A300	260126, 260136, 260140, 260149, 260163, 260165, 260168, 260172, 260177	60 8	9 2	10 9	68	10 6	10 6	3 10	14 7	15 4	16	10 9	6340	200	9
30	XP	Box, Stl., Racks, 50K, (Auto Hoods) C	A300	260127, 260129, 260132, 260144	60 8	9 2	10 9	68	10 6	10 6	3 10	14 7	15 4	16	10 9	6340	200	4
31	XP	Box, Stl., Racks, 50K, (Misc. Auto Parts) C	A300	260128, 260135, 260169, 260178, 260184, 260187, 260194	60 8	9 2	10 9	68	10 6	10 6	3 10	14 7	15 4	16	10 9	6340	200	7
32	XP	Box, Stl., Racks, 50K, (Auto Axles) C	A300	260133, 260134, 260154, 260156, 260161, 260162, 260164, 260170, 260171, 260173, 260176, 260186	60 8	9 2	10 9	68	10 6	10 6	3 10	14 7	15 4	16	10 9	6340	180	12
33	XP	Box, Stl., Racks, 50K, (Auto Motors) C	A300	260137, 260139, 260146, 260160, 260166, 260167, 260193	60 8	9 2	10 9	68	10 6	10 6	3 10	14 7	15 4	16	10 9	6340	200	7
34	XP	Box, Stl., Racks, 50K, (Auto Wheels) C	A300	260153	60 8	9 2	10 9	68	10 6	10 6	3 10	14 7	15 4	16	10 9	6340	200	1
35	XL	Box, Stl., Cush. Underfr., 25K C	A330	264500-264715	60 8	9 2	11 4	68	10	10 8	2 4	14 9	15 6	10	11	6516	140	209
36	XL	Box, Stl., Cush. Underfr., 25K ■F	A330	264716-264900	60 8	9 2	11 6	68	10	10 6	3 6	15	15 6	10	11 1	6445	186	180
37	XL	Box, Stl., Cush. Underfr., 25K	A330	264723	60 8	9 2	11 6	68	10	10 6	3 6	15	15 6	10	11 1	6445	179	1
38	XL	Box, Stl., Cush. Underfr., 50K ■F	A330	265000-265199	60 8	9 4	11 6	68 4	10	10 8	3 6	15	15 6	10	10 10	6217	185	139
39	XL	Box, Stl., Cush. Underfr., Considered Part of Car: 90 Shipper Owned Pallets, 50K, Assigned Service F	A330	265001, 265003-265007, 265011, 265012, 265018, 265020, 265023, 265029, 265030, 265034, 265036, 265038, 265039, 265042, 265051, 265058, 265063, 265089, 265099, 265104, 265105, 265109, 265125, 265129, 265134, 265141-265143, 265145, 265147, 265162, 265167, 265171, 265173, 265175, 265182, 265197	60 8	9 4	11 6	68 4	10	10 8	3 6	15	15 6	10	10 10	6217	185	42
40	XP	Box, Stl., Cush. Underfr., Racks, 50K, (Misc. Auto Parts) F	A300	265021, 265022, 265025, 265049, 265055, 265076, 265082, 265092, 265137, 265163, 265170, 265179	60 8	9 4	11 6	68 4	10	10 8	3 6	15	15 6	10	10 10	6217	185	12
41	XL	Box, Stl., Cush. Underfr., 54 Pallets, 27 Plywood Sheets, 20 Dor-Ker Fillers, 50K F	A330	265053, 265056, 265078, 265102	60 8	9 4	11 6	68 4	10	10 8	3 6	15	15 6	10	10 10	6217	185	4
42	XL	Box, Stl., Cush. Underfr., Load Dividers, Plug Doors, 50K ■F	A330	265700-265799	60 8	9 4	10 11	68 4	9 6	10 7	15 2	14 4	15 6	10	10 10	6217	180	82
43	XL	Box, Stl., Cush. Underfr., Load Dividers, Plug Doors, Considered Part of Car: 27 to 48 Shipper Owned Pallets Per Car, 50K, Assigned Service F	A330	265703, 265750, 265751	60 8	9 4	10 11	68 4	9 6	10 7	15 2	14 4	15 6	10	10 10	6217	180	3
44	XL	Box, Stl., Cush. Underfr., Load Dividers, Plug Doors, Supplemental Blkhds Consisting of Corrugated Spacers & Pressboard Sheets, Considered Part of Car: 80 Pieces Corrugated Cardboard, 50K, Assigned Service F	A330	265709, 265711, 265728, 265733, 265737, 265747, 265769	60 8	9 4	10 11	68 4	9 6	10 7	15 2	14 4	15 6	10	10 10	6217	180	7

CONTINUED ON FOLLOWING PAGE

"MP"

Line No.	A.A.R. Mech. Desig.	Description (See Explanation Pages for Abbreviations & Symbols)	A.A.R. Car Type Code	Numbers (▶Change from Previous Issue)	Inside Length	Inside Width	Inside Height	Outside Length	Width At Eaves or Top of Sides or Platform	Extreme Width	Height To Extreme Width	Height To Eaves or Top of Sides or Platform	To Extreme Height	Door Width of Open'g	Door Height of Open'g	Cubic Feet Level Full	Lbs. (000)	No. of Cars
1	XL	Box, Stl., Cush. Underfr., Load Dividers, Plug Doors, Considered Part of Car: 52 Shipper Owned Pallets, 50K, Assigned Service ...F	A330	265713	60 8	9 4	10 11	68 4	9 6	10 7	15 2	15 4	15 6	10	10 10	6217	180	1
2	XL	Box, Stl., Cush. Underfr., Load Dividers, Considered Part of Car: 60 Shipper Owned Pallets &/or 40 Separators & 20 Dividers, 50K, Assigned Service ...F	A330	265714, 265739, 265758	60 8	9 4	10 11	68 4	9 6	10 7	15 2	15 4	15 6	10	10 10	6217	180	3
3	XL	Box, Stl., Cush. Underfr., Load Dividers, Plug Doors, Considered Part of Car: 58 to 60 Shipper Owned Pallets, 50K, Assigned Service ...F	A330	265777, 265794	60 8	9 4	10 11	68 4	9 6	10 7	15 2	15 4	15 6	10	10 10	6217	180	2
4	XL	Box, Stl., Cush. Underfr., Load Dividers, Plug Doors, 50K ...■F	A330	265800-265899	60 8	9 4	11	68 3	9 6	10 8	15	15 3	15 6	10 6	11	6260	180	87
5	XL	Box, Stl., Cush. Underfr., Load Dividers, Considered Part of Car: 52 Pallets, 50K, Private Service ...F	A330	265812, 265863, 265877	60 8	9 4	11	68 3	9 6	10 8	15	15 3	15 6	10 6	11	6260	180	3
6	XL	Box, Stl., Cush. Underfr., Load Dividers, Plug Doors, Considered Part of Car: 27 to 48 Shipper Owned Pallets Per Car, 50K, Assigned Service ...F	A330	265821, 265841, 265884	60 8	9 4	11	68 3	9 6	10 8	15	15 3	15 6	10 6	11	6260	180	3
7	XL	Box, Stl., Cush. Underfr., Load Dividers, Plug Doors, Considered Part of Car: 60 Shipper Owned Pallets, Assigned Service ...F	A330	265847, 265892	60 8	9 4	11	68 3	9 6	10 8	15	15 3	15 6	10 6	11	6260	180	2
8	XL	Box, Stl., Cush. Underfr., Load Dividers, Plug Doors, Considered Part of Car: 80 Pieces Corrugated Cardboard, Assigned Service ...	A330	265853	60 8	9 4	11	68 3	9 6	10 8	15	15 3	15 6	10 6	11	6260	180	1
9	XL	Box, Stl., Cush. Underfr., Load Dividers, Plug Doors, Considered Part of Car: 58 to 60 Shipper Owned Pallets Per Car, 50K, Assigned Service ...F	A330	265855, 265879, 265886, 265899	60 8	9 4	11	68 3	9 6	10 8	15	15 3	15 6	10 6	11	6260	180	4
10	XL	Box, Stl., Cush. Underfr., 2 Blkhds, 50K ...■F	A330	265900-266149	60 9	9 6	11	68 3	10 5	10 8	15	15 4	15 6	16 8	11	6350	178	243
11	XL	Box, Stl., Cush. Underfr., 2 Blkhds, Considered Part of Car: 52 Pallets, 50K ...F	A330	265910	60 9	9 6	11	68 3	10 5	10 8	15	15 4	15 6	16 8	11	6350	178	1
12	XL	Box, Stl., Cush. Underfr., 2 Blkhds, Considered Part of Car: 60 Pallets, 50K ...F	A330	266138, 266149	60 9	9 6	11	68 3	10 5	10 8	15	15 4	15 6	16 8	11	6350	178	2
13	XL	Box, Stl., Cush. Underfr., Load Dividers, 50K ...■F	A330	▶266150-266349	60 9	9 6	11	69 4	10	10 8	15	15 4		16	11	6350	180	191
14	XL	Box, Stl., Cush. Underfr., Load Dividers, Considered Part of Car: 60 Pallets, 50K, Assigned Service	A330	▶266174, 266194, 266233, 266279, 266317, 266324	60 9	9 6	11	69 4	10	10 8	15	15 4		16	11	6350	180	6
15	XL	Box, Stl., Cush. Underfr., Load Dividers, Considered Part of Car: 52 Pallets, 50K, Assigned Service	A330	▶266238	60 9	9 6	11	69 4	10	10 8	15	15 4		16	11	6350	180	1
16	XL	Box, Stl., Aux. Doors Closed, 25K ...■F	A330	267000-267040	60 8	9 2	11 6	68	10	10 6	3 6	15	15 6	10	11 1	6445	186	35
17	XM	Box, Stl., Aux. Doors Closed, 25K	B309	267015	60 8	9 2	11 6	68	10	10 6	3 6	15	15 6	10	11 1	6445	186	1
18	XP	Box, Stl., Racks, 25K, (Auto Transmissions) ...F	A300	267024, 267028	60 8	9 2	11 6	68	10	10 6	3 6	15	15 6	10	11 1	6445	186	2
19	XP	Box, Stl., Racks, Aux. Doors Closed, 25K, (Auto Motors) ...F	A300	267033, 267040	60 8	9 2	11 6	68	10	10 6	3 6	15	15 6	10	11 1	6445	186	2
20	XP	Box, Stl., Cush. Underfr., 25K, (Misc. Auto Parts) ...■F	A330	267041-267103	60 8	9 2	11 6	68	10	10 6	3 6	15	15 6	16 1	11 1	6445	186	58
21	XM	Box, Stl., 25K	B309	267049, 267074	60 8	9 2	11 6	68	10	10 6	3 6	15	15 6	16 1	11 1	6445	186	2
22	XL	Box, Stl., Cush. Underfr., 25K ...F	A330	267104-267113	60 8	9 2	11 6	68	10	10 6	3 6	15	15 6	16 1	11 1	6445	186	10
23	XP	Box, Stl., Cush. Underfr., 25K, (Misc. Auto Parts) ...F	A300	267114	60 8	9 2	11 6	68	10	10 6	3 6	15	15 6	16 1	11 1	6445	186	1
24	XP	Box, Stl., Cush. Underfr., Double Plug Doors, 50K, (Misc. Auto Parts) ...C	A300	267350-267360	60 9	9 1	10 9	68 2	10 7	10 3	14	14	15 6	16 1	10 9		158	11
25	XL	Box, Stl., End of Car Cushioning, Hi-Cube, 50K, 6"X11" Journals ...F	A330	269000-269004	60 9	9 7	12 8	67 6	10 1	10 9	5 6	16 7	16 10	10	12 7	7568	80	5
26	XL	Box, Stl., End of Car Cushioning, Hi-Cube, 50K, 6"X11" Journals ...F	A330	269009-269013	60 9	9 7	12 8	67 6	10 1	10 9	5 6	16 8	16 10	10	12 7	7568	80	5
27	XL	Box, Stl., End of Car Cushioning, Hi-Cube, 50K, 6"X11" Journals ...F	A330	269014-269039	60 10	9 6	12 8	67	10 7	10 8	5 7	16 5	17	10	12 8	7633	80	26
28	XP	Box, Stl., Cush. Underfr., Plug Doors, 25K, (Misc. Auto Parts) ...C	A300	270000-270099	60 9	9 2	10 9	67 11	9 10	10 4	2 8	14 8	15 4	16	10 9	6232	200	1
29	XP	Box, Stl., Racks, 25K, (Auto Hoods)	A300	270517, 270549	60 9	10 6	10 6	68	10 6	10 6	3 10	14 7	15 4	16	10 9	6340	200	2
30	XP	Box, Stl., 25K, (Misc. Auto Parts)	A300	▶270553-270569	59 9	9 1	10 9	68	10 6	10 6	3 10	14 7	15 4	16	10 9	5840	200	3
31	XP	Box, Stl., Cush. Underfr., Plug Doors, 25K, (Misc. Auto Parts) ...F+	A400	271000-271034	86 6	9 2	12 9	93 8	9 11	9 11	3 4 / 15 6	16 10	17	20	12 9	10000	110	31
32	XP	Box, Stl., Cush. Underfr., Plug Doors, 25K, (Misc. Auto Parts) ...F+	A400	271066-271082	86 6	9 2	12 9	93 8	9 11	9 11	3 4 / 15 6	16 10	17	20	12 9	10000	110	17
33	XP	Box, Stl., Cush. Underfr., Plug Doors, 25K, (Misc. Auto Parts) ...F+	A400	271510-271749	86 6	9 2	12 9	93 8	9 11	9 11	15 6 / 3 4	16 10	17	20	12 9	10000	142	236
34	XP	Box, Hi-Cube, Cush. Underfr., 25K, (Misc. Auto Parts)	A400	271824-271829	86 6	9 2	13 2	93 8	9 11	9 11	15 6	16 10	17	20	12 9	10000	141	6
35	XP	Box, Stl., Cush. Underfr., 2 Plug Doors, 25K, (Misc. Auto Parts) ...F+	A400	272000-272020	86 6	9 2	13 2	93 8	9 11	9 11	16 10	16 10	17	20	12 9	10000	102	20
36	XP	Box, Stl., Cush. Underfr., 25K, (Misc. Auto Parts)	A400	272051, 272052	86 6	9 2	13 2	93 8	9 11	9 11	15 6	16 10	17	20	12 9	10000	94	2
37	XP	Box, Hi-Cube, Cush. Underfr. ...F+	A400	274500-274506	86 6	9 2	12 9	92 7	9 10	9 11	15 6	16 9	17	20	12 9	10000	145	7
38	XM	Box, Stl., Stagg. Doors	B209	350800-350849	50 6	9 2	10 6	54 4	9 4 / 10 6	10 8	3 4	14 5 / 13 6	15	15 2	9 11	4860	110	7
39	XM	Box, Stl.	B209	350850-350899	50 6	9 2	10 6	54 4	9 4 / 10 6	10 8	3 4	14 5 / 13 6	15	15 2	9 11	4860	110	7
40	XM	Box, Stl., Stagg. Doors ...■	B209	▶350900-351099	50 6	9 2	10 6	54 4	9 4 / 10 6	10 8	3 4	14 5 / 13 6	15	15 1	9 10	4860	110	13
41	XL	Box, Stl., Stagg. Doors, Racks, (Auto Parts)	A230	350982, 350989, 351075, 351081	50 6	9 2	10 6	54 4	9 4 / 10 6	10 8	3 4	14 5 / 13 6	15	15 1	9 10	4860	110	4
42	XM	Box, Stl. ...■	B209	▶351100-351699	50 6	9 4	10 6	54 4	9 6 / 10 6	10 8	3 10	14 5 / 13 8	15	15	9 9	4960	110	5
43	XP	Box, Stl., (Carbon Black)	A200	351143, 351162, 351173, 351335, 351405, 351494	50 6	9 4	10 6	54 4	9 6 / 10 6	10 8	3 10	14 5 / 13 8	15	15	9 9	4960	110	6
44	XL	Box, Stl., DF Loaders	A230	351147, 351153, 351170, 351190, 351193, 351196, 351197, 351200, 351213, 351215, 351231, 351233, 351237, 351240, 351244, 351253, 351255, 351273, 351274, 351283, 351285, 351298, 351299, 351301, 351305, 351309, 351312, 351316, 351321, 351325, 351355, 351358-351361, 351373-351375, 351379, 351380, 351400, 351401, 351406, 351413, 351414, 351421, 351425, 351430, 351445-351447, 351449-351451, 351461, 351468, 351482, 351483, 351486, 351489-351492, 351496, 351510, 351521, 351522, 351524, 351532, 351544, 351558, 351567-351569, 351579, 351582, 351583, 351586, 351592, 351612, 351624, 351631, 351634, 351637, 351652, 351653, 351655, 351658, 351672	50 6	9 3	10 6	54 4	9 6 / 10 6	10 8	3 10	14 5 / 13 8	15	15	9 9	4860	110	92
45	XP	Box, Stl., (Wood Chip) ...F	A200	351155, 351189, 351201, 351219, 351223, 351284, 351367, 351397, 351427, 351526, 351548, 351572, 351580, 351603, 351659	50 6	9 4	12 2	54 4	9 6 / 10 6	10 8	3 10	16 1 / 15 6	16 8	15	9 9	5795	110	15

"MP"

Line No.	A.A.R. Mech. Desig.	Description	A.A.R. Car Type Code	Numbers ▶Change from Previous Issue	Inside Length	Inside Width	Inside Height	Outside Length	Width At Eaves or Top of Sides or Platform	Extreme Width	Height from Rail To Extreme Width	To Eaves or Top of Sides or Platform	To Extreme Height	Door Width of Open'g	Door Height of Open'g	Cubic Feet Level Full	Lbs. (000)	No. of Cars
1	LC	Box, Stl., 4 Roof Hatches, (Polyethelene) ...F	L070	351254, 351303, 351350, 351365, 351392, 351437, 351549	50 6	9 4	12 2	54 4	9 6 / 10 6	10 8	3 10	16 1 / 15 4	16 11	15	9 9	5795	110	7
2	XL	Box, Stl., Stagg. Doors, Racks, (Auto Parts)	A230	351262, 351291, 351394, 351459, 351466, 351471, 351539, 351551, 351599, 351604, 351607, 351628, 351636, 351648, 351649	50 6	9 4	10 6	54 4	9 6 / 10 6	10 8	3 10	14 5 / 13 8	15	15	9 9	4960	110	15
3	XM	Box, Stl., Stagg. Doors ■	B209	▶351700-351749	50 6	9 4	10 6	54 4	9 6 / 10 7	10 8	3 10	14 5 / 13 8	15	15	9 9	4960	110	2
4	XL	Box, Stl., Stagg. Doors, DF Loaders	A230	351703, 351705, 351706, 351714, 351716, 351744, 351746	50 6	9 4	10 6	54 4	9 6 / 10 7	10 8	3 10	14 5 / 13 8	15	15	9 9	4860	110	7
5	XM	Box, Stl.	B209	▶351750-351799	50 6	9 2	10 6	54 4	9 4 / 10 6	10 8	3 4	14 5 / 13 6	15	15 2	9 11	4860	110	13
6	XL	Box, Stl.	A230	351800-351824	50 6	9 3	10 6	54 4	9 6 / 10 7	10 8	5 2	14 5 / 14	15 1	8	9 10	4916	110	20
7	XL	Box, Stl.	A230	▶351825-351849	50 6	9 3	10 6	54 4	9 6 / 10 7	10 8	5 2	14 5 / 14	15 1	8	9 10	4906	110	22
8	XM	Box, Stl. ■	B207	▶351850-352092	50 6	9 4	10 6	54 4	9 6 / 10 6	10 8	3 10	14 5 / 13 8	15	8	9 9	4960	110	67
9	XL	Box, Stl., DF Loaders	A230	351850, 351851, 351854, 351860, 351862-351867, 351871, 351873, 351875, 351876, 351880-351885, 351887, 351889, 351890, 351893, 351895, 351898, 351901, 351903-351905, 351907, 351909-351911, 351915-351918, 351920, 351921, 351923-351927, 351930, 351931, 351933, 351934, 351936, 351938, 351939, 351941, 351944-351947, 351952, 351954, 351955, 351957, 351959-351961, 351963-351969, 351972-351974, 351976, 351977, 351980, 351982, 351984-351986, 351990-351996, 351999-352001, 352003, 352007, 352009-352011, 352013, 352014, 352016, 352017, 352019, 352023, 352025-352029, 352032-352034, 352036, 352039, 352040, 352043, 352045, 352046, 352051, 352052, 352054-352056, 352060, 352063, 352066, 352068, 352069, 352073-352077, 352079, 352081, 352084, 352087, 352088	50 6	9 3	10 6	54 4	9 6 / 10 6	10 8	3 10	14 5 / 13 8	15	8	9 9	4860	110	139
10	XM	Box, Stl. ■	B207	352093-352190	50 6	9 4	10 6	54 4	9 6 / 10 6	10 8	5 2	14 5 / 13 8	15 1	8	9 10	4960	110	60
11	XL	Box, Stl., DF Loaders	A230	352095, 352097, 352098, 352102, 352103, 352105, 352113, 352114, 352116, 352118, 352120, 352123, 352125, 352130, 352133, 352134, 352139, 352144, 352146, 352150, 352152, 352154, 352157-352160, 352163, 352173, 352174, 352178, 352180, 352182, 352186	50 6	9 3	10 6	54 4	9 6 / 10 6	10 8	5 2	14 5 / 13 8	15 1	8	9 10	4860	110	33
12	XP	Box, Stl., (Carbon Black)	A200	352096	50 6	9 4	10 6	54 4	9 6 / 10 6	10 8	5 2	14 5 / 13 8	15 1	8	9 10	4960	110	1
13	XL	Box, Stl., DF Loaders ■	A230	▶352191-352804	50 6	9 3	10 6	54 4	9 6 / 10 6	10 8	5 2	14 5 / 13 8	15 1	8	9 11	4906	110	568
14	XM	Box, Stl.	B207	352210, 352452, 352503, 352620, 352665, 352784	50 6	9 3	10 6	54 4	9 6 / 10 6	10 8	5 2	14 5 / 13 8	15 1	8	9 11	4906	110	6
15	XM	Box, Stl., Stagg. Doors, Z-Bar	B209	353000, 353002	50 6	9 4	10 6	54 5	9 4 / 10	10 8	4 7	14 7 / 14	15	15	9 10	4960	110	2
16	XM	Box, Stl., Stagg. Doors, Z-Bar	B209	353080	50 6	9 4	10 6	54 5	9 4 / 10	10 8	4 7	14 7 / 14	15	14 6	9 10	4960	110	1
17	XM	Box, Stl.	B207	353100-353199	50 6	9 4	10 6	54 4	9 6 / 10 8	10 8	6 8	14 5 / 13 7	15 1	8	9 10	4928	110	93
18	XM	Box, Stl.	B208	353200-353799	50 6	9 4	10 6	54 4	9 7 / 10 8	10 8	5 2	14 5 / 13 6	15 1	9	9 11	4988	110	561
19	XM	Box, Stl. ■	B207	353800-354014	50 6	9 2	10 6	54 4	9 4 / 10 6	10 6	6 8	14 5 / 13 7	15	8	9 9	4845	110	186
20	LC	Box, Stl., 8 Roof Hatches, (Calcium Carbonate)	L070	353818, 353866, 353923, 353924	50 6	9 2	10 6	54 4	9 4 / 10 6	10 6	6 8	14 5 / 13 7	15 6	8	9 9	4845	110	4
21	XP	Box, Stl., (Sack Flour)	A200	353822, 353827, 353904, 353905, 354004, 354007	50 6	9 2	10 6	54 4	9 4 / 10 6	10 6	6 8	14 5 / 13 7	15	8	9 9	4845	110	6
22	XM	Box, Stl.	B208	▶354015-354339	50 6	9 2	10 6	54 4	9 4 / 10 6	10 6	6 8	14 5 / 13 7	15	8	9 9	4845	110	306
23	XM	Box, Stl.	B208	354340-354639	50 6	9 4	10 6	54 4	9 6 / 10 8	10 8	13 5	14 5 / 14	15 1	9	9 9	4952	110	286
24	XM	Box, Stl. ■	B209	354650-354749	50 6	9 4	10 6	54 4	9 6 / 10 8	10 8	6 8	14 5 / 13 7	15 1	15	9 10	4928	110	86
25	XL	Box, Stl., DF Loaders	A230	354674, 354677, 354690, 354703, 354707, 354713	50 6	9 3	10 6	54 4	9 6 / 10 8	10 8	6 8	14 5 / 13 7	15 1	15	9 10	4865	110	6
26	XL	Box, Stl., DF Loaders, Shipper Owned: 60 Pallets & 40 Separators & 20 Plywood Dividers, Assigned Service	A230	354699	50 6	9 3	10 6	54 4	9 6 / 10 8	10 8	6 8	14 5 / 13 7	15 1	15	9 10	4865	110	1
27	XM	Box, Stl. ■	B209	354750-354999	50 6	9 4	10 6	54 4	9 7 / 10 8	10 8	5 2	14 5 / 13 7	15 1	15	9 11	4988	110	159
28	XP	Box, Stl., Racks, (Misc. Auto Parts)	A200	354750, 354753, 354758, 354759, 354761, 354765, 354767, 354768, 354771, 354773, 354777, 354778, 354783, 354784, 354793, 354794, 354800, 354801, 354803, 354805, 354809-354811, 354819, 354822, 354823, 354825, 354831, 354839, 354842, 354843, 354846, 354847, 354850, 354851, 354853, 354856, 354858, 354859, 354865, 354867, 354869, 354870, 354875, 354888-354890, 354892, 354893, 354895, 354898, 354899, 354902, 354905, 354909, 354910, 354917, 354926, 354928, 354930, 354941, 354944, 354947, 354948, 354950, 354956-354959, 354961, 354963, 354969, 354981, 354987-354989	50 6	9 4	10 6	54 4	9 7 / 10 8	10 8	5 2	14 5 / 13 7	15 1	15	9 11	4988	110	76
29	XM	Box, Stl.	B207	355000-355299	50 6	9 4	10 6	54 4	9 6 / 10 8	10 8	5 2	14 5 / 13 6	15 1	8	9 11	4988	110	286
30	XM	Box, Stl. ■	B207	355300-355599	50 6	9 4	10 7	54 4	9 6 / 10 6	10 8	5 2	14 5 / 13 8	15 1	8	9 10	4984	110	260
31	XP	Box, Stl., Racks, (Auto Stanchions)	A200	355503	50 6	9 4	10 7	54 4	9 6 / 10 6	10 8	5 2	14 5 / 13 8	15 1	8	9 10	4984	110	1
32	XL	Box, Stl., Aux. Doors Closed	A230	▶355600-355699	50 6	9 3	10 6	54 4	9 6 / 10 6	10 8	5 2	14 5 / 13 8	15 1	8	9 9	4884	110	89
33	XM	Box, Stl. ■	B209	355700-356049	50 6	9 4	10 7	54 4	9 6 / 10 6	10 8	5 2	14 5 / 13 8	15 1	15	9 9	4984	110	238
34	XL	Box, Stl., DF Loaders	A230	355734, 355753, 355781, 355802, 355818, 355832, 355841, 355846, 355859, 355866, 355867, 355870, 355871, 355878, 355888, 355893, 355915, 355917, 355920, 355945, 355950, 355958, 355976, 355978, 355997, 356002, 356011, 356015, 356025, 356026, 356028, 356035, 356040	50 6	9 3	10 7	54 4	9 6 / 10 6	10 8	5 2	14 5 / 13 8	15 1	15	9 9	4884	110	33

See Explanation Pages for Abbreviations & Symbols

CONTINUED ON FOLLOWING PAGE

Line No.	A.A.R. Mech. Desig.	DESCRIPTION (See Explanation Pages for Abbreviations & Symbols)	A.A.R. Car Type Code	NUMBERS ▶Change from Previous Issue	INSIDE Length ft. in.	INSIDE Width ft. in.	INSIDE Height ft. in.	OUTSIDE Length ft. in.	OUTSIDE Width At Eaves or Top of Sides or Platform ft. in.	OUTSIDE Width Extreme Width ft. in.	Height from Rail To Extreme Width ft. in.	Height from Rail To Eaves or Top of Sides or Platform ft. in.	Height from Rail To Extreme Height ft. in.	DOORS Side Width of Open'g ft. in.	DOORS Side Height of Open'g ft. in.	CAPACITY Cubic Feet Level Full	CAPACITY Lbs. (000)	No. of Cars
		"MP"																
1	XP	Box, Stl., Racks, (Auto Hoods)	A200	355746, 355860, 355923, 355938	50 6	9 4	10 7	54 4	9 6 10 6	10 8	5 2	14 5 13 8	15 1	15	9 9	4984	110	4
2	XL	Box, Stl., DF Loaders	A230	355769–355780, 355782–355788, 355790, 355791, 355794, 355796–355799, 355801, 355803, 355804, 355806, 355807, 355809, 355810, 355812, 355836, 355874, 355912, 355921, 356012	50 6	9 3	10 7	54 4	9 6 10 6	10 8	5 2	14 5 13 8	15 1	15	9 9	4906	110	39
3	XM	Box, Stl., Aux. Flush Type Doors: Width 8' & Height 9'9"	B209	▶356050–356099	50 6	9 4	10 6	54 4	9 6 10 8	10 8	5 2	14 5 13 8	15 1	16	9 10	4988	110	48
4	XM	Box, Stl.	B209	▶356100–356199	50 6	9 4	10 6	54 4	9 6 10 7	10 8	5 2	14 5 14	15 1	15	9 9	4959	110	75
5	XM	Box, Stl. ■	B208	▶356800–356899	50 6	9 4	10 6	54 4	10 1	10 9	3 10	14	15 1	9	9 10	4949	154	86
6	LC	Box, Stl., Roof Hatches, Blkhds, [Alcoa at Bauxite-AR]	L070	356600, 356623, 356668	50 6	9 4	10 6	54 4	10 1	10 9	3 10	14	15 1	9	9 10	4949	154	3
7	XP	Box, Stl., Hi-Cube, Plug Doors, End of Car Cush., 50K ....F	A200	364650–364674	50 6	9 6	12 10	58	10	10 8	16	16 3	16 10	16	11 11	6150	154	25
8	XP	Box, Stl., Hi-Cube Plug Doors, End of Car Cushioning, 50K ......F	A200	364675–364724	50 6	9 6	12 10	58	10	10 8	16	16 3	16 10	16	11 11	6150	149	50
9	XP	Box, Stl., Cush. Underfr., Hi-Cube, Plug Doors, High Loads & Loading Patterns, 50K, Not for General Service ....F	A200	364775–364999	50 6	9 6	12 10	58	10	10 8	16	16 3	16 10	16	11 11	6150	154	222
10	XM	Box, Stl., Cush. Underfr., Lading Strap Anchors, 50K ....■	B209	365150–365224	50 6	9 4	10 6	58 2	10	10 7	14 1	14 4	14 11	16	9 10	4960	154	67
11	XM	Box, Stl., Cush. Underfr., Lading Strap Anchors, Aux. Door Blocked, 50K	B207	365171, 365178, 365186, 365221, 365223	50 6	9 4	10 6	58 2	10	10 7	14 1	14 4	14 11	8	9 10	4960	154	5
12	XM	Box, Stl., End of Car Cushioning, 50K ....■	B209	▶365475–365749	50 7	9 4	10 7	58 2	10	10 8	8 3	14	15	16 4	9 11	4954	154	253
13	XP	Box, Stl., End of Car Cush., Considered Part of Car: Shipper Owned Pallets, Assigned Service, 50K	A200	▶365486, 365490, ▶365498, 365517, 365522, 365554, 365579, 365611, 365618, 365643, 365652, 365668, 365683, 365719, 365720, 365738, ▶365740	50 7	9 4	10 7	58 2	10	10 8	8 3	14	15	16 4	9 11	4954	154	17
14	XM	Box, Stl., Cush. Underfr., Lading Strap Anchors, 50K	B209	**365750–366274**	50 6	9 4	10 6	58 4	10	10 8	5 8	14	15	10	9 10	4950	154	518
15	XM	Box, Stl., Lading Band Anchors	B209	**367100–367299**	50 6	9 6	10 7	58 1	10 6	10 8	3 5	13 10	15	16	9 9	5100	154	199
16	XM	Box, Stl., Lading Band Anchors ....E	B209	**367300–367499**	50 6	9 6	11 3	56 1	10 6	10 8	3 5	13 10	15	16	9 9	5397	152	200
17	XM	Box, Stl., Cush. Underfr., Lading Strap Anchors, 50K ....F	B309	**375000–375299**	60 8	9 4	11 6	68 3	9 6	10 8	15	15 3	15 6	16	11	6595	185	294
18	XM	Box, Stl., Cush. Underfr., Lading Strap Anchors, 50K ....F	B309	**375500–375799**	60 8	9 6	11 7	68 3	9 11	10 8	15 3	15 4	15 6	16	11	6660	186	297
19	XM	Box, Cush. Underfr., Sliding Doors, Lading Band Anchors, 50K ...E	B309	**375800–376499**	60 9	9 6	11 6	68 5	10 6	10 8	5 3	15	15 6	16	11	6635	187	699
20	HM	Hop., Stl.	H140	**400269**, 400353, 400373	33	10 4		36 7	10 5	10 5	10 8	10 8	10 8			2191	110	3
21	HT	Hop., Stl.	H250	**520000–520645**	40 8	9 10		44 3	10 5	10 8	10 8	10 8	11 8			3050	154	116
22	HT	Hop., Stl.	H250	**522000–522299**	40 8	9 10		44 3	10 5	10 8	10 8	10 8	11 8			3050	154	34
23	HT	Hop., Stl.	H250	**535000–535199**	40 8	10 4		44 3	10 6	10 6	10 9	10 9	10 9			2760	154	14
24	HT	Hop., Stl.	H250	535200, 535220, 535222, 535233	40 8	10 4		44 3	10 6	10 6	10 9	10 9	10 9			2760	154	4
25	HT	Hop., Stl.	H250	**535850–536099**	40 8	10 4		44 3	10 6	10 6	10 9	10 9	10 9			2760	154	41
26	HT	Hop., Stl.	H250	**536400–537299**	40 8	10 4		44 3	10 6	10 6	10 8	10 8	10 8			2760	154	251
27	HT	Hop., Stl.	H250	**537300–537639**	40 8	10 4		44 3	10 6	10 6	10 8	10 8	10 8			2760	154	98
28	HT	Hop., Stl.	H250	**537640–537699**	40 8	10 4		44 3	10 6	10 6	10 8	10 8	10 8			2760	154	9
29	HT	Hop., Stl.	H250	**537700–538199**	40 8	10 4		44 3	10 6	10 6	10 9	10 9	10 9			2760	154	12
30	HT	Hop., Stl.	H250	**538200–538399**	40 8	10 4		44 3	10 5	10 5	10 8	10 8	10 8			2760	154	13
31	MWB	Hop., Ballast, Stl.	M110	▶565000–565099	40 8	9 8		44 3	10 7	10 7	11 1	11 1	11 1			2795	154	73
32	MWB	Hop., Ballast, Stl.	M110	▶565100–565299	40 8	9 8		44 3	10 7	10 7	11 1	11 1	11 1			2795	154	111
33	MWB	Hop., Ballast, Stl.	M110	▶565300–565599	40 8	10 1		44 2	10 2	10 4		10 8	10 8			2450	154	241
34	HT	Hop., Alum.	H250	570015	43 11	10 4		47 7	10 5			10 8	10 8			3000	154	1
35	HT	Hop., Stl.	H350	▶580000–580299	47 11	9 9		51 8	10 6	10 7		3 6 10 8	11	11		3209	200	280
36	HT	Hop., Stl.	H250	▶580700–580799	47 11	9 9		51 8	10 6	10 7		3 6 10 8	11	11		3209	199	97
37	HT	Hop., Stl. ■	H350	▶580800–581199	47 11	9 9		51 8	10 6	10 7		3 6 10 8	11	11		3209	200	384
38	HTS	Hop., Stl., (Armco Stl. Grinding Balls)	K340	581108, 581131, 581167, 581188	47 11	9 9		51 8	10 6	10 7		3 6 10 8	11	11		3209	200	4
39	HT	Hop., Stl.	H350	587560–587759	47 11	9 9		51 8	10 7	10 7	12	12	12			3737	200	196
40	HMS	Hop., Stl., (Wood Chip) ....F	K120	590000–590029	33	10 4		36 7	10 5	11 1	3 9	15 6	15 7			3572	110	11
41	HTS	Hop., Stl., (Wood Chip) ....■F	K240	▶591000–591255	40 8	10 4		44 3	10 4	11	3 9	15 6	16			4525	154	26
42	HTS	Hop., Stl., (Wood Chip) ....F	K240	591001–591006, 591010, 591012, 591017–591019, 591021, 591034–591037, 591040, 591041, 591047, 591053, 591056, 591058, 591067–591070, 591075, 591076, 591080, 591081, 591083, 591085, 591088, 591091–591094, 591096, 591098, 591101–591104, 591106–591108, 591111, 591114, 591127, 591131, 591156, 591163, 591175, 591218, 591220, 591241, 591254	40 8	10 4		44 3	10 4	11	3 9	15 6	16			4480	154	59
43	HTS	Hop., Stl., (Wood Chip) ....F	K240	591009, 591016, 591020, 591032, 591038, 591044, 591049, 591060, 591062, 591071, 591086, 591087, 591115, 591117–591119, 591121, 591128, 591130, 591132, 591133, 591136, 591139–591141, 591143, 591147–591152, 591155, 591158, 591161, 591164, 591168, 591169, 591172, 591174, 591176–591178, 591180, 591181, 591185–591190, 591192, 591197, 591199, 591200, 591204, 591206, 591208, 591210, 591216, 591217, 591224, 591227–591230, 591233, 591234, 591237–591239, 591242, 591243, 591245, 591248, 591249	40 8	10 4		44 3	10 4	11	3 9	15 6	15 7			4045	154	76
44	HTS	Hop., Stl., (Wood Chip) ....F	K240	591011, 591013, 591022, 591031, 591045, 591051, 591054, 591057, 591061, 591074, 591090, 591112, 591123	40 8	10 4		44 3	10 4	11	3 9	15 6	15 7			3855	154	13
45	HTS	Hop., Stl., (Wood Chip) ....F	K140	591033, 591039, 591043, 591046, 591048, 591050, 591052, 591055, 591059, 591064, 591066, 591072, 591077, 591078, 591082, 591089, 591097, 591099, 591100, 591105, 591109, 591212	40 8	10 4		44 3	10 4	11	3 9	15 6	15 7			4480	110	22
46	HTS	Hop., Stl., (Wood Chip) ....■F	K240	▶591256–591646	40 8	10 4		44 3	10 4	11	3 9	15 6	16			4525	154	236
47	HTS	Hop., Stl., (Wood Chip) ....F	K240	591262, 591268, 591270, 591272, 591273, 591276, 591278, 591279, 591281, 591282, 591284–591286, 591289–591291, 591295, 591297–591299, 591301, 591303, 591305, 591306, 591309, 591311–591315, 591319, 591321–591323, 591327–591330, 591333, 591334, 591336–591338, 591341, 591342, 591344, 591346–591348, 591382, 591383, 591452, 591456, 591472, 591523, 591552, 591581, 591635, 591637, 591646	40 8	10 4		44 3	10 4	11	3 9	15 6	15 7			4045	154	60
48	HTS	Hop., Stl., (Wood Chip) ....F	K240	591340, 591486	40 8	10 4		44 3	10 4	11	3 9	15 6	16			3855	154	2
49	HTS	Hop., Stl., (Wood Chip) ....F	K240	591361–591381, 591384, 591385	40 8	10 4		44 3	10 4	11 1	3 9	15 6	16			4360	154	23

MISSOURI PACIFIC RAILROAD COMPANY — Continued

Line No.	A.A.R. Mech. Desig.	DESCRIPTION (See Explanation Pages for Abbreviations & Symbols)	A.A.R. Car Type Code	NUMBERS ▶Change from Previous Issue	INSIDE Length ft. in.	INSIDE Width ft. in.	INSIDE Height ft. in.	OUTSIDE Length ft. in.	Width At Eaves or Top of Sides or Platform ft. in.	Width Extreme Width ft. in.	Height To Extreme Width ft. in.	Height To Eaves or Top of Sides or Platform ft. in.	Height To Extreme Height ft. in.	DOORS Side Width of Open'g ft. in.	DOORS Side Height of Open'g ft. in.	CAPACITY Cubic Feet Level Full	CAPACITY Lbs. (000)	No. of Cars
		"MP"																
1	HTS	Hop., Stl., (Wood Chip) ....F	K240	591412, 591487, 591489, 591641–591645	40 8	10 4		44 3	10 4	11	3 9	15 6	15 7			4480	154	8
2	HTS	Hop., Stl., (Wood Chip) ....F	K240	592000–592199	69 6	9 1		73 3	9 11	9 11	16 1	16 1	16 1			7000	180	198
3	HTS	Hop., Stl., (Wood Chip) ....F	K240	592200–592399	69 6	9 1		73 3	9 11	9 11	16 1	16 1	16 1			7000	180	200
4	GB	Gond., Stl., Fixed Sides & Ends, Solid Bottom	G112	▶600071–600587	45	9 5	3 9	48 9	10 2	10 4	3 4	7 4	7 4			1634	110	44
5	GB	Gond., Stl., Fixed Sides & Ends, Solid Bottom	G112	600588	45	9 5	3 9	48 9	10 2	10 4	3 4	7 4	7 4			1634	110	1
6	GB	Gond., Stl., Fixed Ends	G112	601750–601829	45	9 5	3 9	48 9	10 4	10 4	3 4	7 4	7 4			1590	110	27
7	GB	Gond., Stl., Fixed Sides & Ends, Solid Bottom ■	G112	601830–602654	45	9 5	3 9	48 9	10 4	10 4	3 4	7 4	7 4			1590	110	384
8	LG	Gond., Stl., Fixed Sides & Ends, Solid Bottom, 10 Containers (Dolomite & Lime)	L016	601866, 601925, 602095, 602299, 602393, 602429, 602507, 602538, 602580, 602601, 602636	45	9 5	3 9	48 9	10 4	10 4	3 4	7 4	7 4			1590	110	11
9	GB	Gond., Stl., Fixed Sides & Ends, Solid Bottom	G112	602655–602732	45	9 5	3 9	48 9	10 4	10 4	3 4	7 4	7 4			1590	110	30
10	GB	Gond., Stl., Fixed Ends, Flat Bottom ■	G312	610000–610789	52 6	9 5	3 9	56 3	10 5	10 5	7 4	7 4	7 5			1856	154	651
11	LG	Gond., Stl., Fixed Ends, Flat Bottom, 10 Shipper Owned Containers, (Dolomite)	L017	▶610368	36 9	9 5	3 9	56 3	10 5	10 5	7 4	7 4	7 5			1856	154	1
12	GB	Gond., Stl., Fixed Ends, Solid Bottom ■	G312	610790–612029	52 6	9 5	3 9	56 3	10 4	10 5	7 4	7 4	7 4			1856	154	901
13	LG	Gond., Stl., Fixed Sides, Solid Ends, Solid Bottom, 9 Containers: Cap. 135 Cubic Ft. Each, (Dolomite)	L016	610791, 610811, 610819, 610826, 610836, 610973, 610994, 611079, 611088, 611120, 611139, 611140, 611147, 611160, 611228, 611256	36 9	9 5	3 9	56 3	10 4	10 5	7 4	7 4	7 4				154	16
14	GB	Gond., Stl., Fixed Ends & Sides, Solid Bottom	G312	612030–612279	52 6	9 5	3 9	56 3	10 4	10 4	7 4	7 4	7 4			1856	154	202
15	GB	Gond., Stl., Fixed Ends, Flat Bottom ■	G312	612280–613174	52 6	9 5	3 9	56 3	10 4	10 4	7 4	7 4	7 4			1856	154	790
16	GBS	Gond., Stl., Fixed Ends, Flat Bottom, 11 Containers, (Coke)	E330	612289, 612294, 612391, 612397, 612457, 612512, 612567, 612579, 612584, 612611, 612622, 612627, 612653, 612703, 612773, 612774, 612847, 612848, 612851, 612856, 612891, 612981, 613008, 613024, 613052, 613057, 613076, 613084, 613088, 613102, 613149	52 6	9 5	3 9	56 3	10 5	10 5	7 4	7 4	7 4			1856	154	31
17	GB	Gond., Stl., Fixed Ends, Flat Bottom	G312	▶613175–613674	52 6	9 5	3 9	56 3	10 5	10 5	7 4	7 4	7 4			1856	154	439
18	GB	Gond., Stl., Fixed Ends, Flat Bottom	G412	630000–630099	65	7 9	3 6	68 9	8 7	8 8	4 3	7 1	7 3			1763	154	99
19	GB	Gond., Stl., Fixed Sides & Ends, Solid Bottom	G312	640000–640199	53	9 6	5	57 6	10 5	10 5	8 4	8 7	8 7			2523	195	199
20	GB	Gond., Stl., Fixed Ends, Flat Bottom	G312	640250–640329	52 2	9 6	4 6	56 11	8 1	10 5	8 1	8 1	8 2			2244	195	79
21	GB	Gond., Stl., Fixed Ends, Flat Bottom ■	G312	640350–640549	53 1	9 6	5	57 5	10 4	10 4	8 7	8 7	8 7			2523	197	195
22	GBS	Gond., Stl., Fixed Ends, Flat Bottom, (Diagonal Plate), [United States Steel], When Empty Return to Agent E.J. & E.R.R. in Gary/IN	E330	640386, 640427, 640449, 640468, 640489	53	9 6	5	57 5	10 4	10 4	8 7	8 7	8 7			2523	197	5
23	GB	Gond., Stl., Fixed Ends, Flat Bottom	G312	640550–640749	53 1	9 6	5	57 1	8 7	10 7		8 7	8 7			2520	196	200
24	GB	Gond., Stl., Fixed Ends, Flat Bottom	G412	650000–650499	65 6	9	5 6	69 11	9 11	9 11	9 1	9 1	9 1			3200	189	500
25	GB	Gond., Stl., Fixed Ends, Flat Bottom, Wood Flr.	G432	650500–650899	65 6	9	5 3	69 11	9 11	9 11	9 1	9 1	9 1			3200	189	400
26	GB	Gond., Stl., Flat Bottom, Drop Ends: Width 8'10"	G332	660000–660099	52 6	9 5	3 9	57 2	10 5	10 8	5 6	7 4	7 7			1856	154	91
27	GB	Gond., Stl., Flat Bottom, Drop Ends: Width 7'2" & Height 3'6"	G432	680000–680049	65	7 9	3 6	70 5	8 7	8 10	6 10	7 3	7 5			1763	150	44
28	GS	Gond.	G282	685000–685099	48 6	9 6	6	52 9	10 6	10 6	10 4	10 4	10 4			2765	154	92
29	GBSR	Gond., 3 Section Removable Roof, Blkhd, (Stl. Mill Products), Inside Width Between Belt Rails 9'1" ■	E340	695000–695099	52 5	9 6	4 6	56 3	10 8	10 8	8 9	8 9	9 8			2242	150	16
30	GB	Gond., Stl.	G332	695000, 695002–695007, 695009–695011, 695013, 695014, 695016–695018, 695020–695023, 695025–695027, 695029–695031, ▶695033, 695034, 695037–695057, 695059–695062, 695064–695067, 695069–695074, 695076–695079, 695081–695085, 695087–695089, 695091–695095, 695097–695099	52 5	9 6	4 6	56 3	10 8	10 8	8 9	8 9	9 8			2242	150	82
31	GBSR	Gond., 3 Section Removable Roof, Blkhd, (Stl. Mill Products), Inside Width Between Belt Rails 9'1" ■	E340	695100–695125	52 5	9 6	4 6	56 3	10 8	10 8	8 9	8 9	9 8			2242	150	4
32	GB	Gond., Stl.	G332	695101–695108, 695110–695113, 695115, 695118–695125	52 5	9 6	4 6	56 3	10 8	10 8	8 9	8 9	9 8			2242	150	21
33	GB	Gond., Stl.	G332	695126–695149	52 5	9 6	4 6	56 3	10 8	10 8	8 9	8 9	9 8			2242	150	17
34	GBSR	Gond., Removable Roof, 4 Stl. Blkhds ■	E340	697050–697149	52 6	9 6	6	61	10	10 8	8 10	10 4				2500	175	98
35	GB	Gond., Stl.	G332	697073, 697139	52 6	9 6	6	61	10	10 8	8 10	10 4				2500	175	2
36	LG	Gond., Stl., Flat Bottom, Fixed Ends, Articulated, Consists of 2- 52'6" Inside Length Gond. Cars Permanently Coupled, Considered Part of Car: Special Stowing Racks, 12 Containers Each, (Concentrates), [Molybdenum Corp.]	L017	699999	52 6	9 5	3 9	112 5	10 4	10 5	7 4	9 5	9 5				308	1
37	LO	Hop., Stl., Stl. Roof	L151	▶700000–700399	29 3	9 5		37 9	7 11 / 9 9	10 2	11 9	13 Eaves / 12 7	13			1892	154	190
38	LO	Hop., Stl., Stl. Roof	L151	700500–700599	29 3	10		37 9	10 1 / 10 8	10 8	12 3	12 6 / 12 3	13 1			2055	154	95
39	LO	Hop., Stl., Stl. Roof	L151	700600–700649⁷	29 3	9 5		37 9	10 3	10 3	12 3	12 2	13 3			2003	154	42
40	LO	Hop., Stl., Stl. Roof	L151	700650–700699	29 3	10		37 9	10 1 / 10 8	10 8	12 3	12 6 / 12 3	13 1			2055	154	49
41	LO	Hop., Stl., Stl. Roof	L151	700700–700899	29 3	10		44 8	10 1 / 10 8	10 8	12 3	12 6 / 12 3	13 1			2072	154	187
42	LO	Hop., Stl., Stl. Roof	L151	700908	31 4	10		43 11	7 11 / 9 9	10 2	10 9	11 9 / 11 4	12 4			2200	154	1
43	HTR	Hop., Stl., Stl. Roof	K230	702167–702199	40 8	10		43 11	7 11 / 9 9	10 2	10 9	11 9 / 11 4	11 9			2955	154	8
44	HTR	Hop., Stl., Stl. Roof	K230	702200–702399	40 8	10 4		44 3	3 / 10 3	10 6	10 8	12 3 / 11	12 3			2760	154	58
45	LO	Hop., Stl., Stl. Roof	L151	702400–702748	35 8	9 10		44 3	9 9	10 6	10 9	12 2	13 4			2680	154	22
46	LO	Hop., Stl., Stl. Roof	L151	702749–702870	35 8	9 10		44 3	9 9	10 6	10 9	12 2	13 4			2680	154	7
47	LO	Hop., Stl., Stl. Roof.	L151	702913, 702933	35 8	9 7		44 3	9 6 / 10 6	10 6	10 8	12 1	13 4			2680	154	2
48	LO	Hop., Stl., Stl. Roof	L151	▶703150–703449	39 10	9 9		48 5	8 8 / 10 6	10 6	12 10	13 1 / 12 10	13 1			2828	154	210
49	LO	Hop., Stl., Stl. Roof	L151	▶703500–703624	39 10	9 9		48 5	8 8 / 10 2	10 2	12 2	13 1 / 12 10	13 1			2828	154	55
50	LO	Hop., Stl., Stl. Roof	L151	▶703625–703754	39 10	9 9		48 5	8 8 / 10 2	10 2	12 2	13 1 / 12 10	13 1			2828	154	52
51	LO	Hop., Stl., Stl. Roof, Combination Keystone Gravity & Enterprise Pneumatic Outlets	L352	704850–704899	41 1	10		49 7	10 1 / 10 8	10 8	12 3	12 6 / 12 3	13 1			3020	154	48
52	LO	Hop., Stl., Stl. Roof	L151	704900–705299	39 10	9 9		48 5	9 7 / 10 2	10 2	12 2	12 8 / 12 3	13 3			2828	154	325
53	LO	Hop., Stl., Stl. Roof	L152	706100–706299	36 11	9 11		46	10 7	10 7	10 7	13 6	14 7			3000	200	197

CONTINUED ON FOLLOWING PAGE

Line No.	A.A.R. Mech. Desig.	DESCRIPTION	A.A.R. Car Type Code	NUMBERS (Change from Previous Issue)	Inside Length	Inside Width	Inside Height	Outside Length	Outside Width At Eaves or Top of Sides or Platform	Outside Extreme Width	Height To Extreme Width	Height To Eaves or Top of Sides or Platform	Height To Extreme Height	Door Width of Open'g	Door Height of Open'g	Cubic Feet Level Full	Lbs. (000)	No. of Cars
		See Explanation Pages for Abbreviations & Symbols			ft. in.	ft. in.	ft. in.	ft. in.	ft. in.	ft. in.	ft. in.	ft. in.	ft. in.	ft. in.	ft. in.			
		"MP"																
1	LO	Hop., Stl., Center Flow	L152	710200–710399	41 3	10 7	....	53 10	7 6	10 8	8 6	14 3	15 1	....	....	3960	200	190
2	LO	Covered Hop., Stl., Trough Hatch	L153	711030–711097	49 9	10 7		54 7	10 1	10 8	8	13 6	15 1			4460	200	64
3	LO	Covered Hop., Stl., Trough Hatch	L153	711630–712329	49 6	10 1		54 3	10 8	10 8	4 11 / 13 10	14	15 1			4427	200	700
4	LO	Hop.	L153	716000–716499	54 7	10		59 3	10 6	10 7	5	14 1	15 1			4740	200	489
5	LO	Hop., Stl.	L153	716900–717299	55 3	10		60	10 1	10 7	8 3	13 5	14 11			4740	200	393
6	LO	Covered Hop., Stl., Trough Hatch	L153	718000–718249	53 3	10 5		58 1	10 1	10 6	9	13 3	15 1			4600	200	249
7	LO	Covered Hop., Stl., Trough Hatch	L153	718250–718299	53 3	10 5		58 1	10 1	10 6	9	13 3	15 1			4600	199	50
8	LO	Hop., Stl., Stl. Roof, Airslide	L451	720000–720174	29 6	9 11		42	10 1	10 8	13 6		14 5			2600	154	165
9	LO	Hop., Stl., Stl. Roof, Airslide	L153	721000–721034	48 11	9 11		53 2	10 1	10 7	13 5	13 10	14 6			4180	190	23
10	LO	Hop., Stl., Stl. Roof, Airslide	L153	721067	48 11	9 11		53 2	10 1	10 7	13 5	13 10	14 6			4180	190	1
11	LO	Covered Hop., Stl., Airslide	L153	721068–721126	48 11	9 11		54 1	10 2	10 8	13 2	13 11	14 6			4180	190	59
12	LO	Covered Hop., Stl., Airslide, Leased from A.R.T.	L153	721127–721151	48 11	9 11		54 1	10 2	10 8	13 2	13 11	14 6			4180	190	25
13	LO	Hop., Stl., Stl. Roof, Dry Flo	L352	722000–722049	40 9	9 11		53 3	10 2 / 10 8	10 8	13 5	13 11 / 13 5	14 6			3500	154	46
14	LP	Rack	L026	725304, 725310, 725345, 725348	37 6	9 1	9 1	44 6	9 9	10	3 1	4 1	12 11				110	4
15	LP	Rack	L026	726000–726499	38	8 8	8 2	45 10	8 8	9 3	10 9	4	12 3				110	450
16	LP	Rack	L026	726500–726599	38	8 8	8 2	45 10	8 8	9 3	10 9	4	12 3				110	100
17	LP	Rack	L026	731000–731099	45	8 8	10 1	52 10	8 8	9 3	12 3	4	14 1				154	98
18	LP	Rack	L026	731100–731199	45	8 8	9 8	52 10	8 8	9 3	12 3	4	12 7				154	98
19	LP	Rack	L026	731189, 731193	45	8 8	8 7	52 10	8 8	9 3	12 3	4	12 7				154	2
20	XMI	Box, Stl., Insulated	B112	775000–775023	40 1	9 2	9 8	44 4	9 10 / 10 5	10 5	4 10	15 .... / 14 2	15 1	8	9 8	3569	110	22
21	XMI	Box, Stl., Insulated	B213	775100–775174	50	8 6	8 10	55 2	9 10	10 8	13 6	13 11	14 10	9	7 9	3753	140	73
22	RBL	Refrig., Stl., Insulated, Cush. Underfr., Plug Doors, Compartmentizer Type Load Dividers, 25K	R106	779800–779999	49 3	9 4	9 10	57 8	9 6 / 10 6	10 8	5 2	14 4 / 13 11	15 1	10	9 4	4402	154	95
23	RBL	Refrig., Stl., Insulated, Cush. Underfr., Considered Part of Car: 52 Shipper Owned Pallets &/or Separators & Dividers, Plug Doors, Compartmentizer Type Load Dividers, 25K, Assigned Service	R106	779801, 779804, 779805, 779811, 779814, 779819, 779826–779828, 779831, 779832, 779836, 779640, 779845, 779852, 779873, 779878, 779683, 779889, 779891, 779894, 779895, 779897, 779904–779906, 779909, 779910, 779912, 779917, 779923, 779925, 779932, 779934, 779938, 779960, 779961, 779965, 779969, 779971, 779975, 779977, 779994, 779996	49 3	9 4	9 10	57 8	9 6 / 10 6	10 8	5 2	14 4 / 13 11	15 1	10	9 4	4402	154	44
24	RBL	Refrig., Stl., Insulated, Cush. Underfr., Plug Doors, Compartmentizer Type Load Dividers, Considered Part of Car: 88 Pallets, 25K, Assigned Service	R106	779803, 779835, 779862, 779958, 779968, 779974, 779992	49 3	9 4	9 10	57 8	9 6 / 10 6	10 8	5 2	14 4 / 13 11	15 1	10	9 4	4402	154	7
25	RBL	Refrig., Stl., Insulated, Cush. Underfr., Plug Doors, Compartmentizer Type Load Dividers, Considered Part of Car: 90-150 Shipper Owned Pallets, Assigned Service, 25K	R106	779806, 779830, 779875, 779888, 779916, 779924, 779956, 779982, 779985, 779989	49 3	9 4	9 10	57 8	9 6 / 10 6	10 8	5 2	14 4 / 13 11	15 1	10	9 4	4402	154	10
26	RBL	Refrig., Stl., Cush. Underfr., Plug Doors, Compartmentizer Type Load Dividers, Considered Part of Car: 56 Shipper Owned Pallets, Assigned Service, 25K	R106	779823, 779856, 779886, 779983	49 3	9 4	9 10	57 8	9 6 / 10 6	10 8	5 2	14 4 / 13 11	15 1	10	9 4	4402	154	4
27	RBL	Refrig., Stl., Insulated, Cush. Underfr., Considered Part of Car: 47 Shipper Owned Pallets &/or Separators & Dividers, Plug Doors, Compartmentizer Type Load Dividers, 25K, Assigned Service	R106	779837, 779839, 779841, 779842, 779846, 779861, 779865, 779874, 779914, 779930, 779943, 779944, 779964, 779967	49 3	9 4	9 10	57 8	9 6 / 10 6	10 8	5 2	14 4 / 13 11	15 1	10	9 4	4402	154	14
28	RBL	Refrig., Stl., Insulated, Cush. Underfr., Plug Doors, Compartmentizer Type Load Dividers, Considered Part of Car: 67 Pallets, 25K, Assigned Service	R106	779843, 779876, 779882, 779919, 779941, 779973, 779981	49 3	9 4	9 10	57 8	9 6 / 10 6	10 8	5 2	14 4 / 13 11	15 1	10	9 4	4402	154	7
29	RBL	Refrig., Stl., Insulated, Cush. Underfr., Plug Doors, Considered Part of Car: Compartmentizer Type Load Dividers & 100 Pallets, 25K, Assigned Service	R106	779866, 779939	49 3	9 4	9 10	57 8	9 6 / 10 6	10 8	5 2	14 4 / 13 11	15 1	10	9 4	4402	154	2
30	RBL	Refrig., Stl., Insulated, Cush. Underfr., Plug Doors, Compartmentizer Type Load Dividers, Supplemental Blkhds Consisting of Corrugated Spacers & Pressboard Sheets, Considered Part of Car: 80 Pieces Corrugated Cardboard, 25K, [Proctor & Gamble]	R106	779870, 779918, 779955, 779959, 779990	49 3	9 4	9 10	57 8	9 6 / 10 6	10 8	5 2	14 4 / 13 11	15 1	10	9 4	4402	154	5
31	RBL	Refrig., Stl., Insulated, Cush. Underfr., Stagg. Doors, Load Dividers, Side Wall Fillers, 25K	R206	780000–780049	50 1	9 3	9 6	57 8	10	10 8	4 2	14 4	15 1	10 6	9 4	4360	140	29
32	RBL	Refrig., Stl., Insulated, Cush. Underfr., Stagg. Doors, Load Dividers, Side Wall Fillers, Considered Part of Car: 50 Shipper Owned Pallets, Assigned Service	R206	780017	50 1	9 3	9 6	57 8	10	10 8	4 2	14 4	15 1	10 6	9 4	4360	140	1
33	RBL	Refrig., Stl., Insulated, Cush. Underfr., Stagg. Doors, Load Dividers, Side Wall Fillers, Considered Part of Car: 47 Shipper Owned Pallets &/or Separators & Dividers, 25K, Assigned Service	R206	780020	50 1	9 3	9 6	57 8	10	10 8	4 2	14 4	15 1	10 6	9 4	4360	140	1
34	XPI	Box, Stl., Insulated	A210	780024, 780045, 780049	50 1	9 3	9 6	57 8	10	10 8	4 2	14 4	15 4	10 6	9 4	4360	140	3
35	RBL	Refrig., Stl., Insulated, Cush. Underfr., Stagg. Doors, Load Dividers, Side Wall Fillers, Considered Part of Car: 52 Shipper Owned Pallets &/or Separators & Dividers, 25K, Assigned Service	R206	780031, 780032, 780034, 780036, 780041–780044, 780048	50 1	9 3	9 6	57 8	10	10 8	4 2	14 4	15 1	10 6	9 4	4360	140	9
36	RBL	Refrig., Stl., Insulated, Cush. Underfr., Stagg. Doors, Load Dividers, Side Wall Fillers, Considered Part of Car: 67 Pallets, 25K, Assigned Service	R206	780038–780040	50 1	9 3	9 6	57 8	10	10 8	4 2	14 4	15 1	10 6	9 4	4360	140	3
37	RBL	Refrig., Stl., Insulated, Cush. Underfr., 25K	R206	780050–780149	50 1	9 3	9 6	57 10	10	10 8	5 7	14 4	15 1	10 6	9 4	4281	154	11
38	RBL	Refrig., Stl., Insulated, Cush. Underfr., Considered Part of Car: 56 Shipper Owned Pallets &/or Separators & Dividers, 25K, Assigned Service	R206	780050–780053, 780055–780059, 780061–780075, 780079, 780082, 780083, 780086, 780088–780090	50 1	9 3	9 6	57 10	10	10 8	5 7	14 4	15 1	10 6	9 4	4281	154	31
39	XPI	Box, Stl., Insulated, Cush. Underfr.	A210	780076	51 1	9 3	9 6	57 10	10	10 8	5 7	14 4	15 1	10 6	9 4	4281	154	1
40	RBL	Refrig., Stl., Insulated, Cush. Underfr., Considered Part of Car: 52 Pallets, 25K, Assigned Service	R206	780095, 780096, 780098, 780099, 780133	50 1	9 3	9 6	57 10	10	10 8	5 7	14 4	15 1	10 6	9 4	4281	154	5
41	RBL	Refrig., Stl., Insulated, Cush. Underfr., Considered Part of Car: 52 Shipper Owned Pallets, 25K, Assigned Service	R206	780100–780107, 780109–780111, 780113–780115, 780117–780119, 780139	50 1	9 3	9 6	57 10	10	10 8	5 7	14 4	15 1	10 6	9 4	4281	154	18
42	RBL	Box, Stl., Insulated, Cush. Underfr., Considered Part of Car: 40 Shipper Owned Pallets, 25K, Assigned Service	R206	780120–780122, 780124–780126	50 1	9 3	9 6	57 10	10	10 8	5 7	14 4	15 1	10 6	9 4	4360	154	6
43	RBL	Refrig., Stl., Insulated, Cush. Underfr., Considered Part of Car: 69 Shipper Owned Pallets, 25K, Assigned Service	R206	780127–780132	50 1	9 3	9 6	57 10	10	10 8	5 7	14 4	15 1	10 6	9 4	4360	154	6
44	RBL	Refrig., Stl., Insulated, Cush. Underfr., Considered Part of Car: 56 Shipper Owned Pallets &/ or Separators & Dividers, 25K, Assigned Service	R206	780135–780138, 780140–780143, 780145–780149	50 1	9 3	9 6	57 10	10	10 8	5 7	14 4	15 1	10 6	9 4	4360	154	13

Line No.	A.A.R. Mech. Desig.	DESCRIPTION (See Explanation Pages for Abbreviations & Symbols)	A.A.R. Car Type Code	NUMBERS (Change from Previous Issue)	INSIDE Length	INSIDE Width	INSIDE Height	OUTSIDE Length	OUTSIDE Width At Eaves or Top of Sides or Platform	OUTSIDE Width Extreme	Height from Rail To Extreme Width	Height from Rail To Eaves or Top of Sides or Platform	Height from Rail To Extreme Height	DOORS Side Width of Open'g	DOORS Side Height of Open'g	CAPACITY Cubic Feet Level Full	CAPACITY Lbs. (000)	No. of Cars
		"MP"																
1	RBL	Refrig., Stl., Insulated, Underfr. Considered Part of Car: 52 Pallets, 25K, Assigned Service	R206	780144	50 1	9 3	9 6	57 10	10	10 8	5 7	14 4	15 1	10 6	9 4	4360	154	1
2	RBL	Refrig., Stl., Insulated, Supplemental Blkhds Consisting of Corrugated Spacers & Pressboard Sheets, 25K, [Proctor & Gamble]	R206	780150-780160	50 1	9 3	9 10	55 8	9 11	10 8	....	14 2	15	12 2	9 4	4582	154	11
3	RBL	Refrig., Stl., Insulated, 25K	R206	780161	50 1	9 3	9 10	55 8	9 11	10 8		14 2	15	12 2	9 4	4582	154	1
4	RBL	Refrig., Cush. Underfr., 25K ■	R206	780375-780473	49 10	9 2	9 4	59 3	10 5	10 8	4 4	14	15 1	10 6	9 4	4410	143	37
5	RBL	Refrig., Cush. Underfr., Considered Part of Car: 52 Shipper Owned Pallets &/or Separators & Dividers, 25K, Assigned Service	R206	780376, 780378, 780382, 780383, 780387-780390, 780396, 780397, 780403, 780406-780413, 780417, 780419, 780420, 780422, 780438, 780440-780443, 780446, 780449, 780450, 780452-780459	49 10	9 2	9 4	59 3	10 5	10 8	4 4	14	15 1	10 6	9 4	4410	143	39
6	RBL	Refrig., Cush. Underfr., Considered Part of Car: 60 Shipper Owned Pallets, 25K, Assigned Service	R206	780386, 780394, 780451	49 10	9 2	9 4	59 3	10 5	10 8	4 4	14	15 1	10 6	9 4	4410	143	3
7	RBL	Refrig., Cush. Underfr., Considered Part of Car: 56 Pallets, 25K, Assigned Service	R206	780414, 780444	49 10	9 2	9 4	59 3	10 5	10 8	4 4	14	15 1	10 6	9 4	4410	143	2
8	RBL	Refrig., Cush. Underfr., Considered Part of Car: 50 Shipper Owned Pallets, 25K, Assigned Service	R206	780415, 780434, 780436, 780437	49 10	9 2	9 4	59 3	10 5	10 8	4 4	14	15 1	10 6	9 4	4410	143	4
9	RBL	Refrig., Cush. Underfr., Considered Part of Car: 56 Pallets, 25K, [Quaker]	R206	780423	49 10	9 2	9 4	59 3	10 5	10 8	4 4	14	15 1	10 6	9 4	4410	143	1
10	RBL	Refrig., Cush. Underfr., Considered Part of Car: 47 Shipper Owned Pallets &/or Separators & Dividers, 25K, Assigned Service	R206	780424	49 10	9 2	9 4	59 3	10 5	10 8	4 4	14	15 1	10 6	9 4	4410	143	1
11	RBL	Refrig., Cush. Underfr., Considered Part of Car: 80 Pieces Corrugated Cardboard, 25K, [Proctor & Gamble]	R206	780439	49 10	9 2	9 4	59 3	10 5	10 8	4 4	14	15 1	10 6	9 4	4410	143	1
12	RBL	Refrig., Cush. Underfr., Side Fillers, Considered Part of Car: 36 Pieces Corrugated Cardboard, 25K, [Proctor & Gamble]	R206	780445, 780448	49 10	9 2	9 4	59 3	10 5	10 8	4 4	14	15 1	10 6	9 4	4410	143	2
13	RBL	Refrig., Stl., Insulated, Cush. Underfr., Considered Part of Car: 90-150 Shipper Owned Pallets, 25K, Assigned Service	R206	780460, 780462, 780463	49 10	9 2	9 4	59 3	10 5	10 8	4 4	14	15 1	10 6	9 4	4410	143	3
14	RBL	Refrig., Cush. Underfr., Side Fillers, Considered Part of Car: 36 Pieces Corrugated Cardboard, 25K, [Proctor & Gamble]	R206	780474	49 10	9	9 4	59 3	10 5	10 8	4 4	14	15 1	10 6	9 4	4410	143	1
15	RBL	Refrig., Stl., Insulated, Cush. Underfr., 50K ■C	R206	780475-780574	50 6	9 2	10	59 4	10 2	10 8	4 5 / 9 4	14 7	15	10 6	10	4648	154	66
16	RBL	Refrig., Stl., Insulated, Cush. Underfr., Considered Part of Car: 56 Shipper Owned Pallets, 50K, Assigned Service C	R206	780475, 780477, 780480-780493, 780506, 780514	50 6	9 2	10	59 4	10 2	10 8	4 5 / 9 4	14 7	15	10 6	10	4648	154	18
17	RBL	Refrig., Stl., Insulated, Cush. Underfr., Considered Part of Car: 52 Shipper Owned Pallets &/or Separators & Dividers, 50K, Assigned Service C	R206	780494, 780495, 780505, 780515, 780521, 780530, 780556, 780561	50 6	9 2	10	59 4	10 2	10 8	4 5 / 9 4	14 7	15	10 6	10	4648	154	8
18	RBL	Refrig., Stl., Insulated, Cush. Underfr., Considered Part of Car: 44 Pallets, 50K, Assigned Service C	R206	780496, 780499	50 6	9 2	10	59 4	10 2	10 8	4 5 / 9 4	14 7	15	10 6	10	4648	154	2
19	RBL	Refrig., Stl., Insulated, Cush. Underfr., Considered Part of Car: 40 Shipper Owned Pallets &/or Separators & Dividers, 50K, Assigned Service	R206	780497	50 6	9 2	10	59 4	10 2	10 8	4 5 / 9 4	14 7	15	10 6	10	4648	154	1
20	RBL	Refrig., Stl., Insulated, Cush. Underfr., Side Fillers Considered Part of Car: 36 Pieces Corrugated Cardboard, 25K, Assigned Service C	R206	780540, 780551, 780562, 780563	50 6	9 2	10	59 4	10 2	10 8	4 5 / 9 4	14 7	15	10 6	10	4648	154	4
21	RBL	Refrig., Stl., Insulated, Cush. Underfr., 50K ■C	R206	780675-780774	50 6	9 4	10 1	59 6	10 2	10 8	4 6 / 13	14 10	15	10 6	10	4775	149	90
22	RBL	Refrig., Stl., Insulated, Cush. Underfr., Considered Part of Car: 47 Pallets, 50K, Assigned Service C	R206	780675, 780676	50 6	9 2	10	59 4	10 2	10 8	4 5 / 9 4	14 7	15	10 6	10	4648	154	2
23	RBL	Refrig., Stl., Insulated, Cush. Underfr., Considered Part of Car: 53 Pallets, 50K, Assigned Service C	R206	780677, 780680, 780684, 780686, 780691-780693	50 6	9 2	10	59 4	10 2	10 8	4 5 / 9 4	14 7	15	10 6	10	4648	154	7
24	RBL	Refrig., Stl., Insulated, Cush. Underfr., Considered Part of Car: 80 Pieces Corrugated Cardboard, 50K, Assigned Service C	R206	780681	50 6	9 4	10 1	59 6	10 2	10 8	4 6 / 13	14 10	15	10 6	10	4775	149	1
25	RBL	Refrig., Stl., Insulated, Cush. Underfr., Plug Doors, 50K	R206	780775-780874	50 7	9 4	10 1	59 7	10 3	10 8	4 4	14 5	15	10 6	10	4760	154	100
26	RBL	Refrig., Stl., Insulated, Cush. Underfr., Considered Part of Car: Shipper Owned Pallets, 25K, Assigned Service ■	R206	786000-786199	50 1	9 3	9 4	59 3	10 5	10 8	4 4	14	15 1	10 6	9 4	4320	143	44
27	RBL	Refrig., Stl., Insulated, Cush. Underfr., Considered Part of Car: 56 Shipper Owned Pallets, 25K, Assigned Service	R206	786000-786014, 786068, 786138	50 1	9 3	9 4	59 3	10 5	10 8	4 4	14	15 1	10 6	9 4	4320	143	17
28	RBL	Refrig., Stl., Insulated, Cush. Underfr., Considered Part of Car: 53 Shipper Owned Pallets, 25K, Assigned Service	R206	786019, 786021, 786024, 786025, 786027, 786030, 786034-786037, 786039, 786041, 786044, 786046, 786051, 786053, 786057-786060, 786070, 786071, 786075, 786077, 786078, 786085, 786097	50 1	9 3	9 4	59 3	10 5	10 8	4 4	14	16 1	10 6	9 4	4320	143	27
29	RBL	Refrig., Stl., Insulated, Cush. Underfr., Considered Part of Car: 47 Shipper Owned Pallets, 25K, Assigned Service	R206	786031, 786045, 786047, 786050, 786076, 786084	50 1	9 3	9 4	59 3	10 5	10 8	4 4	14	16 1	10 6	9 4	4320	143	6
30	RBL	Refrig., Stl., Insulated, Cush. Underfr., Considered Part of Car: 88 Shipper Owned Pallets, 25K, Assigned Service	R206	786079	50 1	9 3	9 4	59 3	10 5	10 8	4 4	14	15 1	10 6	9 4	4320	143	1
31	RBL	Refrig., Stl., Cush. Underfr., Considered Part of Car: 47 Shipper Owned Pallets &/or Inflatable Dunnage Bags, 25K, Assigned Service	R206	786100, 786101, 786105, 786106, 786114, 786115, 786119, 786122, 786125, 786131, 786136, 786137, 786139, 786143, 786144, 786146, 786147, 786150, 786153, 786155, 786160, 786161, 786166, 786170, 786172, 786174, 786175, 786177-786180, 786182, 786187, 786189-786193, 786196-786198	50 1	9 3	9 4	59 3	10 5	10 8	4 4	14	15 1	10 6	9 4	4320	143	41
32	RBL	Refrig., Stl., Insulated, Cush. Underfr., Considered Part of Car: 88 Shipper Owned Pallets &/or Inflatable Dunnage Bags, 25K, Assigned Service	R206	786102, 786103, 786107-786113, 786116-786118, 786120, 786121, 786123, 786124, 786126-786130, 786132-786135, 786140-786142, 786145, 786148, 786149, 786151, 786152, 786154, 786156-786159, 786162-786165, 786167-786169, 786171, 786176, 786181, 786183-786188, 786194, 786195, 786199	50 1	9 3	9 4	59 3	10 5	10 8	4 4	14	15 1	10 6	9 4	4320	143	56
33	RBL	Refrig., Stl., Insulated, Cush. Underfr., Considered Part of Car: 90-150 Shipper Owned Pallets, Assigned Service, 25K	R206	786104	50 1	9 3	9 4	59 3	10 5	10 8	4 4	14	15 1	10 6	9 4	4320	143	1
34	RBL	Refrig., Stl., Insulated, Cush. Underfr., Considered Part of Car: 88 Shipper Owned Pallets &/or Inflatable Dunnage Bags, 25K, Assigned Service ■	R206	786200-786399	51 5	9 3	9 6	59 5	10 1	10 8	12 11	14 2	15	10 6	9 4	4543	154	187
35	RBL	Refrig., Stl., Insulated, Cush. Underfr., Considered Part of Car: 56 Shipper Owned Pallets &/or Inflatable Dunnage Bags, 25K, Assigned Service	R206	786249, 786274, 786395	51 5	9 3	9 6	59 5	10 1	10 8	12 11	14 2	15	10 6	9 4	4543	154	3
36	RBL	Refrig., Stl., Insulated, Cush. Underfr., Considered Part of Car: 47 Shipper Owned Pallets &/or Inflatable Dunnage Bags, 25K, Assigned Service	R206	786300, 786308, 786384, 786390, 786397	51 5	9 3	9 6	59 5	10 1	10 8	12 11	14 2	15	10 6	9 4	4543	154	5
37	RBL	Refrig., Stl., Insulated, Cush. Underfr., Considered Part of Car: 53 Shipper Owned Pallets, 25K, Assigned Service	R206	786305, 786361, 786398	51 5	9 3	9 6	59 5	10 1	10 8	12 11	14 2	15	10 6	9 4	4543	154	
38	RBL	Refrig., Stl., Insulated, Cush. Underfr., Considered Part of Car: 44 Pallets, 25K, Assigned Service	R206	786399	51 5	9 3	9 6	59 5	10 1	10 8	12 11	14 2	15	10 6	9 4	4543	154	1
39	RBL	Refrig., Stl., Insulated, Cush. Underfr., Considered Part of Car: 47 Shipper Owned Pallets, 25K, Assigned Service ■	R206	786400-786499	51 5	9 3	9 6	59 5	10 1	10 8	12 11	14 2	15	10 6	9 4	4462	154	86

CONTINUED ON FOLLOWING PAGE

MISSOURI PACIFIC RAILROAD COMPANY — Continued

Line No.	A.A.R. Mech. Desig.	DESCRIPTION	A.A.R. Car Type Code	NUMBERS ▶Change from Previous Issue	Inside Length	Inside Width	Inside Height	Outside Length	Width At Eaves or Top of Sides or Platform	Extreme Width	Height To Extreme Width	Height To Eaves or Top of Sides or Platform	Height To Extreme Height	Door Width of Open'g	Door Height of Open'g	Cubic Feet Level Full	Lbs. (000)	No. of Cars
		"MP"																
1	RBL	Refrig., Stl., Insulated, Cush. Underfr., Considered Part of Car: 48 Shipper Owned Pallets, 25K, Assigned Service	R206	786404, 786411, 786413, 786414, 786417-786424	51 5	9 3	9 6	59 5	10 1	10 8	12 11	14 2	15	10 6	9 4	4462	154	12
2	RBL	Refrig., Stl., Insulated, Cush. Underfr., Considered Part of Car: Shipper Owned Pallets, 25K, Assigned Service ■	R206	▶786500-786599	51 5	9 3	9 6	59 5	10 1	10 8	12 11	14 2	15	10 6	9 4	4454	154	32
3	RBL	Refrig., Stl., Cush. Underfr., Considered Part of Car: 47 Shipper Owned Pallets, 25K, Assigned Service	R206	786500, 786501, 786503-786509, 786536-786538, 786542, 786545, 786550-786552, 786554, 786557, 786559, 786563, 786566, 786569, 786570, 786573, 786576, 786579, 786586, 786591, 786593	51 5	9 3	9 6	59 5	10 1	10 8	12 11	14 2	15	10 6	9 4	4454	154	30
4	RBL	Refrig., Stl., Insulated, Cush. Underfr., Considered Part of Car: 88 Shipper Owned Pallets, 25K, Assigned Service	R206	786502, 786539, 786540, 786572, 786580, 786585, 786589, 786599	51 5	9 3	9 6	59 5	10 1	10 8	12 11	14 2	15	10 6	9 4	4454	154	8
5	RBL	Refrig., Stl., Insulated, Cush. Underfr., Considered Part of Car: 53 Shipper Owned Pallets, 25K, Assigned Service	R206	786516, 786521, 786526, 786527, 786532, 786533, 786541, 786543, 786546, 786547, 786553, 786555, 786560, 786562, 786564, 786565, 786568, 786571, 786574, 786575, 786577, 786582, 786584, 786587, 786596, 786597	51 5	9 3	9 6	59 5	10 1	10 8	12 11	14 2	15	10 6	9 4	4454	154	26
6	RBL	Refrig., Stl., Insulated, Cush. Underfr., Considered Part of Car: 56 Shipper Owned Pallets, 25K, Assigned Service	R206	▶786524, 786581	51 5	9 3	9 6	59 5	10 1	10 8	12 11	14 2	15	10 6	9 4	4454	154	2
7	RBL	Refrig., Stl., Insulated, Cush. Underfr., Considered Part of Car: 54 Shipper Owned Pallets, 25K, Assigned Service	R206	786583	51 5	9 3	9 6	59 5	10 1	10 8	12 11	14 2	15	10 6	9 4	4454	154	1
8	RBL	Refrig., Stl., Insulated Box, Considered Part of Car: Shipper Owned Pallets, 25K, Assigned Service ■	R206	786600-786699	50 5	9 3	9 6	59 5	10 1	10 8	12 10	14 2	15	10 6	9 4	4454	143	18
9	RBL	Refrig., Stl., Insulated Box, Considered Part of Car: 47 Shipper Owned Pallets, 25K Assigned Service	R206	786600, 786607, 786610, 786624, 786627-786629, 786634, 786638, 786640, 786642, 786645, 786651, 786653, 786656, 786657, 786662, 786664, 786665, 786667-786669, 786671, 786673, 786676, 786677, 786679, 786680, 786682, 786686, 786687, 786693-786695, 786697, 786698	50 5	9 3	9 6	59 5	10 1	10 8	12 10	14 2	15	10 6	9 4	4454	143	37
10	RBL	Refrig., Stl., Insulated, Cush. Underfr., Considered Part of Car: 53 Shipper Owned Pallets, 25K, Assigned Service	R206	786601-786603, 786605, 786609, 786611-786613, 786616, 786618, 786623, 786625, 786630, 786632, 786633, 786635-786637, 786639, 786641, 786644, 786647-786649, 786652, 786654, 786655, 786658-786661, 786663, 786670, 786672, 786678, 786681, 786683, 786685, 786688-786690, 786693	50 5	9 3	9 6	59 5	10 1	10 8	12 10	14 2	15	10 6	9 4	4454	143	42
11	RBL	Refrig., Stl., Insulated, Cush. Underfr., Considered Part of Car: 88 Shipper Owned Pallets, 25K, Assigned Service	R206	786619, 786650, 786675	50 5	9 3	9 6	59 5	10 1	10 8	12 10	14 2	15	10 6	9 4	4454	143	3
12	RBL	Refrig., Stl., Insulated, Cush. Underfr., 50K ■C	R206	794800-794999	60 6	9 2	10	69 6	10 2	10 8	4 5	14 7	15	10 6	10	5583	170	68
13	RBL	Refrig., Stl., Cush. Underfr., Considered Part of Car: 52 Shipper Owned Pallets, 50K, Assigned Service C	R206	794801, 794805, 794808, 794810, 794812, 794867, 794872, 794876, 794881, 794882, 794895, 794915, 794968, 794975, 794977, 794983, 794985, 794986, 794989, 794994	60 6	9 2	10	69 6	10 2	10 8	4 5	14 7	15	10 6	10	5583	170	20
14	RBL	Refrig., Stl., Insulated, Cush. Underfr., Considered Part of Car: 67 Shipper Owned Pallets, 50K, Assigned Service C	R206	794814-794817, 794900-794904, 794906-794910	60 6	9 2	10	69 6	10 2	10 8	4 5	14 7	15	10 6	10	5583	170	14
15	RBL	Refrig., Stl., Insulated, Cush. Underfr., Considered Part of Car: 60 Shipper Owned Pallets &/or Separators & Dividers, 50K, Assigned Service C	R206	794818, 794822, 794824, 794828, 794830, 794832-794836, 794846, 794874, 794937, 794972, 794978	60 6	9 2	10	69 6	10 2	10 8	4 5	14 7	15	10 6	10	5583	170	15
16	RBL	Refrig., Stl., Insulated, Cush. Underfr., Considered Part of Car: 48 Pallets & 24 Separators, 50K, Assigned Service C	R206	794819, 794829, 794916, 794923, 794947, 794953, 794956	60 6	9 2	10	69 6	10 2	10 8	4 5	14 7	15	10 6	10	5583	170	7
17	RBL	Refrig., Stl., Insulated, Cush. Underfr., Considered Part of Car: 104 Shipper Owned Pallets, 25K, Assigned Service C	R206	794821, 794825, 794844, 794869, 794885, 794893, 794924, 794938, 794948, 794969, 794991	60 6	9 2	10	69 6	10 2	10 8	4 5	14 7	15	10 6	10	5583	170	11
18	RBL	Refrig., Stl., Insulated, Cush. Underfr., Supplemental Blkhds Consisting of Corrugated Spacers & Pressboard Sheets, Side Fillers, Considered Part of Car: 36 Pieces Corrugated Cardboard, 25K, Assigned Service C	R206	794831, 794838, 794839, 794875, 794889, 794894, 794899, 794922, 794943, 794951, 794958	60 6	9 2	10	69 6	10 2	10 8	4 5	14 7	15	10 6	10	5583	170	11
19	RBL	Refrig., Stl., Insulated, Cush. Underfr., Considered Part of Car: 52 Shipper Owned Pallets &/or Separators & Dividers, 25K, Assigned Service	R206	794843, 794849, 794851-794856, 794858, 794861, 794862, 794883, 794888, 794897, 794898, 794913, 794917, 794918, 794921, 794929, 794944, 794955, 794976, 794990	60 6	9 2	10	69 6	10 2	10 8	4 5	14 7	15	10 6	10	5583	170	24
20	RBL	Refrig., Stl., Cush. Underfr., Considered Part of Car: 52 Pallets, Assigned Service C	R206	794865, 794868, 794871, 794873, 794891, 794892, 794912, 794931, 794933-794935, 794945, 794950, 794952, 794954, 794967, 794970, 794974, 794982, 794988, 794995, 794997-794999	60 6	9 2	10	69 6	10 2	10 8	4 5	14 7	15	10 6	10	5583	170	24
21	RBL	Refrig., Stl., Insulated, Cush. Underfr., Considered Part of Car: 40 Pallets, 25K, Assigned Service C	R206	794959	60 6	9 2	10	69 6	10 2	10 8	4 5	14 7	15	10 6	10	5583	170	1
22	RBL	Refrig., Stl., Insulated, Cush. Underfr., Considered Part of Car: 60 Pallets, 25K, Assigned Service C	R206	794961	60 6	9 2	10	69 6	10 2	10 8	4 5	14 7	15	10 6	10	5583	170	1
23	RB	Refrig., Stl., Insulated, Cush. Underfr., 25K C	R200	794965	60 6	9 2	10	69 6	10 2	10 8	4 5	14 7	15	10 6	10	5583	170	1
24	FM	Flat, Stl.	F102	800271, 800273, 800274	53 6	10 6		56 9	10 6	10 6	3 2	3 6	3 6				110	3
25	FM	Flat, Stl.	F201	800280-800283	45	9 1		49 2	9 1	10	4 2	4 2	4 2				154	4
26	FM	Flat, Stl.	F201	800286-800289	45	10 6		49 2	10 6	10 6	4 2	4 2	4 2				154	4
27	FM	Flat, Stl.	F201	800291	45	10 6		49 2	10 6	10 6	4 2	4 2	4 2				154	1
28	FM	Flat, Stl.	F201	800292, 800297, 800299, 800301, 800306	43 4	10 6		47	10 6	10 6	4 3	4 3	4 3				154	5
29	FM	Flat, Stl.	F102	800308	53 6	9 4		56 8	10 2	10 2	3 8	3 8	3 8				110	1
30	FM	Flat, Stl.	F101	800450-800458	50	8 2		53 3	9 4	10 3	3 5	3 9	3 9				110	7
31	FM	Flat, Stl., When Load is Centered & Uniformly Distributed in Excess of 44 Linear Ft. Car May Be Loaded to Gross Rail Load of 220000 Lbs. ■	F103	▶815000-815049	60	10 6		63 5	10 6	10 6	3 9	3 9	3 9				110	45
32	FMS	Flat, Stl., (Coil Stl.), When Load is Centered & Uniformly Distributed in Excess of 44 Linear Ft. Car May Be Loaded to Gross Rail Load of 220000 Lbs.	F213	▶815020, 815031, ▶815036, 815042, 815049	60	10 6		63 5	10 6	10 6	3 9	3 9	3 9				154	5
33	FM	Flat, Stl. When Load is Centered & Uniformly Distributed in Excess of 44 Linear Ft. Car May Be Loaded to Gross Rail Load of 220000 Lbs.	F103	▶815050-815149	60	10 6		63 5	10 6	10 6	3 9	3 9	3 9				110	98
34	FM	Flat, Stl., End Cush. ■	F103	818010-818043	60	10 6		64 5	10 6	10 6	3 9	3 9	3 9				147	26
35	FMS	Flat, Stl., End Cush., Tie Down Chains	F113	818010-818013, 818019, 818031, 818041, 818043	60	10 6		64 5	10 6	10 6	3 9	3 9	3 9				147	8
36	FMS	Flat, Stl., End Cush., Tie Down Chains	F113	818044-818046	60	10 6		64 5	10 6	10 6	3 9	3 9	3 9				147	3
37	FM	Flat, Stl., End Cush. C	F103	818100-818108	60	10 6		65	10 6	10 6	3 6	3 6	3 6				150	9
38	FM	Flat, Stl., End Cush. ■	F103	818116-818123	60	10 6		64 4	10 6	10 6	3 6	3 6	3 6				150	5
39	FMS	Flat, Stl., End Cush.	F113	818117, 818119, 818122	60	10 6		64 4	10 6	10 6	3 6	3 6	3 6				150	3
40	FM	Flat, Stl., End Cush.	F203	▶819780-819791	61 4	10 3		65 11	3 9	10 3	3 9	3 9	3 9				193	12
41	FM	Flat, Stl., End Cush.	F203	819800-819839	61 4	10 3		65 8	3 9	10 3	3 9	3 9	3 9				188	40
42	FM	Flat, Stl., End Cush. ■	F203	819900-819999	60	10 6		65		10 6	3 11		5 11				188	97

Line No.	A.A.R. Mech. Desig.	DESCRIPTION See Explanation Pages for Abbreviations & Symbols	A.A.R. Car Type Code	NUMBERS ►Change from Previous Issue	INSIDE Length	INSIDE Width	INSIDE Height	OUTSIDE Length	At Eaves or Top of Sides or Platform	Extreme Width	To Extreme Width	To Eaves or Top of Sides or Platform	To Extreme Height	DOORS Side Width of Open'g	DOORS Side Height of Open'g	Cubic Feet Level Full	Lbs. (000)	No. of Cars
		"MP"																
1	FB	Flat, Stl., Blkhds	F233	819900, 819901, 819924	60	10 6	....	65	....	10 6	3 11	....	5 11	....	....		188	3
2	FBS	Flat, Stl., Blkhds ■	F181	820260-820265	48 6	10 6	6 6	56 9	10 6	10 6	3 9	3 9	10 3				110	4
3	FBS	Flat, Stl., Blkhds, (Brick)	F281	820261, 820262	48 6	10 6	6 6	56 9	10 6	10 6	3 9	3 9	10 3				154	2
4	FBS	Flat, Stl., Blkhds, (Plasterboard) ■	F181	820266-820274	48 6	10 6	8 6	56 9	10 6	10 6	3 9	3 9	10 3				110	7
5	FM	Flat, Stl.	F102	820271	53 6	10 6	8 6	56 9	10 6	10 6	3 9	3 9	10 3				110	1
6	FBS	Flat, Stl., Blkhds	F181	820273	48 6	10 6	8 6	56 9	10 6	10 6	3 9	3 9	10 3				110	1
7	FBS	Flat, Stl., Blkhds, (Plasterboard)	F181	820275-820278	49	10 6	9	56 9	10 6	10 6	3 6	3 9	12 9				110	3
8	FM	Flat, Stl.	F101	820279	49	10 6	9	56 9	10 6	10 6	3 6	3 9	12 9				110	1
9	FBS	Flat, Stl., Blkhds, Removable Side Gates, (Brick)	F181	820280-820290	48 9	8 11	4	56 9	10 6	10 6	3 6	3 9	12 9				110	10
10	FBS	Flat, Stl., (Brick)	F181	820295	46	9 4	3 4	53 3	9 4	10 2	3 5	3 9	7 1				110	1
11	FBS	Flat, Stl., Blkhds, Tie Down Chains ■	F181	820300-820349	48 6	10 6	9	56 8	10 6	10 8	2 9 11 6	3 8	12 8				110	....
12	FBS	Flat, Stl., Blkhds, Removable Side Boards, (Brick)	F181	820300, 820308, 820310, 820312, 820327, 820335	48 6	8 10	3 4	56 8	10 6	10 6	3 7 8	3 8	8				110	6
13	FM	Flat, Stl. ■	F102	820350-820369	53 6	9 4	....	56 8	10 2	10 2	3 8	3 8	3 8				110	1
14	FBS	Flat, Stl., Blkhds, Side Gates, (Brick), Inside Width Shown is Between Side Gates	F181	820350, 820357, 820361, 820369	48 8	8 10	4	56 8	10 2	10 2	3 5	3 8	9 8				110	4
15	FBS	Flat, Stl., Blkhds, (Plasterboard)	F181	820353, 820356	48 6	10 2	6 6	56 8	10 2	10 2	3 5	3 8	10 2				110	2
16	FBS	Flat, Stl., Blkhds, (Plasterboard)	F181	820359, 820365	48 8	10 2	8 6	56 8	10 2	10 2	3 5	3 8	9 8				110	2
17	FBS	Flat, Stl., Blkhds, Cap. of 154000 lbs. is for Uniformly Distributed Load, Tie Down Chains	F282	821000-821049	56 6	10 6	8 6	63 5	10 6	10 6	3 8 12 6	3 8	12 6				154	50
18	FBS	Flat, Stl., Blkhd, Tie Down ■ C	F282	822100-822159	56 6	10 6	10 3	63 5	10 6	10 6	3 5 14	3 9	14				178	43
19	FBS	Flat, Stl., Blkhd, 13 Compts., (Coiled Stl. Rods), [Armco Steel] ... C	F282	822109-822112, 822119, 822124, 822126, 822128, 822131, 822133, 822138, 822139, 822143, 822145, 822146, 822148, 822149	....	8 5	....	63 5	10 6	10 6	3 5 14	3 9	14				178	17
20	FBS	Flat, Stl., End Cush., Blkhd, Tie Down Chains	F282	823000-823039	56 6	10 6	10 3	64 5	10 6	10 6	3 5 14	3 9	14				174	39
21	FBS	Flat, Stl., Blkhd, Tie Down Chains, End Cush. ... C	F282	►823115-823214	56 6	10 6	10 3	64 5	10 6	10 6	3 5 14	3 9	14				174	100
22	FBS	Flat, Stl., Blkhd, Tie Down Chains, End Cush. ... C	F282	►823215-823314	56 6	10 6	10 3	64 5	10 6	10 6	3 5 14	3 9	14				174	99
23	FM	Flat, Stl.	F102	825000-825044	53 6	10 6		56 8	10 6	10 6	3 8	3 8	3 8				110	38
24	FM	Flat, Stl.	F102	825050-825062	53 6	9 4		56 8	10 2	10 2	3 8	3 8	3 8				110	10
25	FMS	Flat, Stl., End Cush.	F113	828000-828062	60	10 6		62 9	10 6	10 6	3 6	3 11	3 11				142	63
26	FMS	Flat, Stl., End Cush.	F219	829900-829907	89	9		92 5	9	9 6	3 4	3 6	3 6				154	8
27	FC	Flat, Stl., ACF 1 Trailer Hitch ■	F871	►833000-833130	50	8 2		53 3	9 4	10 3	3 5	3 9	7 9				110	67
28	FC	Flat, Stl., ACF 1 Trailer Hitch	F871	833000-833005	45	8 2		48 3	9 4	10 3	3 5	3 9	7 9				110	6
29	FM	Flat, Stl.	F101	833046	50	8 2		53 3	9 4	10 3	3 5	3 9	7 9				110	1
30	FC	Flat, Stl. ■ C	F875	838000-838014	85	8 2		88 5	8 11	10 2	4 4	3 6	6 3				158	1
31	LG	Gond., Fixed Ends, 3 Compt., Considered Part of Car: 11-300 Cubic Ft. Rubber Containers, Assigned Service	L018	838001, 838005, 838013	85	8 2	4 6	88 5	9	10 2	4 4	8	10 8				158	2
32	FC	Flat, Stl., ACF Trailer Hitches ... C	F875	838002-838004, 838008-838012, 838014	85	8 2		88 5	8 11	10 2	4 4	3 6	6 3				158	9
33	FW	Flat, Well, See Heavy Cap. Section	F140	850000	42 3	10 2		48 8	10 2			4 5	7 7				110	1
34	FD	Flat, Depressed, See Heavy Cap. Section	F320	863000, 863001	58 3	8 4		61 4	8 4			3 11	6 11				250	2
35	FD	Flat, Depressed, See Heavy Cap. Section	F320	863002	57 9	9		60 10	9	9 7	4	4 3	5 10				250	1
36	FM	Flat, Heavy Duty, See Heavy Cap. Section	F303	865000-865002	35 11 34 11	10		60 6	10	10	4 2	4 2	6 10				600	3
37	FM	Flat, Stl., See Heavy Cap. Section	F302	866000	53	9 9		56 7	9 9	10 3	3 6	3 8	3 8				250	1
38	FA	Flat, Stl., End Cush. ■ C	....	867500-867574	89	8 6		93 4	9 3	10 8	3 10						130	....
39	FA	Flat, Stl., Tri-Level Auto Racks, End Cush.	V682	867501-867503, 867505, 867507-867511, 867513, 867525, 867528, 867532, 867534, 867536, 867539-867545, 867547, 867548, 867550, 867552-867557, 867559-867563, 867565, 867567, 867570, 867572	89	8 6		93 4	9 3	10 8	3 10						130	40
40	FA	Flat, Stl., Bi Level Auto Racks, End Cush.	V582	867504, 867512, 867514-867524, 867526, 867527, 867529-867531, 867533, 867535, 867537, 867538, 867546, 867549, 867551, 867564, 867566, 867568, 867569, 867571, 867573, 867574	89	8 6		93 4	9 3	10 8	3 10						130	32
41	FA	Flat, Stl., Heavy Duty B: Level Auto Racks, End Cush., 3 Compt., Considered Part of Car: 11 Containers, Assigned Service ... C	V582	867506	89	8 6		93 4	9 3	10 8	3 10						130	1
42	LG	Gond., Stl., Fixed Ends, 3 Compt., Considered Part of Car: 11-300 Cubic Ft. Rubber Containers, Assigned Service ... C	L018	867575-867579	85	8 2		88 5	8 11	10 2	4 4	3 6	6 3				88	4
43	FA	Flat, Stl., Bi Level Auto Racks, End Cush. ■ C	V582	868000-868019	89	8 2		93 3	8 11	8 11	3 4	3 4					110	15
44	FA	Flat, Stl., Tri Level Auto Racks, End Cush. ... C	V682	868006, 868016-868019	89	8 2		93 3	8 11	8 11	3 4	3 4					110	5
45	FA	Flat, Stl., End Cush. ■ C	....	868020-868117	89 1	8 6		93 5	9 1	10 8	4 2	4 2					120	9
46	FA	Flat, Stl., Tri Level Auto Racks, End Cush.	V682	868020, 868021, 868024-868034, 868036-868038, 868079-868087, 868089, 868090, 868093-868096, 868098, 868100, 868103, 868107, 868111-868113, 868115, 868116	89 1	8 6		93 5	9 1	10 8	4 2	4 2					120	40
47	FA	Flat, Stl., Bi Level Auto Racks, End Cush.	V582	868039, 868042-868049, 868051, 868053-868062, 868064, 868066-868071, 868076-868078, 868091, 868092, 868097, 868101, 868102, 868104, 868108-868110, 868114, 868117	89 1	8 6		93 5	9 1	10 8	4 2	4 2					120	41
48	GBSR	Gond., Stl., Cush. Underfr., Sectioned Removable Canopy Type Covers, (Coil Stl.)	E240	950000-950049	49 11	7 11		59		10 7	4		14 4				189	49
49	FA	Flat, Stl., End Cush. ■ C	....	992000-992097	89 1	8 6		93 5	9 1	10 8	4 2	4 2					120	
50	FA	Flat, Stl., Tri Level Auto Racks, End Cush. ... C	V682	992003	89 1	8 6		93 5	9 1	10 8	4 2	4 2					120	1
51	FA	Flat, Stl., Bi Level Auto Racks, End Cush. ... C	V582	992019, 992020	89 1	8 6		93 5	9 1	10 8	4 2	4 2					120	2
52	FCS	Flat, Stl., Winches, Tie Down Chains, 2 Removable Pedestals, Bridge Plates, End Cush.	F087	995000, 995001	89 1	8 6		93 5	9 1	10 8	4 2	4 2					145	2
53	FM	Flat, Articulated	F209	999900	85 11	10 6		89 2	10 6	10 6	3 10	3 10	5 4				160	1
54	FM	Flat, Stl., Articulated	F209	999950	85 11	9 3		89 2	9 3	10 2	3 6	3 10	5 4				160	1
		Total																36162

CONTINUED ON FOLLOWING PAGE

127

A P P E N D I X   I I

L o c o m o t i v e   D i a g r a m s

The locomotive diagrams on the following pages have been selected from official Missouri Pacific records and are representative of the wide variety of steam and diesel locomotives in MoPac service over the years.

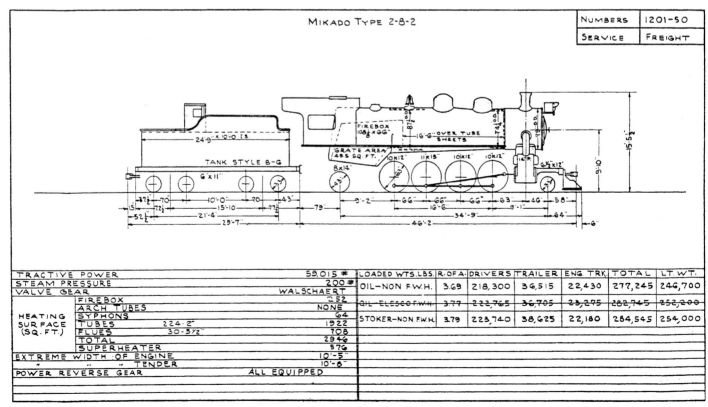

MIKADO TYPE 2-8-2

NUMBERS	1201-50
SERVICE	FREIGHT

TRACTIVE POWER		59,015 #	LOADED WTS.LBS.	R.OF A.	DRIVERS	TRAILER	ENG. TRK.	TOTAL	LT. WT.
STEAM PRESSURE		200 #	OIL—NON F.W.H.	3.69	218,300	36,515	22,430	277,245	246,700
VALVE GEAR		WALSCHAERT							
HEATING SURFACE (SQ. FT.)	FIREBOX	252	OIL-ELESCO F.W.H.	3.77	222,765	36,705	23,275	282,745	252,200
	ARCH TUBES	NONE							
	SYPHONS	64	STOKER—NON F.W.H.	3.79	223,740	38,625	22,180	284,545	254,000
	TUBES 224-2"	1922							
	FLUES 30-5½"	708							
	TOTAL	2946							
	SUPERHEATER	576							
EXTREME WIDTH OF ENGINE		10'-5"							
" " TENDER		10'-6"							
POWER REVERSE GEAR		ALL EQUIPPED							

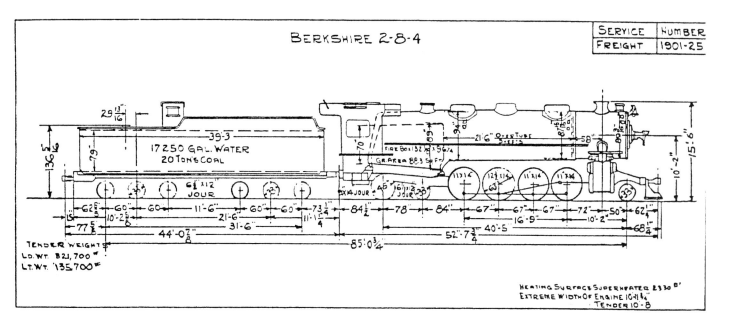

BERKSHIRE 2-8-4

SERVICE	NUMBER
FREIGHT	1901-25

17250 GAL. WATER
20 TONS COAL

TENDER WEIGHTS
LD. WT. 321,700#
LT. WT. 135,700#

HEATING SURFACE SUPERHEATER 2330 □'
EXTREME WIDTH OF ENGINE 10'11¼"
TENDER 10'-8"

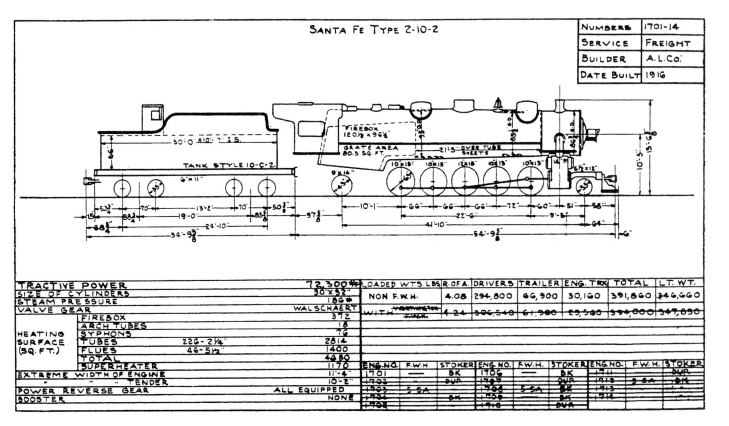

SANTA FE TYPE 2-10-2

NUMBERS	1701-14
SERVICE	FREIGHT
BUILDER	A.L.Co.
DATE BUILT	1916

TANK STYLE 10-C-2

FIREBOX 120⅛ x 96¼
GRATE AREA 80.3 SQ. FT.

TRACTIVE POWER		72,300#
SIZE OF CYLINDERS		30"x32"
STEAM PRESSURE		186#
VALVE GEAR		WALSCHAERT
HEATING SURFACE (SQ. FT.)	FIREBOX	372
	ARCH TUBES	18
	SYPHONS	76
	TUBES 226-2¼	2814
	FLUES 46-5½	1400
	TOTAL	4680
	SUPERHEATER	1170
EXTREME WIDTH OF ENGINE		11'-4"
" TENDER		10'-2"
POWER REVERSE GEAR		ALL EQUIPPED
BOOSTER		NONE

LOADED WTS LBS	R. OF A.	DRIVERS	TRAILER	ENG. TRK	TOTAL	LT. WT.
NON F.W.H.	4.08	294,800	66,900	30,160	391,860	346,660
WITH WORTHINGTON F.W.H.	4.24	306,540	61,900	25,560	394,000	347,850

ENG. NO.	F.W.H	STOKER	ENG. NO.	F.W.H	STOKER	ENG. NO.	F.W.H.	STOKER
1701	—	BK	1706		BK	1711		DUP
1702		DUP	1707		DUP	1712	5-SA	BK
1703	5-SA	BK	1708	5-SA	BK	1713		—
1704		BK	1709		BK	1714		—
1705			1710		DUP			

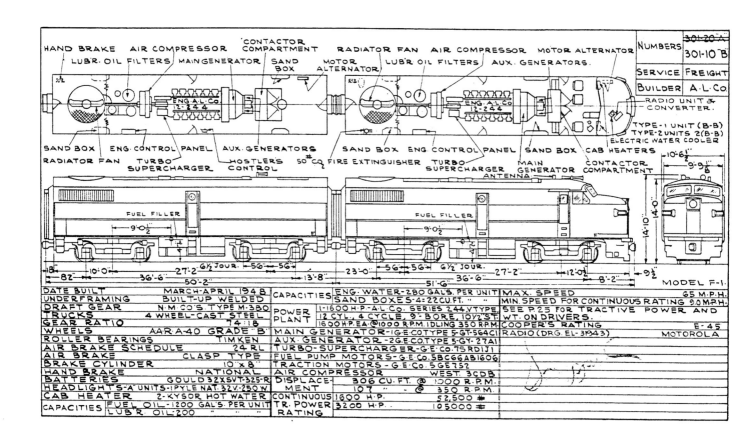

HAND BRAKE AIR COMPRESSOR CONTACTOR COMPARTMENT RADIATOR FAN AIR COMPRESSOR MOTOR ALTERNATOR
LUB'R. OIL FILTERS MAIN GENERATOR SAND BOX MOTOR ALTERNATOR LUB'R OIL FILTERS AUX. GENERATORS.

ENG. A.L.Co 12-244 ENG. A.L.Co 12-244

SAND BOX ENG. CONTROL PANEL AUX. GENERATORS SAND BOX ENG. CONTROL PANEL SAND BOX CAB HEATERS
RADIATOR FAN TURBO-SUPERCHARGER HOSTLER'S CONTROL 50 CO₂ FIRE EXTINGUISHER TURBO-SUPERCHARGER MAIN GENERATOR CONTACTOR COMPARTMENT
ANTENNA

FUEL FILLER 9'-0½" FUEL FILLER 9'-0½"

18" 10'-0" 36'-6" 27'-2" 6½" JOUR. 56" 56" 13'-8" 23'-0" 56" 56" 6½" JOUR. 36'-6" 27'-2" 12'-0½" 8'-2" 9½"
82" 50'-2" 51'-6"

	NUMBERS	301-20 A
		301-10 B
	SERVICE	FREIGHT
	BUILDER	A.L.Co.

RADIO UNIT & CONVERTER.
TYPE-1 UNIT (B-B)
TYPE-2 UNITS 2(B-B)
ELECTRIC WATER COOLER
10'-6½" 9'-9⅝" 14'-0" 14'-10" 9½"

MODEL F-1.

					MAX. SPEED	65 M.P.H.
DATE BUILT	MARCH-APRIL 1948	CAPACITIES	ENG. WATER-280 GALS. PER UNIT		MIN. SPEED FOR CONTINUOUS RATING 9.0 M.P.H.	
UNDERFRAMING	BUILT-UP WELDED		SAND BOXES-4:22 CU.FT. "			
DRAFT GEAR	N.M.CO'S TYPE M-380	POWER PLANT	1-1600 H.P.-A.L.Co. SERIES 244 V TYPE		SEE P.25 FOR TRACTIVE POWER AND	
TRUCKS	4 WHEEL-CAST STEEL		12 CYL, 4 CYCLE, 9" BORE, 10½" ST.		WT. ON DRIVERS.	
GEAR RATIO	74:18		1600 H.P. EA.@1000 R.P.M. IDLING 350 R.P.M.			
WHEELS	A.A.R. A-40 GRADE "B"	MAIN GENERATOR-1 G.E. CO. TYPE 5-GT-564C1			COOPER'S RATING	E-45
ROLLER BEARINGS	TIMKEN	AUX. GENERATOR-2 G.E. CO. TYPE 5-GY-27A1			RADIO (DRG. EL-31943)	MOTOROLA
AIR BRAKE SCHEDULE	24 RL	TURBO-SUPERCHARGER-G.E.Co.75 RDIJ1				
AIR BRAKE	CLASP TYPE	FUEL PUMP MOTORS-G.E.Co. 5BC66AB1606				
BRAKE CYLINDER	10"X8"	TRACTION MOTORS-G.E.Co. 5 GE 752				
HAND BRAKE	NATIONAL	AIR COMPRESSOR	WEST. 3CDB			
BATTERIES	GOULD 32XSVT-325-R	DISPLACEMENT	306 CU.FT. @ 1000 R.P.M.			
HEADLIGHTS-A UNITS-1 PYLE NAT. 32 V-250 W			107 - @ 350 R.P.M.			
CAB HEATER	2-KYSOR HOT WATER	CONTINUOUS	1600 H.P.	52,500 #		
CAPACITIES	FUEL OIL-1200 GAL'S PER UNIT	TR. POWER RATING	3200 H.P.	105000 #		
	LUB'R. OIL:200 " "					

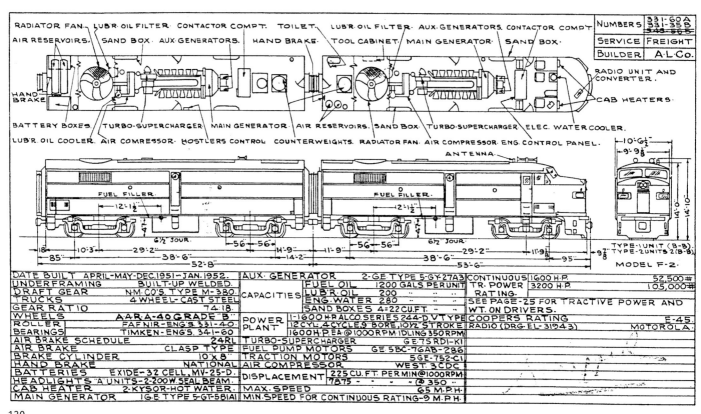

RADIATOR FAN. LUB'R. OIL FILTER. CONTACTOR COMPT. TOILET. LUB'R. OIL FILTER. AUX. GENERATORS. CONTACTOR COMPT.
AIR RESERVOIRS. SAND BOX. AUX. GENERATORS. HAND BRAKE. TOOL CABINET. MAIN GENERATOR. SAND BOX.
HAND BRAKE

BATTERY BOXES. TURBO-SUPERCHARGER. MAIN GENERATOR. AIR RESERVOIRS. SAND BOX. TURBO-SUPERCHARGER. ELEC. WATER COOLER.
LUB'R. OIL COOLER. AIR COMPRESSOR. HOSTLERS CONTROL. COUNTERWEIGHTS. RADIATOR FAN. AIR COMPRESSOR. ENG. CONTROL PANEL.
ANTENNA

FUEL FILLER 12'-1½" FUEL FILLER 12'-1½"

18" 10'-3" 29'-2" 38'-6" 47" 56" 56" 14'-9" 14'-2" 11'-9" 56" 56" 6½" JOUR. 47" 38'-6" 29'-2" 11'-9" 95" 9½"
85" 52'-8" 53'-6"

	NUMBERS	331-60 A
		331-35 B
		343-36 B
	SERVICE	FREIGHT
	BUILDER	A.L.Co.

RADIO UNIT AND CONVERTER.
CAB HEATERS.
10'-6½" 9'-9⅝" 14'-0" 14'-10" 9½"
TYPE-1 UNIT (B-B)
TYPE-2 UNITS 2(B-B)

MODEL F-2.

					CONTINUOUS	1600 H.P.	52,500 #
DATE BUILT	APRIL-MAY-DEC.1951-JAN.1952.	AUX. GENERATOR	2-G.E. TYPE 5-GY-27A3		TR. POWER RATING	3200 H.P.	105,000 #
UNDERFRAMING	BUILT-UP WELDED.		FUEL OIL	1200 GALS. PER UNIT			
DRAFT GEAR	N.M.CO'S. TYPE M-380.	CAPACITIES	LUB'R. OIL	200 "	SEE PAGE-25 FOR TRACTIVE POWER AND		
TRUCKS	4 WHEEL-CAST STEEL		ENG. WATER	280 "	WT. ON DRIVERS.		
GEAR RATIO	74:18.		SAND BOXES 4-22 CU.FT. "				
WHEELS	A.A.R. A-40 GRADE "B"	POWER PLANT	1-1600 H.P. ALCO. SERIES 244-D.V TYPE		COOPERS RATING		E-45
ROLLER BEARINGS	FAFNIR-ENG'S 331-40.		12 CYL. 4 CYCLE, 9" BORE, 10½ STROKE		RADIO (DRG. EL-31943)		MOTOROLA.
	TIMKEN-ENG'S 341-60.		1600 H.P. EA.@1000 RPM IDLING 350 RPM				
AIR BRAKE SCHEDULE	24RL	TURBO-SUPERCHARGER	GE.75 RDI-K1				
AIR BRAKE	CLASP TYPE	FUEL PUMP MOTORS	GE.5BC-76AB-286				
BRAKE CYLINDER	10"X8"	TRACTION MOTORS	5 GE-752-C1				
HAND BRAKE	NATIONAL	AIR COMPRESSOR	WEST. 3CDC				
BATTERIES	EXIDE-32 CELL, MV-25-D.	DISPLACEMENT	225 CU.FT. PER MIN@1000 RPM				
HEADLIGHTS 'A' UNITS-2-200 W. SEAL BEAM.			7875 - @ 350				
CAB HEATER	2-KYSOR-HOT WATER.	MAX. SPEED	65 M.P.H.				
MAIN GENERATOR	1 G.E. TYPE 5-GT-581A1	MIN. SPEED FOR CONTINUOUS RATING-9 M.P.H.					

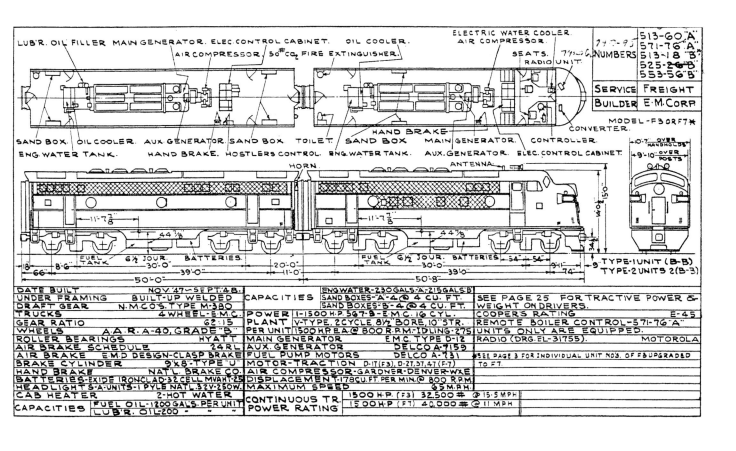

Top callouts (left unit): LUB'R. OIL FILLER. MAIN GENERATOR. ELEC. CONTROL CABINET. OIL COOLER. AIR COMPRESSOR. 50# CO₂ FIRE EXTINGUISHER. ELECTRIC WATER COOLER. AIR COMPRESSOR. SEATS. RADIO UNIT.

Bottom callouts: SAND BOX. OIL COOLER. AUX. GENERATOR. SAND BOX. TOILET. SAND BOX. MAIN GENERATOR. CONTROLLER. ENG. WATER TANK. HAND BRAKE. HOSTLERS CONTROL. ENG. WATER TANK. AUX. GENERATOR. ELEC. CONTROL CABINET. HAND BRAKE. HORN. ANTENNA.

NUMBERS	513-60 A
	571-76 A
	513-18 B
	525-2GB B
	553-56 B
SERVICE	FREIGHT
BUILDER	E.M.CORP.

MODEL-F3 OR F7*
CONVERTER.

10'-7" OVER HANDHOLDS
9'-10" OVER POSTS

TYPE-1 UNIT (B-B)
TYPE-2 UNITS 2(B-B)

DATE BUILT	NOV.'47-SEPT.'48.	CAPACITIES	ENG.WATER-230 GALS.'A':215GALS'B'	SEE PAGE 25 FOR TRACTIVE POWER &
UNDER FRAMING	BUILT-UP WELDED		SAND BOXES-'A'-4@ 4 CU.FT.	WEIGHT ON DRIVERS.
DRAFT GEAR	N.M.CO'S. TYPE M-380		SAND BOXES-'B'-4 @ 4 CU.FT.	
TRUCKS	4 WHEEL-E.M.C.	POWER	1-1500 H.P. 567-B-E.M.C. 16 CYL.	COOPER'S RATING E-45
GEAR RATIO	62:15	PLANT	V-TYPE, 2 CYCLE, 8½"BORE,10"STR.	REMOTE BOILER CONTROL-571-76 'A'
WHEELS	A.A.R. A-40, GRADE "B"	PER UNIT	1500 H.P. EA.@ 800 R.P.M.-IDLING 275	UNITS ONLY ARE EQUIPPED.
ROLLER BEARINGS	HYATT	MAIN GENERATOR	E.M.C. TYPE D-12	RADIO (DRG. EL-31755). MOTOROLA
AIR BRAKE SCHEDULE	24 RL	AUX. GENERATOR	DELCO A-7159	
AIR BRAKE	E.M.D DESIGN-CLASP BRAKE	FUEL PUMP MOTORS	DELCO A-731	*SEE PAGE 3 FOR INDIVIDUAL UNIT NO.S OF F3 UPGRADED
BRAKE CYLINDER	9"x8"-TYPE "U"	MOTOR-TRACTION	D-17(F3), D-27,37,47(F-7)	TO F7.
HAND BRAKE	NAT'L. BRAKE CO.	AIR COMPRESSOR-GARDNER-DENVER-WXE	
BATTERIES-EXIDE IRONCLAD-32 CELL MVAH-25		DISPLACEMENT-178 CU.FT. PER MIN.@ 800 R.P.M.	
HEADLIGHTS-'A' UNITS-1 PYLE NAT'L 32 V-250W.		MAXIMUM SPEED 65 M.P.H.	
CAB HEATER	2-HOT WATER	CONTINUOUS TR. POWER RATING	1500 H.P. (F3) 32,500 # @ 15.5 MPH
CAPACITIES	FUEL OIL-1200 GALS. PER UNIT		1500 H.P. (F7) 40,000 # @ 11 MPH
	LUB'R. OIL-200 - " "		

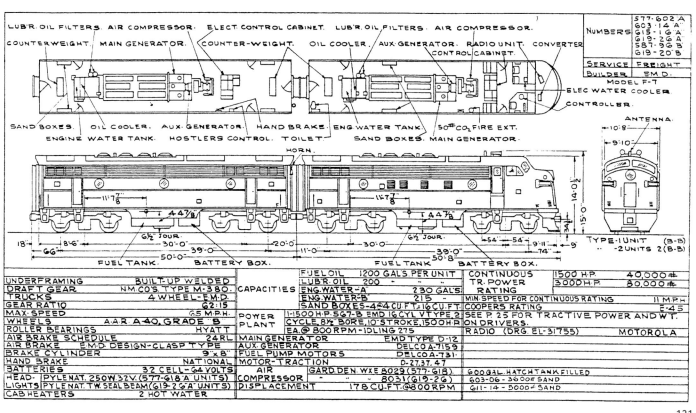

Top callouts (left unit): LUB'R. OIL FILTERS. AIR COMPRESSOR. ELECT. CONTROL CABINET. LUB'R. OIL FILTERS. AIR COMPRESSOR. RADIO UNIT. CONVERTER. COUNTERWEIGHT. MAIN GENERATOR. COUNTER-WEIGHT. OIL COOLER. AUX. GENERATOR. CONTROL CABINET.

Bottom callouts: SAND BOXES. OIL COOLER. AUX. GENERATOR. HAND BRAKE. ENG. WATER TANK. 50# CO₂ FIRE EXT. ENGINE WATER TANK. HOSTLERS CONTROL. TOILET. SAND BOXES. MAIN GENERATOR. HORN.

NUMBERS	577-602 A
	603-14 A
	615-16 A
	587-96 B
	619-20 B
SERVICE	FREIGHT
BUILDER	EM.D.

MODEL-F-7
ELEC. WATER COOLER.
CONTROLLER.
ANTENNA.

TYPE-1 UNIT (B-B)
-2 UNITS 2(B-B)

UNDERFRAMING	BUILT-UP WELDED	CAPACITIES	FUEL OIL 1200 GALS. PER UNIT	CONTINUOUS TR. POWER RATING	1500 H.P. 40,000 #
DRAFT GEAR	N.M.CO'S. TYPE M-380.		LUB'R. OIL 200 - " "		3000 H.P. 80,000 #
TRUCKS	4 WHEEL-E.M.D.		ENG.WATER-'A' 230 GALS.	MIN.SPEED FOR CONTINUOUS RATING 11 M.P.H.
GEAR RATIO	62:15		ENG.WATER-'B' 215 "	
MAX. SPEED	65 M.P.H.		SAND BOXES-4@4 CU.FT.=16 CU.FT.	COOPERS RATING E-45
WHEELS	A.A.R. A-40, GRADE "B"	POWER PLANT	1-1500 H.P. 567-B EMD 16 CYL V TYPE,2	SEE P. 25 FOR TRACTIVE POWER AND WT.
ROLLER BEARINGS	HYATT		CYCLE,8½" BORE,10 STROKE,1500 H.P.	ON DRIVERS.
AIR BRAKE SCHEDULE	24 RL		EA.@ 800 RPM-IDLING 275	RADIO (DRG. EL-31755) MOTOROLA
AIR BRAKE	E.M.D. DESIGN-CLASP TYPE	MAIN GENERATOR	EMD TYPE D-12	
BRAKE CYLINDER	9"x8"	AUX. GENERATOR	DELCO A-7159	
HAND BRAKE	NATIONAL	FUEL PUMP MOTORS	DELCO A-731.	
BATTERIES	32 CELL-64 VOLTS	MOTOR-TRACTION	D-27,37,47	
HEAD-	PYLE NAT. 250W.32V. (577-618 'A' UNITS)	AIR COMPRESSOR	GARD.DEN. WXE 8029 (577-618)	600 GAL. HATCH TANK FILLED
LIGHTS	PYLE NAT. T.W. SEAL BEAM (619-2G 'A' UNITS)		" 8031 (619-2G)	603-06 - 3600# SAND
CAB HEATERS	2 HOT WATER	DISPLACEMENT	178 CU.FT.@ 800 RPM	611-14 - 5000# SAND

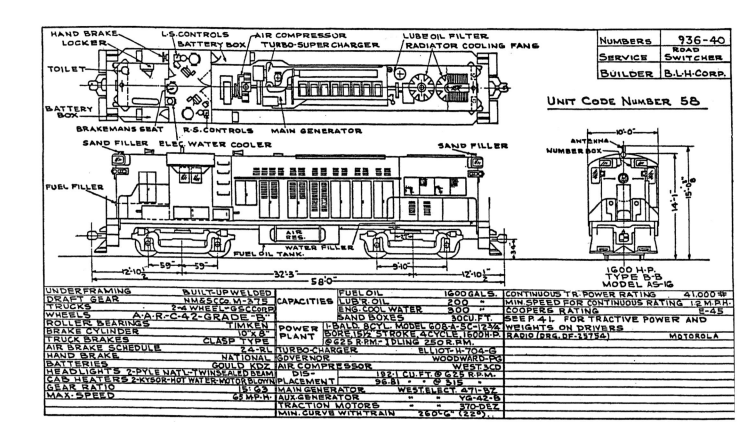

UNIT CODE NUMBER 58

1600 H.P.
TYPE B-B
MODEL AS-16

UNDERFRAMING	BUILT-UP WELDED		FUEL OIL	1600 GALS.	CONTINUOUS TR. POWER RATING	41,000 #
DRAFT GEAR	NM&S.CO. M-375	CAPACITIES	LUB'R. OIL	200 "	MIN. SPEED FOR CONTINUOUS RATING	12 M.P.H.
TRUCKS	2-4 WHEEL-GSC Corp		ENG. COOL WATER	300 "	COOPERS RATING	E-45
WHEELS	A·A·R·C-42-GRADE "B"		SAND BOXES	30 CU. FT.	SEE P. 41. FOR TRACTIVE POWER AND
ROLLER BEARINGS	TIMKEN	POWER PLANT	1-BALD. 8 CYL. MODEL 608-A-5C-12¾ BORE, 15½" STROKE, 4 CYCLE, 1600 H.P. @ 625 R.P.M.- IDLING 250 R.P.M.		WEIGHTS ON DRIVERS
BRAKE CYLINDER	10"x 8"				RADIO (DRG. DF-25754)	MOTOROLA
TRUCK BRAKES	CLASP TYPE				
AIR BRAKE SCHEDULE	24-RL		TURBO-CHARGER	ELLIOT-H-704-G	
HAND BRAKE	NATIONAL		GOVERNOR	WOODWARD-PG	
BATTERIES	GOULD KDZ		AIR COMPRESSOR	WEST. 3CD	
HEADLIGHTS 2-PYLE NAT'L-TWIN SEALED BEAM			DIS-	192.1 CU. FT. @ 625 R.P.M.	
CAB HEATERS 2-KYSOR-HOT WATER-MOTOR BLOWN			PLACEMENT	96.81 " " @ 315	
GEAR RATIO	15:63		MAIN GENERATOR	WEST. ELECT. 471-BZ	
MAX·SPEED	65 M.P.H.		AUX. GENERATOR	YG-42-B	
			TRACTION MOTORS	370-DEZ	
			MIN. CURVE WITH TRAIN	260'-6" (22°)	

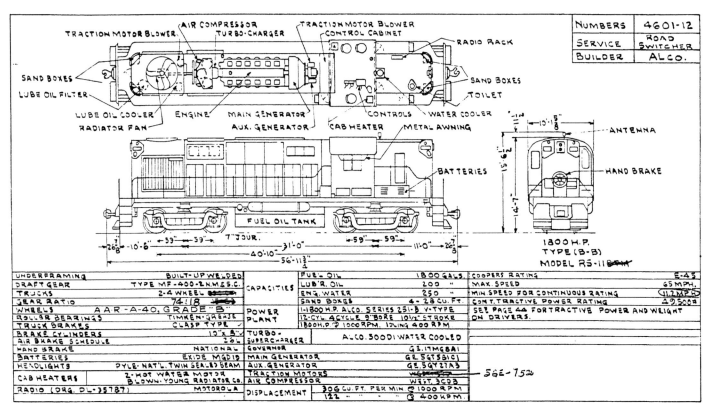

NUMBERS	4601-12
SERVICE	ROAD SWITCHER
BUILDER	ALCO.

1800 H.P.
TYPE (B-B)
MODEL RS-11

UNDERFRAMING	BUILT-UP WELDED		FUEL OIL	1800 GALS.	COOPERS RATING	E-45
DRAFT GEAR	TYPE MF-400-2 N.M.&S.C.	CAPACITIES	LUB'R. OIL	200 "	MAX. SPEED	65 MPH.
TRUCKS	2-4 WHEEL		ENG. WATER	250 "	MIN SPEED FOR CONTINUOUS RATING	11.2 MPH.
GEAR RATIO	74:18		SAND BOXES	4-28 CU. FT.	CONT. TRACTIVE POWER RATING	49,500 #
WHEELS	AAR-A-40, GRADE "B"	POWER PLANT	1-1800 H.P. ALCO. SERIES 251-B V-TYPE		SEE PAGE 44 FOR TRACTIVE POWER AND WEIGHT
ROLLER BEARINGS	TIMKEN GREASE		12-CYL. 4 CYCLE 9" BORE 10½" STROKE		ON DRIVERS.
TRUCK BRAKES	CLASP TYPE		1800 H.P. @ 1000 RPM, IDLING 400 RPM		
BRAKE CYLINDERS	12"x 5"	TURBO-	ALCO. 500 DI WATER COOLED		
AIR BRAKE SCHEDULE	26L	SUPERCHARGER			
HAND BRAKE	NATIONAL		GOVERNOR	G.E. 17 MG8A1	
BATTERIES	EXIDE MGD19		MAIN GENERATOR	G.E. 5GT581C1	
HEADLIGHTS	PYLE NAT'L. TWIN SEALED BEAM		AUX. GENERATOR	G.E. 5GY27A3	
CAB HEATERS	2-HOT WATER MOTOR BLOWN, YOUNG RADIATOR CO.		TRACTION MOTORS		SEE-752
			AIR COMPRESSOR	WEST. 3CD	
RADIO (DRG. DL-35787)	MOTOROLA	DISPLACEMENT	306 CU.FT. PER MIN @ 1000 RPM		
			122 " " @ 400 RPM.		

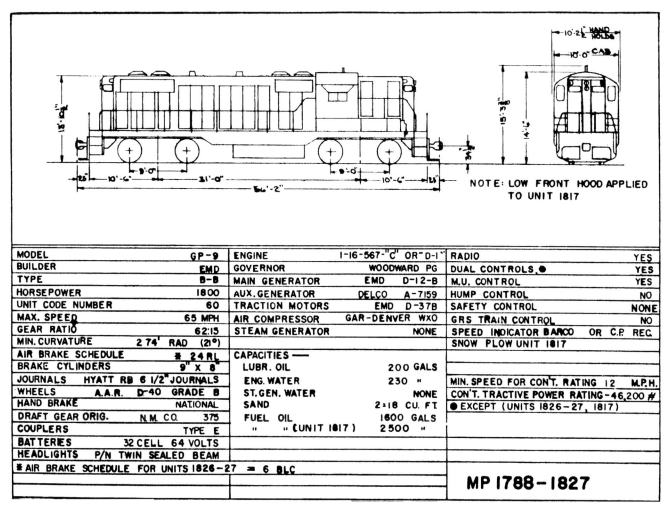

NOTE: LOW FRONT HOOD APPLIED
TO UNIT 1817

MODEL	GP-9	ENGINE	1-16-567-"C" OR "D-1"	RADIO	YES
BUILDER	EMD	GOVERNOR	WOODWARD PG	DUAL CONTROLS ●	YES
TYPE	B-B	MAIN GENERATOR	EMD D-12-B	M.U. CONTROL	YES
HORSEPOWER	1800	AUX. GENERATOR	DELCO A-7159	HUMP CONTROL	NO
UNIT CODE NUMBER	60	TRACTION MOTORS	EMD D-37B	SAFETY CONTROL	NONE
MAX. SPEED	65 MPH	AIR COMPRESSOR	GAR-DENVER WXO	GRS TRAIN CONTROL	NO
GEAR RATIO	62:15	STEAM GENERATOR	NONE	SPEED INDICATOR BARCO OR C.P. REC.	
MIN. CURVATURE	274' RAD (21°)			SNOW PLOW UNIT 1817	
AIR BRAKE SCHEDULE	# 24 RL	CAPACITIES —			
BRAKE CYLINDERS	9" X 8"	LUBR. OIL	200 GALS	MIN. SPEED FOR CON'T. RATING 12 M.P.H.	
JOURNALS HYATT RB 6 1/2" JOURNALS		ENG. WATER	230 "	CON'T. TRACTIVE POWER RATING-46,200 #	
WHEELS A.A.R. D-40 GRADE B		ST. GEN. WATER	NONE	● EXCEPT (UNITS 1826-27, 1817)	
HAND BRAKE	NATIONAL	SAND	2=18 CU. FT		
DRAFT GEAR ORIG. N.M.CO. 375		FUEL OIL	1600 GALS		
COUPLERS	TYPE E	" " (UNIT 1817)	2500 "		
BATTERIES 32 CELL 64 VOLTS					
HEADLIGHTS P/N TWIN SEALED BEAM					
# AIR BRAKE SCHEDULE FOR UNITS 1826-27 = 6 BLC					

MP 1788-1827

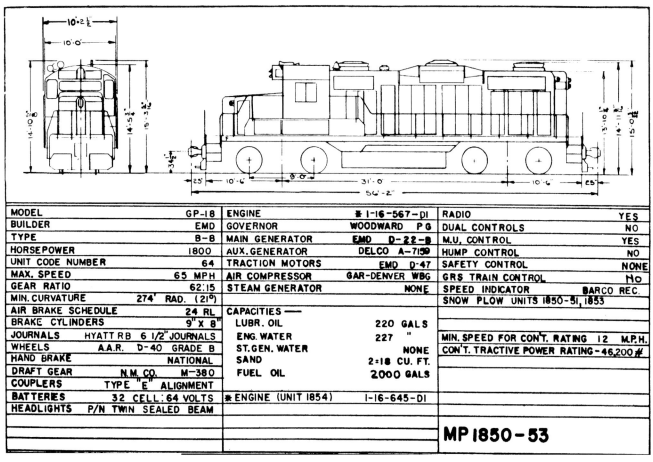

MODEL	GP-18	ENGINE	# 1-16-567-D1	RADIO	YES
BUILDER	EMD	GOVERNOR	WOODWARD PG	DUAL CONTROLS	NO
TYPE	B-B	MAIN GENERATOR	EMD D-22-B	M.U. CONTROL	YES
HORSEPOWER	1800	AUX. GENERATOR	DELCO A-7159	HUMP CONTROL	NO
UNIT CODE NUMBER	64	TRACTION MOTORS	EMD D-47	SAFETY CONTROL	NONE
MAX. SPEED	65 MPH	AIR COMPRESSOR	GAR-DENVER WBG	GRS TRAIN CONTROL	No
GEAR RATIO	62:15	STEAM GENERATOR	NONE	SPEED INDICATOR BARCO REC.	
MIN. CURVATURE	274' RAD. (21°)			SNOW PLOW UNITS 1850-51, 1853	
AIR BRAKE SCHEDULE	24 RL	CAPACITIES —			
BRAKE CYLINDERS	9" X 8"	LUBR. OIL	220 GALS		
JOURNALS HYATT RB 6 1/2" JOURNALS		ENG. WATER	227 "	MIN. SPEED FOR CON'T. RATING 12 M.P.H.	
WHEELS A.A.R. D-40 GRADE B		ST. GEN. WATER	NONE	CON'T. TRACTIVE POWER RATING-46,200 #	
HAND BRAKE	NATIONAL	SAND	2=18 CU. FT.		
DRAFT GEAR N.M.CO. M-380		FUEL OIL	2000 GALS		
COUPLERS TYPE "E" ALIGNMENT					
BATTERIES 32 CELL 64 VOLTS		# ENGINE (UNIT 1854)	1-16-645-D1		
HEADLIGHTS P/N TWIN SEALED BEAM					

MP 1850-53

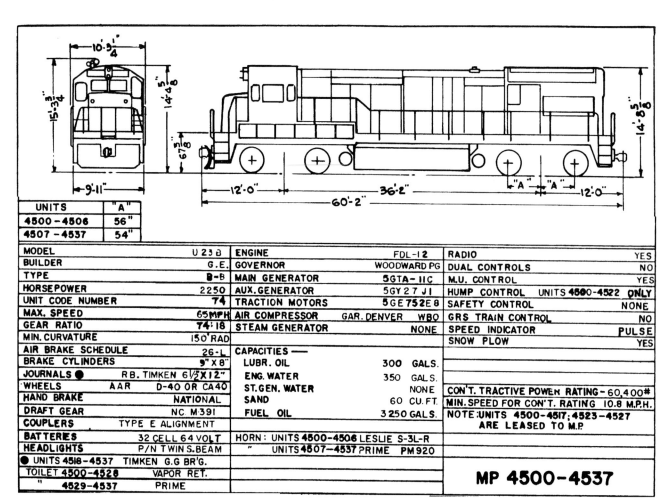

UNITS	"A"
4500-4506	56"
4507-4537	54"

MODEL	U 23 B	ENGINE	FDL-12	RADIO	YES
BUILDER	G.E.	GOVERNOR	WOODWARD PG	DUAL CONTROLS	NO
TYPE	B-B	MAIN GENERATOR	5GTA-11C	M.U. CONTROL	YES
HORSEPOWER	2250	AUX.GENERATOR	5GY27J1	HUMP CONTROL UNITS 4500-4522	ONLY
UNIT CODE NUMBER	74	TRACTION MOTORS	5GE752E8	SAFETY CONTROL	NONE
MAX. SPEED	65MPH	AIR COMPRESSOR	GAR.DENVER WBO	GRS TRAIN CONTROL	NO
GEAR RATIO	74:18	STEAM GENERATOR	NONE	SPEED INDICATOR	PULSE
MIN. CURVATURE	150° RAD			SNOW PLOW	YES
AIR BRAKE SCHEDULE	26-L	CAPACITIES —			
BRAKE CYLINDERS	9"X8"	LUBR. OIL	300 GALS.		
JOURNALS ●	R.B. TIMKEN 6½X12"	ENG. WATER	350 GALS.		
WHEELS	AAR D-40 OR CA40	ST.GEN. WATER	NONE	CON'T. TRACTIVE POWER RATING-60,400#	
HAND BRAKE	NATIONAL	SAND	60 CU.FT.	MIN.SPEED FOR CON'T. RATING 10.8 M.P.H.	
DRAFT GEAR	NC M-391	FUEL OIL	3250 GALS.	NOTE:UNITS 4500-4517; 4523-4527	
COUPLERS	TYPE E ALIGNMENT			ARE LEASED TO M.P.	
BATTERIES	32 CELL 64 VOLT	HORN : UNITS 4500-4506 LESLIE S-3L-R			
HEADLIGHTS	P/N TWIN S.BEAM	" UNITS 4507-4537 PRIME PM920			
● UNITS 4518-4537 TIMKEN G.G BR'G.					
TOILET 4500-4528	VAPOR RET.			**MP 4500-4537**	
" 4529-4537	PRIME				

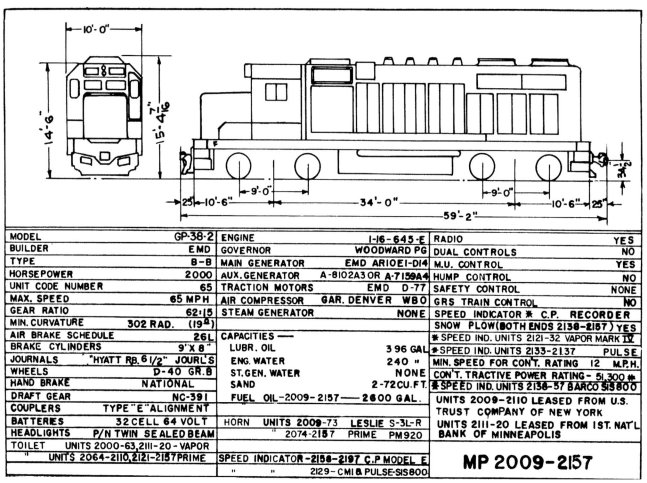

MODEL	GP-38-2	ENGINE	1-16-645-E	RADIO	YES
BUILDER	EMD	GOVERNOR	WOODWARD PG	DUAL CONTROLS	NO
TYPE	B-B	MAIN GENERATOR	EMD AR10E1-D14	M.U. CONTROL	YES
HORSEPOWER	2000	AUX.GENERATOR	A-8102A3 OR A-7159A4	HUMP CONTROL	NO
UNIT CODE NUMBER	65	TRACTION MOTORS	EMD D-77	SAFETY CONTROL	NONE
MAX. SPEED	65 MPH	AIR COMPRESSOR	GAR. DENVER WBO	GRS TRAIN CONTROL	NO
GEAR RATIO	62:15	STEAM GENERATOR	NONE	SPEED INDICATOR ✱ C.P. RECORDER	
MIN. CURVATURE	302 RAD. (19°)			SNOW PLOW(BOTH ENDS 2138-2157) YES	
AIR BRAKE SCHEDULE	26L	CAPACITIES —		✱ SPEED IND. UNITS 2121-32 VAPOR MARK Ⅳ	
BRAKE CYLINDERS	9"X8"	LUBR. OIL	396 GAL	✱SPEED IND. UNITS 2133-2137 PULSE	
JOURNALS	"HYATT RB.6½" JOURL'S	ENG. WATER	240 "	MIN. SPEED FOR CON'T. RATING 12 M.P.H.	
WHEELS	D-40 GR.B	ST.GEN. WATER	NONE	CON'T. TRACTIVE POWER RATING- 51,300 #	
HAND BRAKE	NATIONAL	SAND	2-72CU.FT.	✱SPEED IND. UNITS 2138-57 BARCO SIS800	
DRAFT GEAR	NC-391	FUEL OIL-2009-2157—2600 GAL.		UNITS 2009-2110 LEASED FROM U.S.	
COUPLERS	TYPE "E" ALIGNMENT			TRUST COMPANY OF NEW YORK	
BATTERIES	32 CELL 64 VOLT	HORN UNITS 2009-73 LESLIE S-3L-R		UNITS 2111-20 LEASED FROM 1ST. NAT'L	
HEADLIGHTS	P/N TWIN SEALED BEAM	" 2074-2157 PRIME PM920		BANK OF MINNEAPOLIS	
TOILET UNITS 2000-63,2111-20 - VAPOR					
" UNITS 2064-2110,2121-2157 PRIME		SPEED INDICATOR -2158-2197 C.P MODEL E		**MP 2009-2157**	
		" " 2129-CMI & PULSE-SIS800			

134

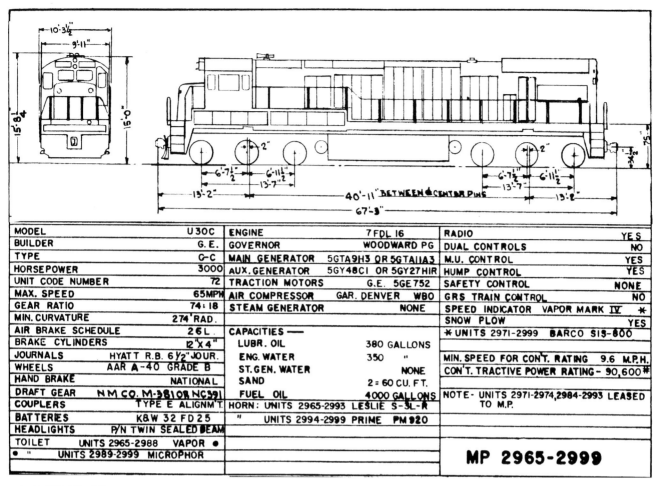

MODEL	U 30C	ENGINE	7 FDL 16	RADIO	YES
BUILDER	G. E.	GOVERNOR	WOODWARD PG	DUAL CONTROLS	NO
TYPE	C-C	MAIN GENERATOR	5GTA9H3 OR 5GTA11A3	M.U. CONTROL	YES
HORSEPOWER	3000	AUX. GENERATOR	5GY48C1 OR 5GY27HIR	HUMP CONTROL	YES
UNIT CODE NUMBER	72	TRACTION MOTORS	G.E. 5GE752	SAFETY CONTROL	NONE
MAX. SPEED	65MPH	AIR COMPRESSOR	GAR. DENVER WBO	GRS TRAIN CONTROL	NO
GEAR RATIO	74:18	STEAM GENERATOR	NONE	SPEED INDICATOR VAPOR MARK IV ✱	
MIN. CURVATURE	274'RAD.			SNOW PLOW	YES
AIR BRAKE SCHEDULE	26L	CAPACITIES —		✱ UNITS 2971-2999 BARCO SIS-800	
BRAKE CYLINDERS	12"X 4"	LUBR. OIL	380 GALLONS		
JOURNALS	HYATT R.B. 6½"JOUR.	ENG. WATER	350 "	MIN. SPEED FOR CONT. RATING 9.6 M.P.H.	
WHEELS	AAR A-40 GRADE B	ST. GEN. WATER	NONE	CONT. TRACTIVE POWER RATING - 90,600#	
HAND BRAKE	NATIONAL	SAND	2 = 60 CU. FT.		
DRAFT GEAR	N M CO. M-3810R NC391	FUEL OIL	4000 GALLONS	NOTE- UNITS 2971-2974,2984-2993 LEASED	
COUPLERS	TYPE E ALIGNM'T.	HORN: UNITS 2965-2993 LESLIE S-3L-R		TO M.P.	
BATTERIES	K&W 32 FD 25	" UNITS 2994-2999 PRIME PM920			
HEADLIGHTS	P/N TWIN SEALED BEAM				
TOILET UNITS 2965-2988 VAPOR ●				**MP 2965-2999**	
● " UNITS 2989-2999 MICROPHOR					

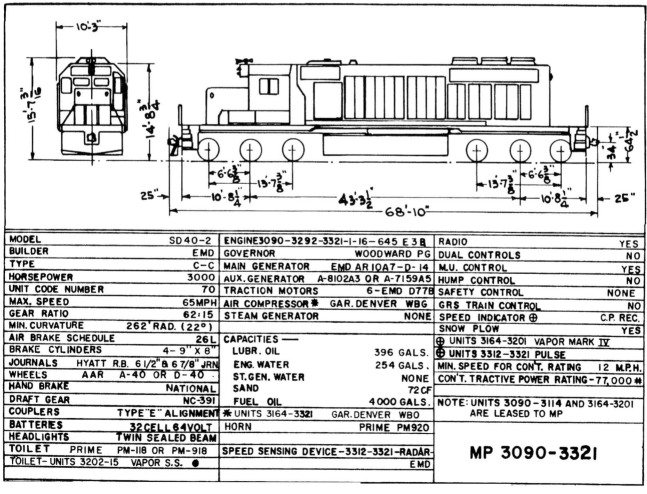

MODEL	SD40-2	ENGINE3090-3292-3321-1-16- 645 E 3 B		RADIO	YES
BUILDER	EMD	GOVERNOR	WOODWARD PG	DUAL CONTROLS	NO
TYPE	C-C	MAIN GENERATOR	EMD AR10A7-D-14	M.U. CONTROL	YES
HORSEPOWER	3000	AUX. GENERATOR	A-8102A3 OR A-7159A5	HUMP CONTROL	NO
UNIT CODE NUMBER	70	TRACTION MOTORS	6-EMD D77B	SAFETY CONTROL	NONE
MAX. SPEED	65MPH	AIR COMPRESSOR ✱	GAR. DENVER WBG	GRS TRAIN CONTROL	NO
GEAR RATIO	62:15	STEAM GENERATOR	NONE	SPEED INDICATOR ⊕	C.P. REC.
MIN. CURVATURE	262'RAD. (22°)			SNOW PLOW	YES
AIR BRAKE SCHEDULE	26L	CAPACITIES —		⊕ UNITS 3164-3201 VAPOR MARK IV	
BRAKE CYLINDERS	4-9"X 8"	LUBR. OIL	396 GALS.	⊕ UNITS 3312-3321 PULSE	
JOURNALS	HYATT R.B. 6 1/2"& 6 7/8" JRN	ENG. WATER	254 GALS.	MIN. SPEED FOR CONT. RATING 12 M.P.H.	
WHEELS	AAR A-40 OR D-40	ST. GEN. WATER	NONE	CONT. TRACTIVE POWER RATING-77,000#	
HAND BRAKE	NATIONAL	SAND	72 CF		
DRAFT GEAR	NC-391	FUEL OIL	4000 GALS.	NOTE: UNITS 3090-3114 AND 3164-3201	
COUPLERS	TYPE "E" ALIGNMENT	✱ UNITS 3164-3321 GAR.DENVER WBO		ARE LEASED TO MP	
BATTERIES	32CELL 64VOLT	HORN	PRIME PM920		
HEADLIGHTS	TWIN SEALED BEAM				
TOILET PRIME PM-118 OR PM-918		SPEED SENSING DEVICE-3312-3321-RADAR-		**MP 3090-3321**	
TOILET- UNITS 3202-15 VAPOR S.S. ●		EMD			

B I B L I O G R A P H Y

Various Public Relations and Industrial Relations documents including early history, employee training and development, operations, and marketing research, Missouri Pacific Lines, 1980s.

We Can Help You Switch to Coal, Public Relations Dept., Missouri Pacific Railroad.

"Coal Traffic," *Mo-Pac News*, September, 1975, Missouri Pacific Railroad.

"First Coal Unit Trains Go On Mine to River Run," *Mo-Pac News*, September, 1966.

"New Coal Dock on MoPac Lines," *Mo-Pac News*, March, 1979.

"New Unit Coal Trains," *Mo-Pac News*, March-April, 1980.

Through Freight Train Schedules, Missouri Pacific Railroad, 1950s thru 1980s.

Missouri Pacific Railroad, various division and system timetables from 1962 through No. 18, October 25, 1981.

Missouri Pacific Railroad System Timetable No. 1, April 28, 1985.

Railway Age, various 1925 through 1982.

Tardy, Randy, "MoPac Unveils New Mainline in East," *Arkansas Democrat*, Little Rock, Arkansas, February 21, 1982.